Teaching Mathematics

THIRD EDITION

TEACHING MATHEMATICS

A Sourcebook of Aids, Activities, and Strategies

Max A. Sobel and Evan M. Maletsky

Montclair State University

ALLYN AND BACON

Boston • London • Toronto • Sydney • Tokyo • Singapore

Vice President, Editor in Chief, Education: Sean W. Wakely
Series Editor: Frances Helland
Editorial Assistant: Bridget Keane
Marketing Managers: Ellen Dolberg and Brad Parkins
Editorial Production Service: Chestnut Hill Enterprises, Inc.
Manufacturing Buyer: Suzanne Lareau
Cover Administrator: Jennifer Hart

Internet: www.abacon.com

Between the time Website information is gathered and published, some sites may have closed. Also, the transcription of URLs can result in typographical errors. The publisher would appreciate notification where these occur so that they may be corrected in subsequent editions.

Library of Congress Cataloging-in-Publication Data

Sobel, Max A.
    Teaching mathematics : a sourcebook of aids, activities, and strategies / Max A. Sobel and Evan M. Maletsky. – 3rd ed.
        p.   cm.
    ISBN 0-205-29256-9
    1. Mathematics–Study and teaching (Secondary)   I. Maletsky, Evan M.   II. Title.
QA11.S663 1999
510'.71'2–dc21   98-8469
                                                                          CIP

Printed in the United States of America

10 9 8 7 6 5 4 3 2 1   03 02 01 00 99 98

CONTENTS

Preface   ix

PREFACE

Teaching Mathematics: A Sourcebook of Aids, Activities, and Strategies has been designed for use by teachers of mathematics as well as teachers in training. It treats the art of teaching through a series of motivational ideas suitable for many grade levels and abilities, and includes a discussion of activities, materials, and manipulatives suitable for classroom use. When necessary, required subject matter content is covered as well.

The first two editions of *Teaching Mathematics* were written in response to the many teachers and students of mathematics who attended lectures, courses, and workshops given by the authors but who were unable to find appropriate materials in a single convenient source. The authors collaborated to provide a collection of teaching aids, activities, and strategies suitable for elementary and secondary mathematics classes. Attention is given to contemporary topics such as technology and fractals, and to pedagogical issues such as the use of manipulatives, the importance of forming connections, and cooperative learning techniques.

In this revised and expanded third edition, changes have been made based on the suggestions of users of the last two editions, students and teachers alike. It also reflects the recommendations of such major professional groups as the National Council of Teachers of Mathematics (NCTM), located at 1906 Association Drive, Reston, Virginia, 22091. A complete listing of all their publications is available by writing to NCTM or by contacting their website (**www.nctm.org**).

In the first three chapters, we address the general question of the art of teaching mathematics, with specific attention given to the role, importance, methods, and techniques of motivation. Many educators agree that motivation is the key to success for both teaching and learning mathematics, and that sufficient time must be provided in the daily lesson plan to be certain that students are suitably motivated. This point of view, prevalent in the first two editions, is given emphasis in this third edition as well.

Problem solving emerged in the 1980s as a major concern for mathematics educators, captured our attention in the 1990s as well, and promises to be at the core of mathematics curricula in the twenty-first century. Thus Chapter 3 is devoted specifically to strategies in this important topic. However, problem solving is addressed throughout every chapter of this third edition.

A major theme of the 1990s dealt with technology. With this in mind, this current edition addresses the use of graphing calculators and computers in the curriculum, and also provides suggestions for the use of the Internet as a source of information for both students and teachers as well.

In Chapters 4 through 7 we focus on specific aids and activities in arithmetic, algebra, geometry, and probability and statistics with a separate chapter devoted to each of these four areas. These chapters provide numerous motivational ideas and explore key subject matter topics in some detail. Appropriate classroom activities and experiments are identified with detailed descriptions on the construction and use of related models and aids. Extensive attention is given the use of manipulatives both in the hands of the student and in those of the teacher. These not only offer concrete models for the presentation of new concepts, but can be used to expand and reinforce established concepts by helping students to see familiar topics in new and different ways. Attention is given in these chapters to the use of the overhead projector as well as to suggested applications using the graphing calculator and computer.

Chapter 8 is new to this edition. It emphasizes selected concepts from discrete mathematics and presents the topic of fractals with teaching instructions for this contemporary addition to the curriculum. Numerous computer-generated pieces of art help set the stage for this presentation. Although given primary emphasis in Chapters 1 to 3, the idea of motivation continues to be an underlying theme of Chapters 4 through 8. Ideas are presented from the point of view of generating attention, interest, and surprise, and many are tied to problem-solving situations. These are important aspects of successful teaching, and they can be nurtured through the effective and imaginative use of aids and activities in the classroom. This in turn enables students to see ideas presented in new and different ways and helps to foster creative thinking, perhaps the most critical of all the mathematical skills.

Most of the material that appears in this book has been presented and tested in a variety of ways. Some of the content is based on talks given by the authors at state, regional, and national conferences throughout the country. Many of the ideas concerning the use of multisensory aids have been used by the authors in various undergraduate and graduate courses in mathematics education that they have taught at Montclair State University and elsewhere. Furthermore, most of the laboratory and discovery activities included in this edition have been used by the authors in numerous junior and senior high school mathematics classes that they have taught, as well as in workshops conducted for teachers of such classes, and reflect the feedback received from such use.

A leading educator once said that we have done a reasonably good job in the past in teaching better mathematics but that it is equally important to learn how to teach mathematics better. It is the sincere hope of both authors that the material and ideas presented in this book will enable teachers of mathematics to improve their pedagogical skills and thus better motivate their students to learn the required subject matter. It is in this sense that the authors fondly and encouragingly dedicate this third edition to the thousands of teachers and students whom they have had the good fortune to meet and teach throughout their collective careers, spanning a period of 50 years. We hope that this volume serves as one small contribution to the big and exciting task of teaching mathematics better.

Finally, we would like to thank Miriam A. Leiva, University of North Carolina–Charlotte, and Michael Mikusa, Kent State University, for reviewing this edition.

Teaching Mathematics

1

THE ART OF TEACHING

Teachers must know their stuff.
They must know the pupils whom they are stuffing.
Above all else, they must know how to stuff them artistically.

This job description for teachers summarizes the essential ingredients for the successful teaching of mathematics. It is the last item of this list that is the primary focus of this first chapter, and indeed of the entire book. As teachers, we all strive to perfect our artistry in "stuffing" our students with appropriate, contemporary mathematics. This artistry is especially important when we attempt to motivate our students and to challenge the many reluctant learners who cross our paths daily. In this first chapter we list a number of guiding principles involved in the art of teaching, and then elaborate on these in later chapters with reference to specific subject-matter areas.

Most teachers have their own "bag of tricks" that works for them. However, all conscientious teachers constantly search for new ideas and techniques to adopt in their classrooms. Thus it is hoped that the collection of items presented in this chapter, and throughout the book as well, may provide some additional insights and procedures that teachers of mathematics will find useful in their daily teaching.

1.1 START THE PERIOD IN AN INTERESTING WAY

There are far too many teachers of mathematics who rely on a single universal lesson plan which, for a 45-minute period, proceeds as follows:

30 minutes—review yesterday's assignment
10 minutes—introduce the new lesson
5 minutes—have students begin the next assignment

Such an approach, followed daily, can only be classified by the three D's:

Dull
Deadly
Destructive of all interest

Although it is essential to review most assignments that are given, a teacher need not begin every lesson in this manner, and certainly should not devote the major portion of every class to such a review. The first five minutes of a period often spell the difference between the success or the failure of a lesson. Thus it is imperative that some thought be given to imaginative ways to begin so as to capture student attention and interest.

Start with a Challenging Question

An interesting question can often serve as one of the most effective ways to start or end a class. A thought-provoking question is posed and students are given an opportunity to guess, discuss, and debate the answer. Then, with teacher guidance, appropriate methods are considered for the solution of the problem. Of course the question should be designed so that its solution requires the class to employ mathematical content and methods appropriate to the curriculum and level of instruction at hand.

Consider, for example, a seventh-grade class studying a unit on our decimal system of notation. The teacher wishes to provide some review of fundamental computation, and also hopes to develop an appreciation of the meaning of very large numbers. An interesting question that could be used to start the class is the following:

> **I've just decided to count to one million.**
>
> **1, 2, 3, 4, 5, . . .**
>
> **How long will it take me?**

Some students will begin to make random guesses. After a few of these have been offered and recorded, remind the class members that they really do not yet have adequate information for solving this problem. For example, they have not been told the rate at which you will count nor whether you will count without stopping. Tell them that you will count at the rate of one number per second and will not stop until the task has been completed. Then ask for guesses again.

Of course there will always be one bright student who gives the answer as 1 million seconds! Give credit for this response, but then ask for the answer in more commonly understood units of time, such as days, weeks, months, or years. At this point it is extremely important to *allow students to guess before they compute.* A heated discussion among students concerning their guesses is the best way to motivate them to perform the computation necessary to pro-vide the correct answer.

A word of caution should be inserted here. Occasionally one meets a class where most attempts at motivation seem to fail. After discussion of the vari-ous guesses for the time it takes to count to 1 million, you must lead the class to discover the computational method used to find the correct answer. If, at this point, the class is not really interested in the correct answer, there is hardly any purpose in pursuing the matter further. It is for this reason that it is important to generate sufficient discussion in advance so that students are eager to learn the solution.

This problem provides an excellent opportunity to emphasize the skills of estimation. To change 1,000,000 seconds to days we need to complete this computation:

$$\frac{1,000,000}{60 \times 60 \times 24}$$

For a quick estimate, round 24 to 25 and note the results:

$$\frac{1,000,000}{60 \times 60 \times 25} = \frac{1,000,0\cancel{00}}{6\cancel{0} \times 6\cancel{0} \times 25} = \frac{\overset{400}{\cancel{10,000}}}{36 \times \underset{1}{\cancel{25}}} = \frac{400}{36}$$

Since $\frac{400}{36}$ is somewhat greater than 10, a very good estimate would be 11 days. The actual answer is approximately $11\frac{1}{2}$ days.

Provide Challenges

There are many interesting and challenging questions that can be used to stimulate discussion at the start of a period and that can also help motivate a review of computational skills. Here are just a few illustrations; others appear elsewhere in the text and within the Exercises. The reader is urged to guess and estimate the answer for each of the following so as to experience the thought processes that students might encounter. Begin a collection of such challenging questions in an index card file.

1. Consider 1 million pennies piled one on top of another. Would the pile be higher than the ceiling of your classroom?
   higher than the school flagpole?
   higher than the Empire State Building?
   higher than the moon?
2. One million $1 bills are placed end to end on the ground. How far would they reach? Across a football field? Across the state? Across the United States? Around the world?

3. I'm going to snap my fingers. One minute later I'll snap them again. Then 2 minutes later I'll snap them again. Then I'll wait 4 minutes to snap them; then 8 minutes, 16 minutes, and so on. Each time I double the number of minutes in the interval between snaps. At this rate, how many times will I snap my fingers in one year?
4. What historical event happened approximately 1 billion seconds ago?
5. How many pencils, laid end to end, would be needed to reach from New York City to San Francisco? List the assumptions you make in estimating your answer. (Be prepared for the student who responds that one pencil is all you need if it is long enough!)

As a final example, consider an eighth-grade class that is studying a unit on measurement. Here is an interesting question that could be used to start the class:

Look at our classroom. Do you think we could fit 1 million basketballs into this room?

How about 1 million baseballs?

One million table-tennis balls?

One million marbles?

One million pennies?

For a classroom of average size the guess is often between 1 million table-tennis balls and 1 million pennies. After time for discussion, the class should be asked to determine a procedure by which to approximate the correct answer. One possibility might be to bring an empty shoebox to class and fill it up with table-tennis balls. Then use a tape measure and approximate the volume of the room. By comparing the volume of the room with the volume of the shoebox, one can obtain a fair approximation of the number of table-tennis balls that could fit into the room.

Another question that could be used to serve the same purpose, or could be given as an assignment, is to determine the approximate weight of 1 million pennies. Questions of this type generally serve to set the stage for interesting class discussions that make students look forward to attending their mathematics class . . . a place where exciting things happen!

1.2 USE HISTORICAL TOPICS WHEN APPROPRIATE

Too many of our students think of mathematics as a very dull subject, and they picture mathematicians as hermits who spend their lives buried in mountains of figures. One interesting way to make mathematics come alive is to make frequent use of historical items that help to show that mathematicians are human beings, with mortal weaknesses and interests. Books on the history of mathematics are excellent sources for such items, many of which can be appropriately used to introduce or to supplement particular topics in the classroom.

Anecdotes about Mathematicians

Karl Gauss

Make a list of birthdates of famous mathematicians and celebrate these dates when they arrive. For example, on April 30 you might consider a birthday party for the German mathematician Karl Friedrich Gauss (1777–1855), considered by many to have been one of the three greatest mathematicians of all times, along with Archimedes and Newton. Gauss has been honored by having his picture on both stamps and coins in his native country.

It is claimed that young Gauss was a precocious youngster with a born flair for mathematics. To keep him suitably occupied, his teacher in elementary school told Gauss to write the numbers from 1 to 100 and to find their sum. In a flash Gauss is supposed to have given the answer as 5050. It is further claimed that he did so by mentally recognizing this pattern:

$$1 + 2 + 3 \cdots \cdots \cdots \cdots \cdots + 98 + 99 + 100$$

$$1 + 100 = 101$$
$$2 + 99 = 101$$
$$3 + 98 = 101$$

Since there are 50 pairs that each add to 101, the total sum is 50×101 or 5050! Today we use the formula $S = \dfrac{n(n+1)}{2}$ for the sum of the first n successive counting numbers.

Leonhard Euler

On April 15 celebrate the birthday of one of the most prolific mathematicians of all times, Leonhard Euler (1707–1783). His contributions are so extensive that one can be found for almost any level of instruction. A few are noted below, along with a picture of a stamp produced in his honor in Switzerland.

Euler was the first to use the symbol π.

He was the first to use i for $\sqrt{-1}$.

He was the first to use e for the special irrational transcendental number 2.718281... which is the limit of $\left(1 + \dfrac{1}{n}\right)^n$ as n becomes large without bound.

The discovery of this very interesting relationship among e, π, and i is also credited to Euler:

$$e^{\pi i} + 1 = 0$$

Euler published a list of 30 pairs of *amicable numbers*. (See Exercise 8 at the end of this chapter.)

For a challenging question to start the period, ask the class why Euler was wrong when he thought that he had found a formula that would generate only *prime numbers* for integral values of n. (See Exercise 2.)

$$n^2 - n + 41$$

Another interesting contribution made by Euler was the following square array that gives a sum of 260 for each horizontal row and vertical column. What is especially interesting about this array is that a chess knight can begin at the square marked 1, and can then land on each number through 64, in numerical order, by using L-shaped moves. Students who are chess players will enjoy confirming this fact, and performing "magic" tricks by memorizing the moves that successively produce the 64 numbers of the square.

1	48	31	50	33	16	63	18
30	51	46	3	62	19	14	35
47	2	49	32	15	34	17	64
52	29	4	45	20	61	36	13
5	44	25	56	9	40	21	60
28	53	8	41	24	57	12	37
43	6	55	26	39	10	59	22
54	27	42	7	58	23	38	11

Note how the movement of the knight on a grid relates to the eight symmetries of a square. Consider a knight on square 4. It can move to squares 47, 51, 3, 15, 9, 41, 53, and 5, as shown below on the left. Compare the other moves to the move from square 4 to square 5. These moves can be shown as eight tetrominoes that correspond to the eight rotations and reflections on the square shown on the right.

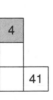

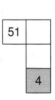

Identity

90° rotation
counterclockwise

180° rotation
counterclockwise

270° rotation
counterclockwise

Vertical
axis
reflection

Horizontal
axis
reflection

Positive
diagonal
reflection

Negative
diagonal
reflection

Pierre Fermat

Unsolved and impossible problems are usually of great interest to mathematics students. Every teacher of geometry has had experience with would-be angle trisectors, students who attempt the impossible. (See Activity 14.) When studying the Pythagorean theorem, point out that $x^2 + y^2 = z^2$ has many integer solutions for x, y, and z, such as 3, 4, 5 and 5, 12, 13. Then tell this interesting anecdote about the problem known as **Fermat's Last Theorem.**

Pierre de Fermat (1601–1665) claimed that there do not exist positive integers, x, y, and z such that $x^n + y^n = z^n$, for $n > 2$. Fermat claimed that he had discovered a proof of the impossibility of this relation but that the margin of his book was too narrow to include it. Many mathematicians throughout the ensuing centuries have struggled, unsuccessfully, trying to prove Fermat's conjecture.

In the early 1900s, a professor of mathematics in Darmstadt, Germany, Paul Wolfskehl, spent many long hours in a vain attempt to prove Fermat's Last Theorem. He was also disappointed in love, and so decided to end his life. Being a methodical man, he wrote a suicide note specifying the date and hour that he would commit the act. Within a few hours of the appointed time he decided to occupy his final hours by one last look at Fermat's Theorem. It is said that he became so engrossed once again in the problem that his appointed suicide hour passed by unnoticed, whereupon he tore up his note and began life with renewed energy. When Wolfskehl finally died in 1908 he left a will that provided 100,000 marks to the first one to prove Fermat's Theorem.

There are many ways that the creative teacher can use this story to generate interest in a classroom. For example, the story of Paul Wolfskehl can be an exciting introduction to the study of the Pythagorean theorem. Just start with a simulated newspaper headline on the chalkboard or bulletin board that states

MATHEMATICS SAVES A LIFE!

This same story has yet another happy ending. In 1997 the Wolfskehl prize, then valued at $50,000, was indeed awarded. Two years earlier, in 1995, Dr. Andrew Wiles, a British mathematician working at Princeton University, finally proved Fermat's conjecture. He spent a good part of his lifetime working on the proof, and, in its final form, it took about 200 pages to complete. The brilliant proof itself used many new mathematical methods and others only recently developed. Today, most believe that Fermat thought he actually had a proof but there was some unknown flaw in his thinking. Of course, this remains just a conjecture. But as for Fermat, his last theorem is no longer a conjecture. After more than 350 years of searching, a complete proof has been found and it is now truly a theorem. As a final note to this story, the King

Faisal Foundation in Saudi Arabia declared Professor Wiles to be the winner of the 1998 King Faisal International Prize of $200,000!

The history of mathematics is rich with such interesting anecdotes about mathematicians that can be used to generate interest in a topic under study in the classroom. Here are a few more examples.

Maria Agnesi

Maria Gaetana Agnesi (1718–1799) was a somnambulist who often solved problems in her sleep and awoke to find the completed solutions on her desk in the morning! She is probably best known for a curve, now known as the "Witch of Agnesi," that she discussed in detail. Secondary students can be asked to sketch this curve.

$$y = \frac{a^3}{a^2 + x^2}$$

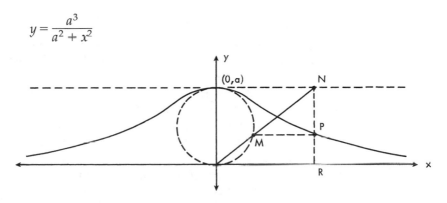

The curve is the locus of points P that may be found geometrically as follows. Draw a circle with diameter of length a that passes through the origin and the point $(0, a)$. Draw a secant from the origin that meets the circle at point M and meets the line through $(0, a)$, parallel to the x-axis, at N. Draw the segment NR perpendicular to the x-axis. Then draw a line segment through point M, parallel to the x-axis, to locate the point P.

Lorenzo Mascheroni

Lorenzo Mascheroni (1750–1800) proved that all Euclidean construction can be completed with a compass alone. (It is understood that two points determine a unique line, but that the line itself cannot be drawn.) This mathematician met Napoleon during his conquest of Italy and was challenged to show how a circle can be divided into four equal parts by compass alone. Both the story and the problem are excellent items to incorporate into a lesson for a geometry class studying constructions.

As a simple example of a Mascheroni construction, consider the problem of finding a point C, collinear with two given points A and B, such that $AB = BC$.

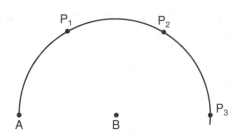

Using B as center, and AB as radius, swing an arc. Then begin at A and mark off points P_1, P_2, P_3,..., using the same radius. The point P_3 will be the required point.

Using the Internet

There are numerous sources on the Internet that mathematics teachers can use or can refer their students to use on a variety of topics. For example, there is a website that will provide information on the search for the largest known prime, with updates on an almost daily basis. Thus, as of the writing of this text, the largest known prime was $2^{3021377} - 1$ which is a number that is 909,526 digits long. Undoubtedly, by the time this text is read, a new prime will have been discovered. Apparently there are worldwide volunteers who are participating in the Great Internet Mersenne Prime Search (GIMPS) and can be reached at this website: **www.mersenne.org/prime.htm**

A number of the form $2^n - 1$, n a counting number, is called a *Mersenne number* and is called a **Mersenne prime** if $2^n - 1$ is prime. The prime number cited above happens to be the 37th known Mersenne prime.

Two very helpful websites are those of the major professional associations for mathematics teachers. Through these, readers can obtain information about the organizations themselves, as well as a very large collection of mathematics books and publications suitable for their professional use.

National Council of Teachers of Mathematics: **www.nctm.org**
Mathematical Association of America: **www.maa.org**

Birthdates of famous mathematicians can be used to motivate a discussion of their lives and works, and can often be related to the topic of the day. Using the Internet, students can find a calendar that will allow them to discover birthdates for every day of the year! A convenient source to start such a search is to use this website:

www.yahoo.com/science/mathematics/history

Following is a representative list of some of the most important mathematicians in history, together with their dates of birth.

Jan. 3   Sonya Kovalevsky (1850–1891)
Jan. 23   Davis Hilbert (1862–1943)
Feb. 19   Nicolaus Copernicus (1473–1543)
Mar. 3   Georg Cantor (1845–1918)
Mar. 14   Albert Einstein (1879–1955)
Mar. 23   Emmy Noether (1882–1935)
Apr. 1   Sophie Germain (1776–1831)
Apr. 15   Leonhard Euler (1707–1783)
Apr. 30   Karl Friedrich Gauss (1777–1855)
May 16   Maria Gaetana Agnesi (1718–1799)
May 26   Abraham De Moivre (1667–1754)
June 19   Blaise Pascal (1623–1662)
July 1   Gottfried Leibniz (1646–1716)
Aug. 5   Neils Henrick Abel (1802–1829)
Aug. 20   Pierre de Fermat (1601–1665)
Sept.17   Bernhard Riemann (1826–1866)
Oct. 25   Evariste Galois (1811–1832)
Nov. 17   August Möbius (1790–1868)
Dec. 2   Nicolai Lobachevsky (1792–1856)
Dec. 25   Isaac Newton (1642–1727)

A similar listing for major contributions in the development of computers can be of interest to students. Including two from the preceding list, the following individuals played key roles in bringing about our current age of technology. Suggest that your students find the major contributions made by each.

Howard Aiken (1900–1973)
Charles Babbage (1791–1871)
J. Presper Eckert (1919–   )
Herman Hollerith (1860–1929)
Joseph Jacquard (1752–1834)
Gottfried Leibniz (1646–1716)
Augusta Ada Byron Lovelace (1815–1852)
John Mauchly (1907–1980)
John Napier (1550–1617)
John Von Neumann (1903–1957)
Blaise Pascal (1623–1662)

Quotable Quotes

Quotations from famous mathematicians can be displayed in class and used as the basis for classroom discussion, research, and writing assignments. For example, in 387 B.C., the Greek philosopher Plato founded his famous Academy in Athens for the pursuit of philosophical and scientific inquiry. Over its door was the motto:

"Let no one ignorant of geometry enter here."

Here are several other noteworthy quotes:

"Mathematics is the queen of the sciences, and arithmetic is the queen of mathematics." (Karl Friedrich Gauss)

"God created the natural numbers; everything else is man's handiwork." (Leopold Kronecker)

"Give me a place to stand and a lever long enough and I will move the earth." (Archimedes)

"Number rules the universe." (The Pythagoreans)

"There is no royal road to geometry." (Menaechmus)

"Imagination is more important than knowledge." (Albert Einstein)

"One thing I know and that is that I know nothing." (Socrates)

"Mathematics is the only infinite human activity." (Paul Erdos)

1.3 MAKE EFFECTIVE USE OF MANIPULATIVE AIDS

The chapters that follow provide numerous suggestions for aids that can be used in the mathematics classroom to promote learning. The major emphasis throughout is on aids that the teacher can produce with a minimum of time and effort as opposed to more costly commercial products. Although many of the latter are worthwhile, most teachers of mathematics are more receptive to the use of aids if they can be quickly assembled and used.

Tower of Hanoi

The Tower of Hanoi is a famous mathematical problem that students enjoy trying to solve. Although some students can easily construct display-size models for use in class, it can be played using any three objects of different size, such as a quarter, nickel, and penny.

First explain the rules for playing. The Tower of Hanoi puzzle consists of three disks of decreasing size, with the largest on the bottom. The object of the game is to transfer the disks from one peg position to another in the fewest possible moves, using these rules:

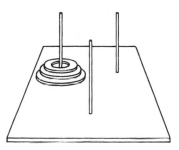

1. Move only one disk at a time.
2. No disk may be placed on top of one smaller than itself.

After explaining the rules of the game, students should be allowed to try to complete the game using three coins and three possible positions, as in the next figure. The three coins must be moved from position *A* to either *B* or *C*, using the rules given above. With three objects, only 7 moves are needed.

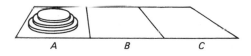

A   *B*   *C*

After students are successful at completing the game in 7 moves, let them attempt the game using four objects. This can be tried using a quarter, a nickel, a penny, and a dime. For four objects, and using the same rules, 15 steps are necessary. For five objects, 31 steps are needed. In general, for n objects, $2^n - 1$ steps are needed. See if students can discover this rule by themselves.

An ancient Hindu legend states that Brahma placed 64 disks of gold in the temple at Benares and called this the tower of Brahma. The priests were told to work continuously to transfer the disks from one pile to another in accordance with the rules set forth earlier. The legend states that the world would vanish when the last move was made. The minimum number of moves to complete this task is $2^{64} - 1$. Ask students to estimate this value and how long it would take to complete this task at the rate of one move per second. It is interesting to note that

$$2^{64} - 1 = 18{,}446{,}744{,}073{,}709{,}551{,}615$$

The world seems safe from destruction!

Paper-Folding and Cutting Activities

A sheet of paper can also be a simple, handy aid for the mathematics teacher. Paper-folding activities frequently stimulate interest in geometry as well as provide challenging problems. For example, when studying equilateral triangles, students can explore methods for constructing one by folding paper using the shorter edge as one side:

| Start with one edge as a side. | Fold the perpendicular bisector of that edge. | Locate the vertex on that bisector. | Fold through that point to complete the equilateral triangle. |

Another activity with paper might involve an informal proof, as in this illustration of the Pythagorean theorem:

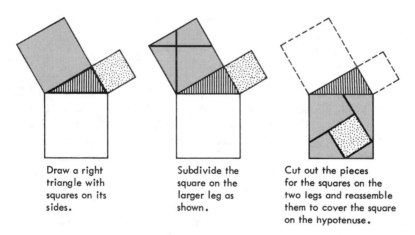

| Draw a right triangle with squares on its sides. | Subdivide the square on the larger leg as shown. | Cut out the pieces for the squares on the two legs and reassemble them to cover the square on the hypotenuse. |

At a more advanced level, the teacher can introduce the topic of finding the sum of an infinite geometric series by duplicating an experiment that is said to have been carried out by Archimedes. Begin with a square sheet of paper and consider this as having an area of one square unit. Cut the paper in half, and place one half on the desk. Cut the remaining piece in half so as to obtain two pieces, each with an area of $\frac{1}{4}$ square unit. Place one of these pieces on the desk. Continue cutting in this manner until the piece that remains in your hand is too small to handle, but imagine the process going on forever. Then note that the sum of the areas of the pieces represent

$$\frac{1}{2} + \frac{1}{4} + \frac{1}{8} + \frac{1}{16} + \frac{1}{32} + \frac{1}{64} + \frac{1}{128} + \cdots$$

which, in the limit, is equal to the original area of one square unit.

It is illuminating for students also to see this sequence of successive sums appear on the screen of a graphing calculator. Thus have them begin with the sum $\frac{1}{2} + \frac{1}{4}$. Then add and enter the sums obtained by adding $\frac{1}{8}, \frac{1}{16}, \frac{1}{32}, \ldots$, in order, and note the partial sums as they approach 1. The screen may look like this:

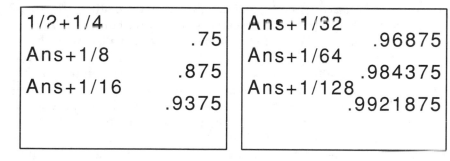

```
1/2+1/4
            .75
Ans+1/8
            .875
Ans+1/16
          .9375
```

```
Ans+1/32
            .96875
Ans+1/64
          .984375
Ans+1/128
         .9921875
```

By the time they have added the first twenty terms in this geometric sequence, the sum to six decimal places is already 0.999999. These approaches provide the necessary motivation to introduce the formula for the sum of any such infinite geometric series where a is the first term, r is the common ratio, and $|r| < 1$:

$$S = a + ar + ar^2 + ar^3 + ar^4 + \cdots = \frac{a}{1-r}$$

For the series shown at the top of the next page,

$$a = \frac{1}{2}, r = \frac{1}{2}, \text{ and } S = \frac{\frac{1}{2}}{1 - \frac{1}{2}} = 1$$

The reader should attempt to expand this activity by dividing the original unit square into thirds. Place two of these pieces on the desk and cut the remaining piece into thirds again. Continue in this manner so that each of the two piles has an area equal to the sum

$$\frac{1}{3} + \frac{1}{9} + \frac{1}{27} + \frac{1}{81} + \dots$$

Since there are two equal piles, each must have one half of the original area of 1. Hence, the sum shown must equal $\frac{1}{2}$. Now try to generalize this procedure by considering divisions of the original piece of paper into fourths, fifths, and so on.

Using a Piece of String

What uses can the teacher find for a piece of string in the mathematics class? Come to class with a piece stuffed in your pocket and start pulling it out. Ask each student to guess at the length before he or she sees it all. Obviously, the answers will vary widely. As the rest is pulled out for them to see, students again guess at the length. The answers will still vary, probably more than the students themselves would expect. Next they are asked to guess how many times it will fit around a dollar bill and a basketball. Once the actual length is given, the ends are tied together and students are asked for the dimensions of the largest square and equilateral triangle that can be formed from it. As a last activity, the teacher can go from one student to the next throughout the entire class asking for a different set of dimensions for a rectangle or an isosceles triangle that can be formed with the string. With a simple piece of string, students can become actively involved and motivated to a further study of measurement. See page 221 for a specific application with classroom results.

1.4 MAKE PROVISIONS FOR STUDENT DISCOVERY

Conflicting points of view exist concerning the role of discovery in the teaching of mathematics. Some claim that skills and concepts are best learned when students are allowed to make significant discoveries on their own. On the other hand, others feel that many students, especially slow learners, learn best by means of a teacher-oriented show-and-tell approach. Regardless of which position one takes, it is clear that discovery techniques can be used effectively to stimulate and maintain interest in mathematics. Furthermore, such approaches help to develop the type of creativity and originality that is important for a student's future success in mathematics.

The famous French mathematician René Descartes (1596–1650) concluded his book *La Geometrie* with this comment:

I hope that posterity will judge me kindly, not only as to the things which I have explained, but also as to those which I have intentionally omitted so as to leave to others the pleasure of discovery.

In our desire to impart knowledge to our students, we must not fail to make provisions for them to participate in and to enjoy this all-important pleasure.

Actually there are two different types of discovery approaches that can be used in the classroom: *guided discovery* and *creative discovery.*

Guided Discovery

Most classroom situations lend themselves best to the guided discovery approach, in which the teacher leads a class along the right path, allowing for discussion, but rejecting incorrect attempts, asking leading questions, and introducing key ideas as necessary. It is a cooperative venture that becomes more and more exciting as the final result comes into view.

The following three examples should serve to illustrate guided discovery approaches that can be utilized in the classroom with most students.

Example 1. A class is asked to find this sum:

$$\frac{1}{1\cdot 2} + \frac{1}{2\cdot 3} + \frac{1}{3\cdot 4} + \cdots + \frac{1}{99\cdot 100}$$

The task appears to be tedious, if not impossible. The teacher suggests that one problem-solving strategy is to consider a smaller version of the problem. Thus the class is led to consider the first term, the first two terms, the first three terms, and so on, looking for a pattern in the successive sums:

$$\frac{1}{1\cdot 2} = \frac{1}{2}$$

$$\frac{1}{1\cdot 2} + \frac{1}{2\cdot 3} = \frac{2}{3}$$

$$\frac{1}{1\cdot 2} + \frac{1}{2\cdot 3} + \frac{1}{3\cdot 4} = \frac{3}{4}$$

At this point the teacher asks the class to guess the sum of the first four terms, pointing out the pattern if necessary. Hopefully there will be members of the class who will guess that it will be $\frac{4}{5}$. This answer is confirmed by actual computation. Finally, the class should be ready to guess that the answer to the given problem is $\frac{99}{100}$. Of course, it is important to point out that this is just a conjecture and not a proof. Note that in this case if the sums were to be found in decimal form, using a calculator, the revealing pattern would never have been seen.

We can prove this sum of $\frac{99}{100}$ by elementary methods. First we need to recognize these relationships, which also lend themselves to discovery approaches.

$$\frac{1}{1\cdot 2} = \frac{1}{2} = \frac{1}{1} - \frac{1}{2} \qquad \frac{1}{2\cdot 3} = \frac{1}{6} = \frac{1}{2} - \frac{1}{3} \qquad \frac{1}{3\cdot 4} = \frac{1}{12} = \frac{1}{3} - \frac{1}{4}$$

In general, we have the following:

$$\frac{1}{n(n+1)} = \frac{1}{n} - \frac{1}{n+1}$$

which can easily be established by combining the terms on the right. Now we can write the given series as follows:

$$\left(1 - \frac{1}{2}\right) + \left(\frac{1}{2} - \frac{1}{3}\right) + \left(\frac{1}{3} - \frac{1}{4}\right) + \cdots + \left(\frac{1}{98} - \frac{1}{99}\right) + \left(\frac{1}{99} - \frac{1}{100}\right)$$

Finally, note that every term except the first and last subtract out, giving this sum:

$$1 - \frac{1}{100} = \frac{99}{100}$$

Example 2. As has already been stated, it is important that students recognize that a conjecture is not a proof, and that without a proof there is no guarantee that a pattern will continue forever. Thus it is worthwhile to occasionally display a pattern that fails after a certain point. One of the most dramatic ones concerns the maximum number of regions into which a circle can be divided by connecting points on the circle. Consider the following apparent pattern:

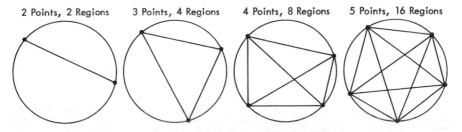

2 Points, 2 Regions   3 Points, 4 Regions   4 Points, 8 Regions   5 Points, 16 Regions

In summary:

Number of Points	Number of Regions
2	2
3	4
4	8
5	16

What is your conjecture about the number of regions expected for six points connected in all possible ways? Test your conjecture on another circle. The apparent answer is 32. However, much to everyone's surprise, the maximum number of regions possible with six points proves to be only 31! In general, the maximum number of regions that can be obtained for n points can be found by this expression:

$$\frac{n^4 - 6n^3 + 23n^2 - 18n + 24}{24}$$

Example 3. Assume you earn $1 on the first day of a job. The second day you are paid $2, the third day $4, the fourth day $8, and so on. Each day, our salary is twice that of the preceding day. You plan to stay on the job for 15 days and wish to know what your total earnings will be. The specific amounts for each day could be listed, and their sum found, but you ask the class to discover a method for finding the sum without actually adding the 15 amounts.

An important problem-solving strategy is to consider a small portion of a problem at a time, as was done in Example 1. That is, consider what the total salary will be for 1 day, 2 days, 3 days, 4 days, and then for 5 days.

For 1 day	For 2 days	For 3 days	For 4 days	For 5 days
1	1	1	1	1
Total 1	2	2	2	2
	Total 3	4	4	4
		Total 7	8	8
			Total 15	16
				Total 31

At this point the class is asked to observe relationships. With teacher assistance they should note these facts:

The salary for 2 days ($3) is $1 less than the salary for the third day ($4).

The salary for 3 days ($7) is $1 less than the salary for the fourth day ($8).

The salary for 4 days ($15) is $1 less than the salary for the fifth day ($16).

The salary for 5 days ($31) is $1 less than the salary for the sixth day ($32).

The discovery is made that the total salary for n days is 1 less than that for the $(n + 1)$ day. To find the salary for 15 days, add

$$1 + 2 + 4 + 8 + 16 + 32 + 64 + 128 + 256 + 512$$
$$+ 1024 + 2048 + 4096 + 8192 + 16{,}384$$

This sum is 1 less than the next term: $2 \times 16{,}384 - 1 = 32{,}767$. Thus the total salary for 15 days is $32,767.

At another level of instruction, students might note that we are dealing here with powers of 2:

Day 1	1	2^0	
Day 2	2	2^1	
Day 3	4	2^2	The sum of the entries for
Day 4	8	2^3	the first n days is $2^n - 1$.
$\vdots$			
Day n	...	2^{n-1}	
Day $n + 1$	...	2^n	

Creative Discovery

Many mathematics textbooks claim to utilize a discovery approach. However, it is difficult to do so in a text where final results must be stated. Thus most discovery techniques must come about through the direction of the classroom teacher. However, at its purest level we have creative discovery, wherein a teacher presents a situation to a class and allows the students to explore on their own, using only their intuition and past learning, with little or no guided direction. Such a *cooperative learning* approach is especially well suited to the gifted student and provides the type of experience that is necessary for later independent research.

Essentially, the creative discovery approach says

Here's a situation . . . explore it.

Most students are disturbed by such an instruction because it is foreign to the traditional approaches that they have encountered in the past. Here are several examples of this approach.

Example 1. Students are given this triangular array of numbers:

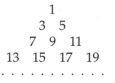

They are then asked to make discoveries about it, without any further direction. Among the many discoveries that might be made is the fact that the sum of the numbers in each successive row represents the cubes of the counting numbers: 1, 8, 27, 64, . . . Can you make some other discoveries?

Example 2. Consider this table of counting numbers:

1	2	3	4	5	6	7	8	9	10
11	12	13	14	15	16	17	18	19	20
21	22	23	24	25	26	27	28	29	30
31	32	33	34	35	36	37	38	39	40
41	42	43	44	45	46	47	48	49	50
51	52	53	54	55	56	57	58	59	60
61	62	63	64	65	66	67	68	69	70
71	72	73	74	75	76	77	78	79	80
81	82	83	84	85	86	87	88	89	90
91	92	93	94	95	96	97	98	99	100

Students are given the table and asked to see what discoveries they can make. A few of the possibilities are given below; the reader will be asked to search for others in the exercises.

1. The multiples of 9 fall on a diagonal line, as do the multiples of 11. Locate all the numbers the sum of whose digits is equal to 10.
2. For any rectangular array of numbers within the table, the sums of the entries in opposite corners are equal. That is,

⟨72⟩	73	74	⟨75⟩
82	83	84	85
⟨92⟩	93	94	⟨95⟩

$$72 + 95 = 167 = 75 + 92$$

Does this rule work for the entire table?

3. For any square array of nine numbers, the sum of all entries is equal to nine times the number in the center of the square.

47	48	49
57	⟨58⟩	59
67	68	69

$$47 + 48 + 49 + 57 + 58 + 59 + 67 + 68 + 69 = 522 = 9 \times 58$$

Can you find a similar rule for any square array of 25 numbers?

Example 3. A more sophisticated example of the creative discovery approach can be given to an eleventh- or twelfth-grade class that has already studied a unit of work on arithmetic and geometric series. The teacher proceeds to tell the class about the infinite tree. This tree looks like any other tree but grows in a very interesting manner. The first day the tree grows 1 foot. The second day two new branches grow, each $\frac{1}{2}$ foot in length and at right angles to each other. The next day two new branches appear at each terminal point, again at right angles to one another but only $\frac{1}{4}$ foot in length. This continues forever! This is what the tree looks like during the first four days of growth.

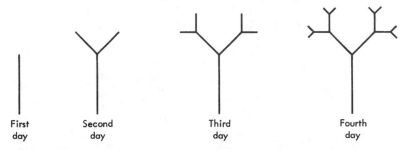

First day   Second day   Third day   Fourth day

At this point in the typical mathematics class the teacher would ask the students to prove certain given relationships. But using a creative discovery approach, the teacher terminates the story of the infinite tree by asking the students to discover whatever they can about it, offering no further clues or direction. Among the many interesting items that students may discover, using only right-triangle relationships and knowledge of geometric series, is that the tree has a limiting finite height of $\frac{4 + \sqrt{2}}{3}$ feet and a limiting breadth of $\frac{2(\sqrt{2} + 1)}{3}$ feet, even though there are an infinite number of branches with a total length that is also infinite. (See Exercise 9.) This can be a difficult problem for most students, so it is well to start the process in class. Use this sequence of figures to show total heights for each of the first four days. The Pythagorean theorem is used to find the vertical heights from the diagonal branches.

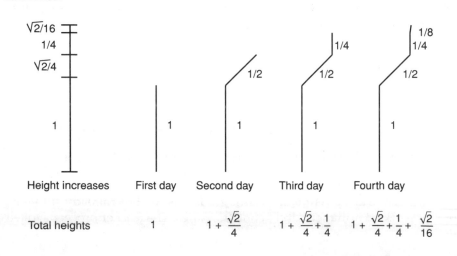

Total heights	1	$1 + \dfrac{\sqrt{2}}{4}$	$1 + \dfrac{\sqrt{2}}{4} + \dfrac{1}{4}$	$1 + \dfrac{\sqrt{2}}{4} + \dfrac{1}{4} + \dfrac{\sqrt{2}}{16}$

Continuing in this manner, the limiting height can be expressed as

$$1 + \frac{\sqrt{2}}{4} + \frac{1}{4} + \frac{\sqrt{2}}{16} + \frac{1}{16} + \frac{\sqrt{2}}{64} + \frac{1}{64} + \cdots$$

which can be written as the sum of these two infinite geometric series:

$$\left(1 + \frac{1}{4} + \frac{1}{16} + \cdots\right) + \sqrt{2}\left(\frac{1}{4} + \frac{1}{16} + \frac{1}{64} + \cdots\right)$$

A similar problem is that of the infinite snowflake. It hits the ground in the shape of an equilateral triangle. Thereafter, each second a new equilateral triangle emerges in the middle third of each side, continuing forever. This is what the first three stages look like:

Once again the student is asked to discover whatever he or she can about the infinite snowflake, with no teacher direction. The first task is to visualize how the snowflake continues to change, from stage to stage, ad infinitum. We now know that the limit figure for this process is based on a *fractal*. Chapter 8 deals in detail with similar iteration activities and the resulting fractal patterns.

Among the many interesting facts that can be discovered about this changing snowflake curve is that there is no limiting perimeter but that there is a limiting area, $\frac{2}{5}n^2\sqrt{3}$ square units, where n is the length of the side of the original equilateral triangle. (See Exercise 10.)

In closing, it should be noted that the creative discovery approach is especially well suited to gifted students. The average or slow learner can seldom function without any teacher direction at all. For the latter group, it is important that we do not deny them the pleasures of discovery that can be attained through teacher direction.

1.5   END THE PERIOD WITH SOMETHING SPECIAL

This bit of advice is not always easy to follow inasmuch as the supply of truly spectacular items is limited. However, through the years a teacher should be able to collect enough interesting material to avoid ending classes in the traditional way: "Begin your homework." With less than five minutes left in the period, this suggestion is seldom effective nor met with enthusiasm!

Introducing some special item during the last few minutes of a class can make students regret that it has come to a close. Hopefully they will walk out talking about the exciting things that happen in their mathematics period . . . and hopefully their enthusiasm will carry over to the next day when they will be eager to return for more.

The Game of 50

The Game of 50 is designed for two players. An effective way to introduce the game is to announce that you are the world champion at this game, and that you are willing to have a student challenge you. Then allow one or two students to compete with you during the last few minutes of the period each day for several days. Continue until someone in the class notes the pattern you use for winning and is able to win the game.

Rules for Playing
The game is played using the numbers 1, 2, 3, 4, 5, and 6. The two players alternate in selecting numbers, and the first to reach 50 wins. As each new number is selected, it is added to the sum of the previously selected numbers. For example, if the student goes first and selects 3, the teacher might then select 6, to give a sum of 9. If the student then selects 5, the total is 14, and it becomes the teacher's turn to go. The game continues in this manner until one player becomes the winner by reaching 50.

Strategy
Actually this game is an excellent way to illustrate the problem-solving strategy of working backwards. Analysis of the game shows that you can always reach 50 if you first reach 43. (Regardless of what number your opponent selects then, you can choose a number to obtain 50.) Working backwards, you can reach 43 if you can get to 36. Continuing in this way, the following "winning numbers" are obtained:

$$1, 8, 15, 22, 29, 36, 43, 50$$

Thus the strategy for winning is to go first and begin with 1. Thereafter, select the complement of your opponent's number relative to 7. That is, if your opponent selects 4, you choose 3; if your opponent selects 2, you choose 5; and so forth. If your opponent goes first and does not know the rules for winning, choose your numbers so as to reach one of the winning numbers as soon as you can.

Extensions

Many variations of this game are possible. A similar game is played by using a set of 16 cards consisting of the four aces, four 2's, four 3's, and four 4's. (An ace counts as 1.)

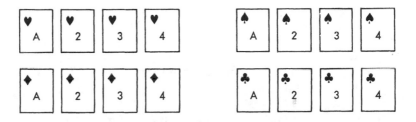

Players alternate selecting one card at a time from the pile of 16 cards, face up, without replacements. As before, cumulative sums are kept. The winner is the first person to select a card that brings the total to exactly 22, or forces the opposing player to go over 22. The set of winning numbers for this game is

$$2, 7, 12, 17, 22$$

The strategy for winning is to go first and begin with 2. Thereafter, select the complement of your opponent's number relative to 5. That is, if your opponent picks 4, you choose 1, and so forth. However, in this case this is not a foolproof strategy because the number of cards is limited. Suppose that your opponent repeatedly chooses 3. This would force you to repeatedly choose 2 and you would run out of 2's prior to reaching the objective number of 22. Can you consider alternative strategies for such a situation?

Mathemagic

Many spectacular things can be done by embellishing rather simple mathematical tricks or patterns. Several examples are given below, others are inserted throughout the text, and still others may be found by a careful search of the available literature.

Example 1. A student is asked to go to the board. With the teacher's back turned so as not to see the work, the student is given these instructions:

Write a two-digit number between 50 and 100.
Add 76 to this number.
Cross out the digit in the hundreds place.
Add the crossed out number to the remaining two-digit number.
Subtract this result from the original number.

These are the steps if a student were to begin with the number 83:

Original number: 83
Add 76:   + 76
                                                   159

Cross out and add: $\cancel{1}$59; $59 + 1 = 60$

                                                    83
Subtract from original number: - 60
Result: 23

The interesting thing about this trick is that the final outcome will always be 23, regardless of the number selected by the student, provided that the stated steps are followed. However, it is certainly not very spectacular to conclude by announcing that the final outcome is 23, as interesting as this may be. A far more dramatic approach is the following.

Before coming to class use the edge of a damp piece of soap and write 23 on the back of your hand. When this dries it becomes completely invisible to the student. In class, after completing the puzzle, ask a member of the class to write the final outcome on a piece of paper and fold it. Then carefully burn the paper in some suitable receptacle and wait until the ashes cool off. Finally pick up the ashes and wipe them on the back of your hand, whereupon, as if by magic, the number 23 is clearly outlined for all to see! It has been the experience of the authors that this trick is one that students continue to talk about for many weeks.

As an alternative ending to this trick, use lemon juice and a toothpick to write 23 on a clear sheet of acetate. This will be invisible when placed on an overhead projector. However when ashes are rubbed over the acetate, the number 23 will magically appear!

Example 2. Have each student in the class write a four-digit number, using four different digits. Then form three additional *cyclic numbers* by moving the digit in the thousands place to the hundreds, tens, and units place. Here is an example, using as the initial number 8234:

8234
4823
3482
2348

Have students find the sum of their four numbers.

(For the example above, the sum is 18,887.)

Find the sum of the digits in the original number.

$$(8 + 2 + 3 + 4 = 17)$$

Divide the sum of the numbers by the sum of the digits.

$$(18,887 \div 17 = 1111)$$

Surprisingly, regardless of the original number chosen, the sum will always be 1111!

Example 3. This little trick can attract some real attention. Have all students participate.

STEPS	ILLUSTRATION
1. Begin by writing a three-digit number with all digits different.	257
2. Form all possible two-digit numbers from this number.	25
	27
	52
	57
	72
	75
3. Find the sum of those two-digit numbers.	308
4. Divide the result by the sum of the three original digits.	$2 + 5 + 7 = 14$
	$\begin{array}{r} 22 \\ 14\overline{)308} \\ 28 \\ \hline 28 \\ 28 \\ \hline \end{array}$
The answer will always be 22!	

Here is why this trick works.

Let the number be *abc* with a value of $100a + 10b + c$.

There are six possible two-digit numbers.

$$10a + b$$
$$10a + c$$
$$10b + a$$
$$10b + c$$
$$10c + a$$
$$10c + b$$

The sum simplifies to 22 times $a + b + c$. So obviously, division by the sum of the digits must give 22.

$$20(a + b + c) + 2(a + b + c) = 22(a + b + c)$$

$$\frac{22(a + b + c)}{a + b + c} = 22$$

Introduce this trick and discuss it when studying factoring or the addition of polynomials. Or use it just for fun and challenge your students to find out why it works.

Mathematical Fallacies

Fallacies are generally of interest to mathematics students. An interesting way to end a class period is to announce the recent discovery of a proof that $1 = 2$! This is a standard fallacy that appears in many algebra texts.

Let $a = b$
Then $a \cdot a = a \cdot b$; that is, $a^2 = ab$
By subtraction, $a^2 - b^2 = ab - b^2$
By factoring, $(a - b)(a + b) = b(a - b)$
By division, $a + b = b$
Thus, $b + b = b$ since $a = b$
Finally, $2b = b$ and $2 = 1$

Of course, the fallacy lies in the fact that we divided by 0 in the form of $a - b$. This can lead to a well-motivated discussion of why division by zero is not permissible.

Problem of the Week

An interesting way to end a period is with a Problem of the Day or Problem of the Week. This should be some challenging problem or puzzle with a solution that is not immediately obvious. Students then are given a day or a week to solve it. Reward the first person to submit a correct solution, and provide honorable mention to everyone who submits a solution. Here is one problem that has proven to be quite challenging to students of all ages:

Find the pattern:

$$3 * 4 \rightarrow 5$$
$$4 * 7 \rightarrow 1$$
$$8 * 4 \rightarrow 0$$
$$1 * 2 \rightarrow 9$$

The challenge is to discover how the third number is obtained from the first two numbers. If you know the pattern, then you will be able to complete these statements:

$$5 * 5 \rightarrow ? \qquad 4 * 1 \rightarrow ? \qquad 6 * 2 \rightarrow ?$$

As a tantalizing hint, note that this problem first appeared in a third-grade text! (What computational skills do third graders possess?)

Here are several other problems that can be used as puzzles of the day or of the week.

1. Discover the pattern and find the next two numbers in this sequence:

$$12, 1, 1, 1, 2, 1, \ldots$$

After you have tried various arithmetic possibilities to no avail, consider what connections this sequence may have to other daily activities or experiences.

2. Find the pattern for generating the figures in this chart:

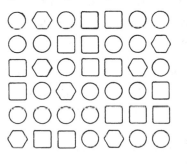

1.6 CONCLUSION

As originally anticipated, a chapter on "The Art of Teaching" is in reality both an impossible and an endless task at the same time! The list of topics that one might include is long and yet can never be all-inclusive. Indeed, an excellent exercise for the reader is to attempt to constantly add to this initial list of items.

Throughout this discussion the personal qualities of the teacher have been bypassed. The easiest way to consider this item is to ask a group of secondary school students to submit an unsigned list of what they consider to be the five most important qualities of a good teacher. The results are predictable. High on the list will be such items as enthusiasm, sincerity, sense of humor, empathy, imagination, and competence. In addition, in their own words, they will say that they like teachers who like to teach.

Thus by our every action we must show our students that we like to teach mathematics. Enthusiasm is contagious, and when teachers demonstrate a sincere interest in both their students and their subject, their classes will seldom ask the embarrassing question, "What good is all this?" The authors of this book sincerely hope that the material in the chapters to follow will help the teacher of mathematics to teach in an exciting, meaningful, and memorable manner.

EXERCISES

1. Show how to use Gauss' method, described on page 5, to find the sum of the first n counting numbers.

2. Test the formula $n^2 - n + 41$ for $n = 1, 2, 3, 4$, and 5. Are the results prime? Try it again for 10, 15, and 20. Are the results still prime? Can you find a value for n for which the formula does *not* produce a prime number?

3. Christian Goldbach (1690–1764) conjectured that every even integer greater than 2 can be expressed as the sum of two prime numbers. To date, this is still an unsolved problem. Show that his conjecture is true for even numbers from 4 through 50.

4. It has been conjectured, but not yet proved, that every odd integer greater than 5 can be expressed as the sum of three prime numbers, not necessarily distinct. Show that this is so for odd integers from 7 through 35.

5. Is has been proved that there is at least one prime number between any counting number n, $n > 1$, and $2n$. Verify this for five specific replacements of n.

6. Explain why the "23" trick described on page 25 works.

7. For the table of counting numbers on page 21, prove algebraically that the product of the entries in diagonally opposite corners of a square array of nine numbers will always differ by 40. Then consider square arrays of 16 numbers. Show that the difference of the products of the entries in opposite corners is constant. What is that constant?

8. Two numbers are said to be **amicable** if the sum of the proper divisors of one number is equal to the other number. (The proper divisors of a number are all the factors of that number except the number itself. For example, the proper divisors of 6 are 1, 2, and 3.) Show that 220 and 284 are amicable numbers. In 1866, a pair of amicable numbers that had not been discovered previously was found by Nicolo Paganini, a 16-year-old boy in Italy. Show that 1184 and 1210 are amicable numbers.

9. For the infinite tree described on page 22, show that the limiting height is $\dfrac{4 + \sqrt{2}}{3}$ feet, and the limiting breadth is $\dfrac{2(\sqrt{2} + 1)}{3}$ feet.

10. For the infinite snowflake described on page 23, show that there is no limiting perimeter but that the limiting area is $\dfrac{2\sqrt{3}}{5}n^2$ square units, where n is the length of a side of the original triangle.

11. Discover the pattern and find the next two numbers in this sequence:

$$0, 6, 20, 42, \ldots$$

12. Look for a pattern and then find the number that should be used in place of the question mark in the following array of numbers:

$$
\begin{array}{cccc}
7 & 4 & 2 & 6 \\
8 & 2 & 4 & 3 \\
5 & 3 & 5 & 7 \\
9 & ? & 2 & 8
\end{array}
$$

13. Consider the distance between two points A and B to be one unit. Show how to use a Mascheroni construction to find a point C such that $AC = \sqrt{3}$.

14. Prepare an ordinary multiplication table for the facts through 10×10. Then discover a way to find the sum of all the entries in the table without actually adding them. (*Hint:* Use the strategy of exploring a simpler, related problem first. Thus consider a table of facts through $2 \times 2, 3 \times 3, 4 \times 4$, etc.)

ACTIVITIES

1. Prepare a set of five questions that can be used in a junior high school mathematics class to promote guessing, and the subsequent discovery of an answer. If possible, test these items in an actual class situation.

2. Consider a ninth-grade general mathematics class of slow learners, and prepare an appropriate set of five questions that promote guessing and then computation of an answer.

3. Prepare a collection of historical anecdotes about mathematicians that could be used in a mathematics classroom to motivate students. Present one of these to your class.

4. Adequate planning is essential to the success of a lesson. Develop a one-period lesson plan for a mathematics class at a designated level that features a discovery approach for a particular concept or skill. List the objectives of your lesson and indicate the manner in which you can evaluate the outcome.

5. Compile a description of at least five different ways that a piece of paper can be used in the mathematics classroom as a visual aid. (Do not neglect graph paper.) Demonstrate one of these to your class.

6. Visit several mathematics classes at different levels of instruction and ask the students to prepare a list of what they consider to be the five most important qualities of a good teacher. Then summarize the results in order of the most frequently mentioned items.

7. Prepare a collection of at least 15 problems or puzzles that can be used effectively to start a mathematics period in an interesting way.

8. Prepare a list of at least 15 challenging problems that can be used as the "Problem of the Week" in a middle school or a senior high school mathematics class.

9. Prepare a collection of arithmetic, algebraic, and geometric fallacies, and present one of these to your class.

10. Variation of the method of reviewing homework assignments is important in order to maintain interest in this portion of a lesson. List at least five different ways that a homework assignment can be reviewed. Be sure to consider the time of the period when the review is to take place.

11. Prepare a report on the activities of several famous mathematicians, both living and dead, male and female. One excellent source of information is a 1996 publication of the National Council of Teachers of Mathematics entitled *Celebrating Women in Mathematics and Science*. Also see the 1995 publication of the Mathematical Association of America entitled *She Does Math*, a collection of real-life problems from women on the job.

12. Describe two distinct problems, one that is suitable for a guided discovery approach and the other that lends itself to a creative discovery approach.

13. Revise the rules given on page 24 for "The Game of 50" to have 100 as the goal. Develop a strategy for winning, and then play the game with some members of your class to demonstrate the winning strategy.

14. Prepare a report on the three famous problems of antiquity: trisection of an angle, duplication of a cube, and squaring of a circle.

15. Contact the National Council of Teachers of Mathematics by using the website given on page 10. Report on any news stories that they are currently featuring, especially the Standards 2000 Project. If you have an e-mail address, sign up for NCTM's *WebNews*, a free service that will provide information on news of interest to teachers of mathematics.

16. Read and report on the book *Fermat's Enigma* by Simon Singh, New York: Walker and Company, 1997.

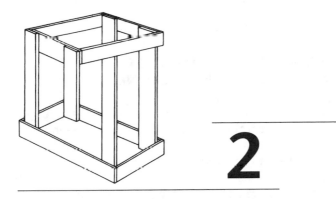

2

MOTIVATING
MATHEMATICAL
LEARNING

Almost every mathematics teacher will agree on the importance of proper motivation for the teaching of mathematics. Students, except for those who seem to have a natural love for the subject, need to have their interest stimulated through suitable teaching techniques and procedures. Only by doing so can we avoid problems such as math anxiety, which has been prevalent for many years.

Students work most effectively if they are truly interested in the subject at hand. However, it is difficult for most teachers to locate a supply of interesting materials and ideas. Many teachers become so involved with the routines of presenting their subject matter that they lack the necessary time and energy to search for motivational items. Nevertheless, there is an abundant supply available; this chapter presents a small sampling that will hopefully encourage the reader to search for additional similar ideas.

The suggestions that follow in this chapter and in subsequent chapters may be used in the classroom in many different ways. Some are helpful to introduce a specific topic, whereas others are designed to show applications of a unit already studied. Many of them are intended for use during the first or last few minutes of a period—to start the class off with a bang and/or to maintain students' attention during those last five minutes before the bell. They are all designed to help develop the idea that mathematics can be both interesting and fun. Hopefully, their use will make students look forward to the mathematics class and feel sorry to see the period end!

2.1 PROVIDE OPPORTUNITIES
FOR GUESSING AND ESTIMATING

We need to focus on the role of students in the learning process, as suggested by constructivist and cooperative learning approaches. Thus it is essential to allow students to become actively involved in a lesson, to discover information on their own, and to connect topics under study to previously learned material and to everyday life situations.

As an interesting example to begin a lesson, consider walking into class with an attache case and asking the students whether or not they think that you could fit one million dollars into the case. First have them vote: yes or no! Then break the class into small groups to discuss the situation and to decide what further information they might need to solve the problem, and where they could find that information. For example, they would need to know the answers for such items as:

(a) the dimensions of the attache case
(b) the largest denomination of the bills that they could use
(c) the dimensions of the bills

Students will eventually discover, possibly at a bank, that a one hundred dollar bill is the largest bill now allowed in circulation, a fact that not too many people know.

Armed with all of this information, students may need to make a scale drawing to see how the bills can be stacked in the attache case and thus arrive at a suitable estimate of the amount of money that can be placed in it. This is an example of a problem whose answer is not generally known, but can be found through a group effort by obtaining the necessary information and using it wisely.

Allowing students the opportunity to guess an answer to a problem not only serves as a strong motivational approach to teaching, but can actually assist with the discovery of a solution. The late mathematician George Polya, famous for his work on problem solving, has said that

"Mathematics in the making consists of guesses."

In order to make a discovery, it is first necessary to make a guess . . . and the guess may be hasty; indeed it should be. These guesses then need to be followed by verification, and this is the hard part of mathematics, the proof in support of a guess. But proof is also the least imaginative part of the process; it is the original intuitive guess that is the creative part of mathematics.

Most adults are afraid to take a guess for fear of being wrong. On the other hand, most adolescents are ready and eager to guess and the teacher should capitalize on this by providing suitable opportunities for intuitive guessing to take place in the classroom.

It is important that students be given sufficient time to formulate guesses and discuss these in class before attempting to find a correct answer through computation. Unless time is taken for this intuitive discussion, the topic serves only to provide a vehicle for computation, and the motivational aspects are lost. Consider, for example, the following problem that could be posed at the start or end of a period in a junior high school class:

Look at this piece of paper that I am holding.

I'm going to put it on the floor and add another piece so as to have two pieces.

Now I'll add two more pieces so as to have four pieces.

Then I'll add four more pieces so as to have eight pieces.

I'll continue this doubling process so as to have 16, 32, etc. pieces.

Assume that I continue this doubling process for 50 times. How high would the pile of paper be?

As indicated in Chapter 1, if the teacher immediately turns to the task of finding an answer by computation, the problem loses all interest to the student. Rather, one should urge students to guess and allow the class to establish the range between the least and the greatest answers given. After the heated discussion that can be expected to ensue, the teacher can encourage suggestions for the arithmetical procedures needed to find the correct answer. This can be done in class if the question is used at the start of a period to motivate a review lesson on computation, or it can be assigned as homework if the problem is given at the end of the period to stimulate interest in mathematics.

Students should be led to realize that in this case, they have insufficient information because they do not know the thickness of the pieces of paper. At this point tell them to assume that the paper was 0.003 inch thick. Then an estimate of the answer can be obtained as follows.

First find the answer in inches.

$$0.003 \times 2^{50} = 0.003 \times 2^{10} \times 2^{10} \times 2^{10} \times 2^{10} \times 2^{10}$$

Since $2^{10} = 1024$, we can estimate 2^{10} as 1000 and write the product as

$$0.003 \times 1000 \times 1000 \times 1000 \times 1000 \times 1000 = 3,000,000,000,000$$

To change this number of inches to feet and then to miles, we need to divide by 12 and by 5280. As an estimate, divide by 10 and 5000:

$$\frac{3,000,000,000,000}{10 \times 5000} = 60,000,000 \text{ miles}$$

Few students will fail to be astounded at this result! Most will recognize the value of this process as a means of obtaining a reasonable estimate of the correct solution. (To the nearest mile, the actual answer is 53,309,562 miles.)

Additional Examples

The following items are representative of the many questions that are suitable to invite guesses, promote discussion and estimation, and motivate students to perform the computation necessary to establish answers. Most of the suggestions offered here are particularly worthwhile for use with groups of slow learners in general mathematics classes inasmuch as these youngsters very much enjoy making guesses and can be stimulated to find answers by appropriate computational procedures. In each case, guess first and then compute.

1. What is the length in inches of a diameter of a penny?
   (a) $\frac{3}{8}$ (b) $\frac{1}{2}$ (c) $\frac{5}{8}$ (d) $\frac{3}{4}$ (e) $\frac{7}{8}$

2. Approximately how many pennies are there in one pound of pennies?
   (a) 100 (b) 150 (c) 200 (d) 250 (e) 300

3. How many pennies must be stacked one on top of the other so that the height of the pile will be equal to the height of a quarter standing on edge?
   (a) 4 (b) 8 (c) 12 (d) 16 (e) 20

4. Estimate which of the following shows the size of a penny.

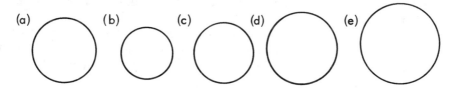

5. How much is a stack of pennies 10 miles high worth?
6. Estimate the dimensions for a box in the shape of a cube that would be just large enough to hold one million pennies.

2.2 MAKE USE OF "MATHEMAGICAL" NOVELTIES

Many motivational ideas are based on "tricks" that can be justified through relatively simple mathematical procedures. Here is an example, together with its mathematical justification.

THE TEACHER SAYS:	THE TEACHER THINKS:
Think of a number.	n
Double the number.	$2n$
Add 7.	$2n + 7$
Subtract 1.	$2n + 6$
Divide by 2.	$n + 3$
Subtract the number you originally started with.	3

At this point everyone in the class is thinking of the number 3. The teacher can then announce that this number is 3, or can continue with several additional operations to arrive at a special number, such as that day's date. This type of activity is very worthwhile to generate interest in mathematics, but it can specifically be used to introduce a unit of work on variables as well as to show an application of the use of variables in algebra

The following collection of mathematical tricks is illustrative of the type suitable for use in the classroom for purposes of motivation. In each case, the reader is invited to discover why the trick works as it does. Most of these explanations are within the grasp of average secondary school students, but even where they are not, it is still worthwhile to use the trick as a means of creating and maintaining interest.

Example 1.

INSTRUCTIONS	ILLUSTRATION
Write a two-digit number between 50 and 100.	78
Add 54.	+ 54
	132
Cross out the hundreds digit, and add it to the remaining two-digit number.	132; 32 + 1 = 33
Subtract your result from the number with which you started.	78
	− 33
The result will always be 45.	45

The final outcome depends upon the number added in the second step. Merely subtract this number from 99 to determine the outcome. In this example, 54 was added in the second step, so the result must be 45. If 84 were to be added in the second step instead of 54, the final result would be 15, regardless of the number between 50 and 100 that was chosen at the start.

In these next tricks, the participant must give the teacher certain information at a given time. Thereafter the teacher uses this information to determine some special number. Often such tricks are used to guess a person's age, as in the next item.

Example 2.

INSTRUCTIONS	ILLUSTRATION
Think of your age (or any other number greater than 9).	14
Multiply by 10.	$14 \times 10 = 140$
From this number subtract the product of any one-digit number and 9. That is, subtract some multiple of 9 from 9 through 81.	$\begin{array}{r} 140 \\ -\ 27 \\ \hline 113 \end{array}$

At this point the teacher asks the student to state the final outcome, 113. To determine the original number, cross out the units digit and add it to the remaining two-digit number. In the example shown, cross out the 3 and then add, to obtain $11 + 3 = 14$, the number started with.

Example 3.

INSTRUCTIONS	ILLUSTRATION
Think of your age.	15
Multiply your age by 2.	$15 \times 2 = 30$
Add 10.	$30 + 10 = 40$
Multiply by 5.	$40 \times 5 = 200$
Add the number of people in your family.	$200 + 4 = 204$
Subtract 50.	$204 - 50 = 154$

Now ask for the final result. The person's age will be represented by the hundreds and tens digit, the number of people in the family by the units digit. For this example, 154 is interpreted to mean an age of 15 and a family size of 4. (It is assumed the size of the family is not greater than 9.)

Many tricks can appear to be quite dramatic through the use of extra showmanship. For example, the next trick begins with a book of 20 matches and requires some burning. Be careful!

Example 4. Hand a student a book of 20 matches, and with your back turned give the following directions.

INSTRUCTIONS	ILLUSTRATION
Pick any number from 1 through 10 and remove that many matches from the book.	Assume that the student removes 8 matches.
Count the remaining matches and find the sum of the two digits in that number.	12 matches remain. The sum of the two digits is 3.
Remove that many more matches.	The student removes 3 more matches.
Burn some of the remaining matches, one at a time and give them to me.	Assume the student chooses to burn 4 of the remaining matches.
You immediately tell the student how many matches are left in the book.	Subtract 4 from 9 to get 5, the number of matches left in the book.

Regardless of how many matches are removed by the student in the first step, there will be exactly 9 left at the end of the third step. So the teacher needs only to subtract the number of burnt matches returned from 9 to find how many remain in the book.

This trick will work as long as the student begins with a collection of 20 items. If there is an objection to the use of matches in the classroom, substitute 20 toothpicks, chips, or pieces of candy instead. If the student starts with 20 candies and returns those that are left at the end, the teacher can "guess" how many were eaten.

The following trick is an interesting one in that it involves two students.

Example 5. Place a pencil and an eraser on the desk, and ask for two volunteers. (We shall call them John and Mary.)

INSTRUCTIONS	ILLUSTRATION
One of you take the pencil, and the other take the eraser. Don't tell me which one takes which object; I'll guess it!	Assume that John takes the pencil and Mary takes the eraser.
The one who took the pencil is assigned the number 7; the one who took the eraser has the number 9. (The teacher does not know who has which number at this stage.)	John begins with 7, and Mary begins with 9.
John, multiply your number by 2. Mary, multiply your number by 3.	John: $7 \times 2 = 14$. Mary: $9 \times 3 = 27$.
Find the sum of these products.	$14 + 27 = 41$.

The teacher now asks for this sum. If the sum is divisible by 3, then Mary took the pencil and John took the eraser. If the sum is not divisible by 3, then John took the pencil and Mary took the eraser. In the example shown, the sum of 41 is not divisible by 3, which indicates that John took the pencil.

Card Tricks

Many card tricks that do not involve sleight of hand are based on some mathematical principle. If used judiciously, one of these can be the dramatic highlight of a lesson. The reader is urged to practice with a deck of playing cards before performing the following trick for a class.

Call a student to the front of the room and begin to count out cards in a row on the desk, facedown. The student is instructed to stop your counting at any number between 1 and 9.

Assume you are told to stop after spreading out seven cards; then the number 7 is the student's "magic number."

Next proceed to spread out 20 additional cards on the desk.

Now instruct the student to count backwards to the seventh card, since 7 was the magic number selected. The student picks up this card and shows it to the class.

Much to everyone's surprise you now announce what the card is! Alternatively, you can place your prediction in a sealed envelope that a student opens and reads to the class.

This is a trick that works automatically provided you know in advance the twenty-first card from the top of the deck. Thus if you wish the final result to be the king of clubs, merely stack the deck in advance so that this card is in the required position. Can you see why this trick always works?

Note that there is nothing special about the number 20 in the procedure described above. For example, in the instructions given, you can spread out 15 additional cards instead of 20, provided you know the sixteenth card in advance.

2.3 INTRODUCE UNUSUAL ARITHMETIC EXPLORATIONS

It has been said that mathematics is not a spectator sport. That is, it is essential that you get your students involved in the lesson at hand as active participants rather than as passive observers. A rich supply of unusual topics in arithmetic exists that can be used for this purpose. Following is a set of representative items that can be used to motivate students in the mathematics classroom, while providing a review of arithmetic fundamentals and other skills as well.

Finger Computation

Finger computation can be counted on to develop interest in most classes. Multiplication by 9 on one's fingers is intriguing and can be accomplished as shown in the following diagrams.

To multiply 3 × 9, bend down the third finger from the left. Then read the answer in groups of fingers on either side of the bent finger.

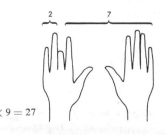

$$3 \times 9 = 27$$

Here are several additional examples:

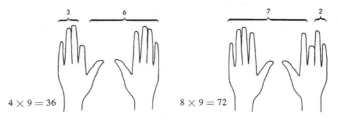

$4 \times 9 = 36$ $8 \times 9 = 72$

Fingers can be used to multiply a two-digit number by 9 provided that the units digit is greater than the tens digit.

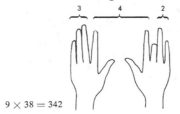

$9 \times 38 = 342$

To multiply 9×38, first put a space after the third finger from the left. Then bend the eighth finger from the left. Read the answer in terms of groups of fingers.

Magic Numbers

The following are not quite as spectacular, but nevertheless are interesting items to use in class.

Example 1. Place this "magic number" for the day on the board:

12,345,679

When the class asks what is magic about this number, proceed to ask row 1 to multiply the number by 9, row 2 to multiply the same number by 18 (2×9), row 3 by 27 (3×9), row 4 by 36 (4×9), and row 5 by 45 (5×9). The following interesting products are obtained:

$$9 \times 12,345,679 = 111,111,111$$
$$18 \times 12,345,679 = 222,222,222$$
$$27 \times 12,345,679 = 333,333,333$$
$$36 \times 12,345,679 = 444,444,444$$
$$45 \times 12,345,679 = 555,555,555$$

This same pattern continues for the remaining multiples of 9 through 81.

Obviously there are many ways in which this example may be used. For example, ask the class if anyone has a favorite or lucky number between 1 and 10. The student who responds with 3 as a lucky number is asked to multiply 12,345,679 by 27 and report on the result; the student who offers 7 as the lucky number is told to multiply 12,345,679 by 63; and so forth. The surprise on the students' faces as they complete the multiplication is rewarding and can be contagious for the rest of the class as well!

Example 2. "Magic numbers" can be used to fascinate students and to motivate them to review arithmetic in a disguised form. As another example, the magic number 15,873 works with multiples of 7. If 15,873 is multiplied by $7 \times n$, where n is a number from 1 through 9, the product consists of repeated n's. An interesting way to use this item in a class is to ask a student to select a favorite number from 1 through 9. Assume the student responds with 8. Then ask the class to multiply 15,873 by 56 (7×8); the product will be 888,888. Here are several additional illustrations:

$$\begin{array}{ll} \begin{array}{r} 15{,}873 \\ \times\ 14 \\ \hline 222{,}222 \end{array} & (7 \times \mathbf{2}) \end{array} \qquad \begin{array}{ll} \begin{array}{r} 15{,}873 \\ \times\ 28 \\ \hline 444{,}444 \end{array} & (7 \times \mathbf{4}) \end{array} \qquad \begin{array}{ll} \begin{array}{r} 15{,}873 \\ \times\ 49 \\ \hline 777{,}777 \end{array} & (7 \times \mathbf{7}) \end{array}$$

There are other such numbers that can be used in a similar fashion. For example, the number 8547 works with multiples of 13 as shown here:

$$\begin{array}{ll} \begin{array}{r} 8547 \\ \times\ 26 \\ \hline 222{,}222 \end{array} & (13 \times \mathbf{2}) \end{array} \qquad \begin{array}{ll} \begin{array}{r} 8547 \\ \times\ 39 \\ \hline 333{,}333 \end{array} & (13 \times \mathbf{3}) \end{array} \qquad \begin{array}{ll} \begin{array}{r} 8547 \\ \times\ 65 \\ \hline 555{,}555 \end{array} & (13 \times \mathbf{5}) \end{array}$$

Shortcuts

Most students find shortcuts to computation quite interesting, and many of these exist. One particularly interesting shortcut enables students to quickly square a number whose units digit is 5. For example:

$$35^2 = \underline{1225} \qquad (3 \times 4 = 12)$$
$$45^2 = \underline{2025} \qquad (4 \times 5 = 20)$$
$$55^2 = \underline{3025} \qquad (5 \times 6 = 30)$$

Note that each product ends with the last two digits as 25. The first two digits represent the product of the tens digit of the original number and its successor. Can you show why this trick works? Try to find additional examples of shortcuts suitable for use in the classroom.

2.4 MAKE USE OF GEOMETRIC CHALLENGES

Every teacher should have his or her own special collection of geometric tidbits—short little puzzles, problems, and curiosities in geometry to warm up the class, to gain attention, to involve, to challenge, to maintain interest, or simply to give a change of pace.

Consider, for example, the following item that can also serve as the problem of the day or week. Two line segments are drawn with their endpoints on different sides on the triangle. Then count the number of sides of the resulting regions and find their sum

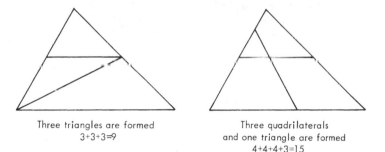

Three triangles are formed
3+3+3=9

Three quadrilaterals
and one triangle are formed
4+4+4+3=15

Representations for 9 and 15 are shown. Now the challenge is to draw other figures to represent each of the numbers between 9 and 15. It is an interesting challenge because, for no special reason, it turns out to be impossible to provide a representation for 12! Occasionally it is useful to have students attempt impossible problems so as to develop the notion that not everything can be established or proved.

A number of geometric guessing activities can lead to interesting discoveries. Most of these can be easily verified by the student through some simple construction or experimentation, as in the following example:

Fold a square piece of paper twice, as shown, and cut off the folded corner. When opened, the paper will have one hole.

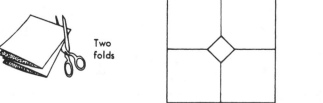

Two
folds

**Three
folds**

Suppose that the paper is folded three times and the folded corner is cut off. How many holes will there be in the paper? How many holes will the paper have if it is folded four times and then the folded corner is cut off? Does the manner in which the paper is folded affect the answer?

Tetratetraflexagons

This amazing little geometric model appears to have just two sides, front and back. But by flexing the model, both sides can be made to disappear. It is called a *tetratetraflexagon* because it can be flexed to show four (tetra) different sides or faces and because it has a four (tetra)-edged rectangular shape.

Constructing and assembling the tetratetraflexagon requires care, patience, and a certain degree of skill, but the effort will be more than repaid by the novelty of the completed model. Students will want their own model to keep.

Step 1. Reproduce the pattern and markings as shown so that each student can get a copy. Starting with small 2-inch squares, the initial pattern will be 6 × 8. The size may be changed, but it is advisable to avoid extremely large or small models.

TETRA- **TETRA-**	**FLEXAGON**	DIRECTIONS: Fold vertically down the center so the two halves are back to back. Carefully separate the two parts of the fold.	
	A new side should appear. Flex it again and you'll find still another side. Remember, don't tear the paper.		You may think that this has just two sides, front and back. If you do, you're wrong!
SIDE 1	When you flex this paper in just the right way, you can make the writing disappear.	Now have fun trying to flex them back! **SIDE 2**	

Step 2. Cut out the pattern. Then repeatedly fold it back and forth along each of the three vertical lines. With a knife or razor blade cut around three sides

of the two center squares, as shown. Be sure not to completely detach them from the rest.

Step 2. Closely follow these assembling instructions.

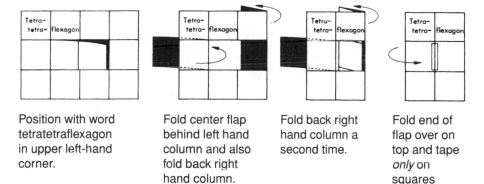

Position with word tetratetraflexagon in upper left-hand corner.	Fold center flap behind left hand column and also fold back right hand column.	Fold back right hand column a second time.	Fold end of flap over on top and tape *only* on squares shown.

Step 3. Follow directions on the tetratetraflexagon for flexing. Be careful that you do not force a fold or tear the paper. By flexing the model twice, both faces with the writing should disappear.

If this flexagon proves interesting, try assembling and flexing a hexa-hexaflexagon—six faces formed from a six-sided polygon.

Polyominoes

A polyomino is merely a set of squares connected along their edges. The simplest form is a single square, called a *monomino.* Two connected squares are called a *domino,* three squares are called a *triomino,* and four connected squares are called a *tetromino.* In this enrichment topic we are concerned with the total number of possible arrangements of such figures that are not congruent to one another.

Classroom Procedures

Supply students with graph paper since this is the most convenient way of drawing and studying polyominoes. Together with the class, demonstrate the following figures and arrangements:

There is only one kind of monomino and one kind of domino. These are familiar shapes.

There are two possible arrangements of triominoes that use three squares.

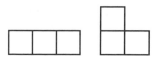

There are five possible tetrominoes.

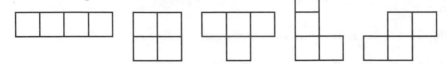

Having given the preceding exposition, ask them to find all the possible pentominoes, figures formed by five squares connected in similar fashion. Caution them not to include any that are congruent to one another but in a different orientation.

Extensions

An obvious extension is to have students search for all possible hexominoes, arrangements of six squares. However, this is a tedious and difficult project inasmuch as there are 35 different hexominoes. This could be a class project where each newly discovered hexomino is placed on the board until all 35 are found.

Another interesting, but difficult extension is to cut out all 12 possible pentominoes and try to arrange them to form a rectangle that is 5 units by 12 units in dimension. This is the basis for a puzzle called *Hex.* Yet another interesting extension is to determine which of the 12 pentominoes can be folded to form a box without a top. A problem such as the following can also be used as a suitable classroom activity after a discussion of polyominoes.

If the patterns below were assembled to form a cube, it would spell MATH around four of its faces.

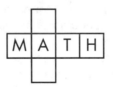

Letter the two patterns below so that they too will spell MATH the same way when assembled. Check your answers by actually forming the cubes.

Letter the following patterns so that each spells MATH when assembled. Cut out the patterns to check your answers.

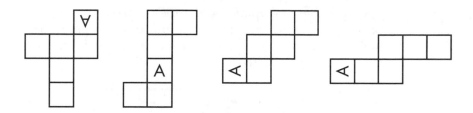

Tessellations

It is apparent to most that squares, rectangles, equilateral triangles, and regular hexagons can be used to tile or tessellate a plane. But students can explore other polygons as well to see if they can be used to form a tessellation.

Classroom Procedures

As an interesting classroom activity, have students cut out of paper some congruent quadrilaterals with no two sides parallel. Then see if they can arrange them to cover the plane without spaces and without overlapping. It will come as a surprise to many that any quadrilateral, convex or concave, can be used for a tessellation. Two are illustrated here. Note that the four angles at each intersection point have the same sizes as the four angles of an individual quadrilateral. Hence, they have a sum of 360° and completely cover the plane about that point.

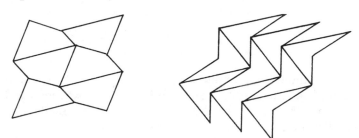

Another way for students to explore tessellations in the classroom is with graph paper or dot paper. Here is one tessellation drawn on graph paper using a hexomino of six squares as the basic shape. Try drawing some other tessellations using the same hexomino.

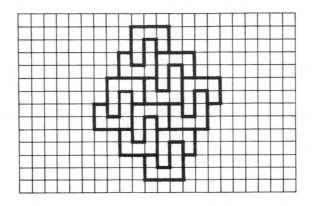

Many artists have used the idea of tessellations in their work. Perhaps the most famous is Maurits Escher (1898-1972). He created elaborate figures that would fit together to form tessellations such as this one. Encourage students to try to create similar tessellations of their own based on equilateral triangles, squares, and regular hexagons.

Extensions

A regular tessellation is made from congruent regular polygons joined side-to-side. Equilateral triangles, squares, and regular hexagons are the only regular polygons that can be used by themselves for a tessellation. A semiregular tessellation uses two or more different regular polygons with sides of the same length in such a way that all vertices are identical. The numerical notation shown for these semiregular tessellations represents the regular polygon arrangement about each vertex.

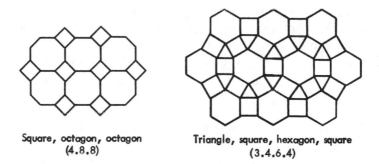

Square, octagon, octagon
(4.8.8)

Triangle, square, hexagon, square
(3.4.6.4)

There are eight semiregular tessellations in all. Two are shown above; two more (4.6.12 and 3.12.12) contain regular dodecagons. See if your students can draw these remaining two pairs using equilateral triangles, squares, and regular hexagons, all with sides of the same length:

1. 3.3.3.4.4 and 3.3.4.3.4
2. 3.6.3.6 and 3.3.3.3.6

Möbius Strips

Discovered by the German mathematician August Möbius, the Möbius strip is a fascinating item that lends itself very well to a worthwhile enrichment topic that can be presented in the form of a laboratory exercise.

Classroom Procedures

Have each student begin with a strip of paper about 20 inches long and 4 inches wide for ease of handling. Mark one end A and the back of the opposite end B as in the figure.

Turn over one end of the paper so as to form a half-twist.

Now join the ends so as to form the figure known as the Möbius strip.

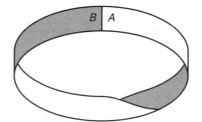

The Möbius strip is a one-sided figure. Start at *A* and draw a line down the middle of the strip. You will ultimately reach *B* without having to cross an edge, even though *B* was on the opposite side of the strip after making the initial half-twist. Now cut the figure down the middle. Instead of two figures as expected, you will end up with one band!

Extensions

Many extensions of this laboratory enrichment topic are possible. A few possibilities are listed.

1. Cut the newly formed figure down the middle again to see what type of figure is obtained, but first ask the class to predict the outcome.
2. Form a new Möbius strip, but this time cut along a line that is approximately one-third of the way across the band.
3. Form a band with two half-twists. Cut it down the center and discover the resulting figure.
4. Repeat the preceding extension, but begin with a band that has three half-twists.

Additional Examples

The geometric examples that follow are but a few of the vast supply available in the literature or ready for the teacher to create. They are ideas for motivation as compared to more extensive classroom activities and experiments such as those found in later chapters. The particular use of these ideas in the mathematics class is left to the imagination of the teacher.

1. Move just three dots to form an arrow painting down instead of up.

2. Form four equilateral triangles with just six toothpicks.

3. How many pennies can you arrange such that each penny touches every other penny?

4. Reposition three of these toothpicks to form a figure that consists of three squares of the same size.

5. Here the letters A through H have been classified with the digits 1, 3, and 5. Discover the pattern and classify the rest of the letters in the alphabet.

6. Without lifting your pencil from the paper, try to draw four connected line segments that pass through all nine points.

2.5 STIMULATE INTEREST WITH MATHEMATICAL RECREATIONS

Most students of mathematics enjoy working with puzzles. Although these are most often recreational in nature, nevertheless there are many other worthwhile outcomes that accrue from the use of suitable puzzles and problems. Appropriate recreational items can be found to stimulate intellectual curiosity, to develop abilities in space perception, to promote discovery, and to develop modes of thinking. The major purpose for their use in the classroom, however, is to motivate the further study of mathematics.

There are a variety of effective ways that mathematical recreations can be used in the classroom. The reader should be able to add to the following list of suggestions:

1. Have one section of the bulletin board or chalkboard entitled "Puzzle of the Week." Each week place a new puzzle or set of puzzles in this spot. Encourage students to submit answers in writing. At the end of the week post a list of the names of all students who submitted correct

solutions. Possibly award a prize for the first correct answer (such as an excuse from homework for one night), or a prize to the student who has the greatest number of correct solutions within each marking period.

2. Place a collection of puzzles on 4 × 6-inch index cards. Any student who completes a classroom assignment or test early is allowed to select a card to use while waiting for the rest of the class to finish their work.
3. Devote the last five minutes of each period to a mathematical recreation.
4. Use the last period before a vacation for recreational activities.
5. On occasion include an interesting puzzle as part of the regular classroom assignment.

The supply of interesting puzzles is almost endless; the following list is representative of the type of puzzle that appears to be of interest to secondary school mathematics students.

1. How can you cook an egg for exactly 15 minutes, if all you have is a 7-minute hourglass and an 11-minute hourglass?
2. How can the water in a full 24-quart can be divided into three equal amounts using three unmarked cans whose capacities are 5, 11, and 13 quarts?
3. Nine coins are in a bag. They all look alike, but one is counterfeit. It weighs less than the others. Use a balance scale and find the fake coin in exactly two weighings.
4. There are 12 coins, of which one is counterfeit, weighing less than the others. Use a balance scale and find the fake coin in exactly three weighings.
5. Use the digits 2, 3, 4, 5, 6, 7, 8, 9, and 10. Place exactly one of these in each position in the figure so that the sum for each row, column, and diagonal is 18.

6. Arrange three piles of toothpicks, chips, or other similar objects so as to have 6 items in pile A, 7 items in pile B, and 11 items in pile C. In exactly three moves you are to attempt to obtain 8 items in each pile. The rules for movement are that you may only move to a pile as many items as are already there, and all items moved must come from a single other pile.
7. Arrange five coins as in the following figure:

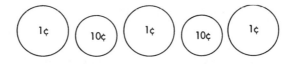

Try to obtain the following arrangement by moving two adjacent coins at a time, but each pair of coins moved must consist of a penny and a dime and must not be interchanged during the move.

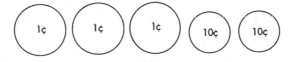

Quite a different type of puzzle that can be both amusing and useful in the mathematics classroom deals with letter and word arrangements and codes. Some are straightforward and reasonably simple, whereas others can tax the most capable. Students enjoy making as well as solving these problems.

8. Can you decipher these alphametics?

Addition: O N E   Subtraction: F I V E
                 T W O   F O U R
           F I V E   O N E
       E I G H T

Many of these puzzle pastimes lend themselves to a series of problems or activities that can be presented to the student in the form of laboratory worksheets or activity cards. Here is one example. Many others can be found in the following chapters.

9. Start with the A on top. Move down to the left or right one letter at a time. The path shown spells out the word ALGEBRA.

How many different paths, from top to bottom, are possible? Do they all spell ALGEBRA?

Some puzzles of a geometric nature simply require great amounts of patience and ingenuity.

10. Loosely tie together the hands of two people with one string looped around the other, as shown. Now get them apart without untying or cutting the string. It can be done!

2.6 USE BULLETIN BOARD DISPLAYS
TO GENERATE INTEREST

In many classrooms the bulletin board can serve as the focal point for exhibits and posters. It can also be used, as is the blackboard, for the actual teaching and on-the-spot development of an idea. Use it to display daily mathematical tidbits, historical quotes, or puzzle problems. Make it the source of enrichment materials related to the unit on hand. Conveniently available in most classrooms, the bulletin board can serve an important role in the overall learning experience. To illustrate the potential of the bulletin board, several illustrations of possible uses are given here.

Optical Illusions

A good topic for a bulletin board display in the mathematics classroom that almost everyone enjoys is optical illusions. They can be effectively exhibited just for fun as well as to convince students that seeing is not always believing. This can be an important point to make in geometry where students are encouraged in their proofs to rely on reason rather than relying too heavily on figures.

Some of the many popular illusions are given in this collection. A new one might be added each week and students encouraged to search for more on their own. These should be placed on the bulletin board to stimulate student discussion and reactions. Ask students to describe what they see.

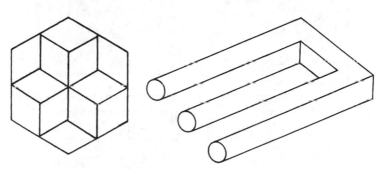

Of course, when the optical illusions are taken down, they should be stored in the box shown here:

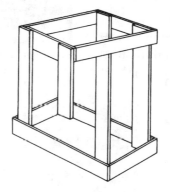

Historical Items

In a slightly different vein, interesting bits from the history of mathematics can be presented via the bulletin board. Stories about Thales, Pythagoras, Euclid, and Archimedes make interesting reading when studying geometry. Or pictures of Descartes, Pascal, and Gauss can be posted when studying coordinate geometry, probability, and complex numbers. Have students interested in philately search out and display some of the stamps relating to mathematics and mathematicians. It is surprising how exciting this can be to some students.

In the illustrations of stamps shown below, the Scott catalog numbers are given in parentheses for each stamp. All the stamps shown are reasonably inexpensive.

Reise (Germany, 779)   Ramanujan (India, 369)

Stevin (Belgium, B321)   Einstein (USA, 1285)

Pascal (France, B181)

Bolyai (Romania, 1345)

Chevyshev
(Russia, 1050)

Descartes (France, 330)

Euler (German Democratic
Republic, A718)

The following stamps can be used to show the general interest that most people have with optical illusions. They can also be shown in conjunction with the figures previously illustrated.

Exploration

Interesting discovery problems can also be illustrated on the bulletin board. One challenging example is the **shortest-path problem.** Three tacks are placed on the bulletin board in a triangular array and a reasonable distance apart. Equipped with a string and a ruler, students try to find the shortest path connecting the points.

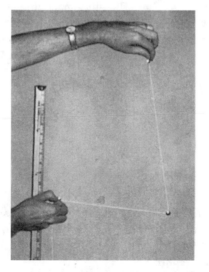

The problem is not as simple as it may sound, but this will make the students only more anxious to try. The solution is somewhat surprising. If the triangle itself contains an angle of 120° or more, the two shortest sides of the triangle form the best path. Otherwise, an intermediate point that forms three 120° angles with the given points locates the shortest connecting path. Notice how the three vertices are connected through a strategically located fourth point.

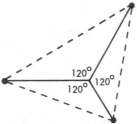

As an extension to this problem, consider the shortest path connecting the four vertices of a square.

2.7 DISCUSS APPLICATIONS OF MATHEMATICAL CONCEPTS

One of the most challenging questions faced by any teacher of mathematics is, "What good is all of this?" Unfortunately, for some topics, we may have to resort to standard answers, such as indicating the future value of the topic in the student's study of mathematics. However, it enhances motivation if we provide meaningful applications of topics under study. For example, during a unit on the conic sections where the ellipse is being studied you can tell the story of the whispering gallery in Washington, D.C. When a person stands at one of the foci of the ellipse and whispers, regardless of the noisy condition of the chamber, someone standing at the other focus can hear the whispered message quite clearly.

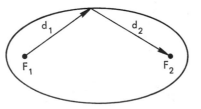

The explanation of this phenomenon is that all sound waves coming from one of the foci will bounce off the sides of the ellipse and pass through the other focus. By the definition of an ellipse, the sum of the two distances in the figure, $d_1 + d_2$, is constant.

At one time one of the authors indicated to an algebra class that this property would apply to an elliptical pool table. Thus if a ball is placed at F_1 and hit hard *in any direction*, it is guaranteed that the ball will hit another one placed at F_2. After class one student indicated that this was the most interesting thing that he had ever learned in all his studies of mathematics!

Before leaving this topic, it should be noted that what is considered to be a genuine application by the teacher is not necessarily one for the student. Thus a student may be quite satisfied to see how mathematics is used to justify a trick or a shortcut, and will be content that this is an application of a topic under study. For example, consider an algebra class that has studied the formula

$$(a - b)(a + b) = a^2 - b^2$$

A real application of this formula for many students is its use to multiply a product such as 78×82 mentally:

$$78 \times 82 = (80 - 2)(80 + 2) = 80^2 - 2^2 = 6396$$

Likewise, students will accept the mathematical explanation of a mathematical trick, such as the one shown on page 37, as a suitable application of a mathematical topic.

Finding suitable applications of mathematics is not a trivial task and is easier for some topics than for others. Here are just a few examples of interesting applications to discuss in class:

Example 1. In the event of an accident, police can estimate the speed of an automobile by measuring the length of the skid marks left when the driver was braking. The speed in miles per hour, s, can be approximated by the formula $s = \sqrt{24d}$, where d is the length of the skid marks in feet. (The constant, 24, will vary in adverse road and weather conditions.)

Example 2. It is known that the air temperature decreases about 5°F for every 1000 feet of altitude. Meteorologists use the following formula to show this relationship:

$$T = t - 5\left(\frac{A}{1000}\right)$$

In this formula, t represents the ground temperature, A is the altitude in feet, and T is the temperature at altitude A, in degrees Fahrenheit.

Example 3. A parabolic surface can be formed by rotating a parabola about its axis. When a source of light is placed at the focus, all light from this source will be reflected in parallel rays, as evidenced by the parabolic reflectors used in headlights and searchlights.

Example 4. It has been determined that the rectangle most pleasing to the eye is one whose dimensions are such that the length is approximately 1.618

times the width. This ratio is referred to as the *golden ratio,* and the rectangle as the *golden rectangle.* Using w as the width and l as the length, the golden rectangle satisfies the following proportion:

$$\frac{w+l}{l} = \frac{l}{w}$$

If $w = 1$, this proportion can be solved to show that $l = \frac{1+\sqrt{5}}{2} = 1.618...$, assuming $l > w$. The dimensions of many famous works of art and historic buildings (such as the Parthenon) are based on this ratio. (See page 155 for a further discussion of the golden ratio.)

Example 5. The property of the ellipse that explains the whispering gallery in Washington is also the basis for the use of the lithotriptor in medicine. A bathtub with an elliptical cross-section is used. Electrical discharges are emitted from one focus of the ellipse, while a patient with kidney stones is placed at the other focus. This serves to disintegrate the kidney stones into small pieces that can then be excreted.

2.8 CONCLUSION

In a sense, there is no real conclusion to the topic of motivation. The items cited in this chapter represent only a small subset of the total ways and means of motivating students. All the material in the remainder of this text may be considered as dealing in some way with the motivation of students in mathematics.

Above and beyond all else, suitable motivation depends upon the enthusiasm and imagination of the teacher. When all is said and done, it is the teacher who counts, and no motivational technique is of value if the teacher does not display his or her genuine interest in the subject at hand.

There is an almost endless supply of topics that are suitable to enrich and motivate mathematics classes at various grade levels as well as at different levels of difficulty. The topics that follow are highly recommended for further exploration.

Ancient Egyptian Mathematics	Fermat's Last Theorem
Card Tricks	Fibonacci Numbers
Conic Sections	Finite Differences
Diophantine Equations	Flatland
Divisibility of Numbers	Flexagons
Euler's Formula	The Four-Color Problem
The Euler Line	The Fourth Dimension

Fractals	Pascal's Theorem
Game of Life	Penrose Tiles
Game Theory	Perfect Numbers
Geometry of Soap Bubbles	Prime Numbers
The Golden Section	Problems of Antiquity
Koenigsberg Bridge Problem	Projective Geometry
Linear Programming	Pythagorean Triples
Linkages	Regular Polygons
Mandelbrot Set	Regular Polyhedrons
Mascheroni's Construction	Relativity
Mathematics and Music	Shortcuts in Computation
Napier's Rods	Tessellations
The Nine-Point Circle	Topology
Nomographs	Trachtenberg System of Computation
The Number *e*	Transfinite Numbers
The Number Pi	Unsolved Problems
Paper Folding	Vectors
Paradoxes	Zeno's Paradoxes

EXERCISES

For Exercises 1–6, first guess and then try to justify your answer with appropriate measurements.

1. The length of a $1 bill is about how many times its width?
   (a) $\frac{5}{3}$ (b) $\frac{6}{3}$ (c) $\frac{7}{3}$ (d) $\frac{8}{3}$ (e) $\frac{9}{3}$

2. About how many pennies would have to be piled on top of one another to reach the ceiling of a room that is 8 feet high?
   (a) 300   (b) 500   (c) 1000   (d) 1500   (e) 2000

3. To the nearest thousand, how many pennies are there in one mile of pennies placed next to each other with their edges touching?
   (a) 20,000   (b) 40,000   (c) 60,000   (d) 80,000   (e) 100,000

4. How much is a stack of pennies 10 miles high worth?
   (a) $1,000   (b) $10,000   (c) $100,000   (d) $500,000   (e) $1,000,000

5. How long would it take to spend $1 million at the rate of $100 every minute?
   (a) 1 day   (b) 1 week   (c) 2 weeks   (d) 1 month   (e) 2 months

6. One million people are lined up with their arms outstretched, fingertip to fingertip. How far will this line of people stretch?
   (a) across the state of Pennsylvania   (b) $\frac{1}{3}$ across the U.S.
   (c) $\frac{1}{2}$ across the U.S.   (d) across the U.S.   (e) around the world

7. Provide a mathematical explanation as to why the match trick illustrated on page 38 works.

8. Explain why the card trick on page 39 works.

9. Within a triangle, draw any two line segments such that their endpoints are points on the triangle. Count the number of sides of the resulting regions and find their sum. Draw figures that illustrate the sums of 10, 11, 13, and 14. (See page 43.)

10. Try the following trick on a friend; then provide a mathematical justification to show why it works. Have your friend roll a die three times and record the results in order. Then give these instructions:

    Multiply the first number by 2.

    Add 5 to the result, and then multiply by 5.

    Add the second number to this product.

    Multiply by 10 and add the third number.

    You then ask your friend to state the final result. From the number mentally subtract 250. The result will be a three-digit number whose digits represent the original three numbers. (Instead of tossing three dice, you can merely have your friend think of a three-digit number.)

11. Arrange the numerals 1 through 8 in the figure so that no two consecutive integers touch at a side or on a corner.

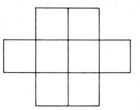

12. Arrange eight coins as in this figure:

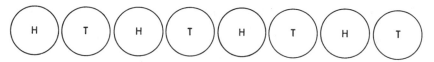

    Moving two adjacent coins at a time, try to obtain the following arrangement:

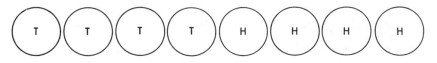

13. Draw a square, number eight pieces of paper, and arrange them as shown in the figure on the left. By sliding only one piece at a time into an open square, arrange the pieces as shown in the figure on the right.

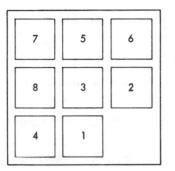 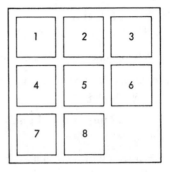

14. Eleven toothpicks are arranged as shown to give five triangles.

    (a) Remove one toothpick to show four triangles.
    (b) Remove two toothpicks to show four triangles.
    (c) Remove two toothpicks to show three triangles.
    (d) Remove three toothpicks to show three triangles.

15. A coin is in a "cup" formed by four matchsticks. Try to get the coin out of the cup by moving only two matchsticks to form a congruent cup but in a new position.

ACTIVITIES

1. Prepare a set of multiple-choice questions similar to those found on page 36 that requires one to guess and estimate about familiar objects.

2. Prepare a collection of magic tricks that are based on some mathematical principle. Demonstrate at least one of these in class.

3. Search for other examples of the use of fingers in completing computations.

4. Prepare a collection of various computational shortcuts. Demonstrate at least one of these in class.

5. Prepare a bulletin board display suitable for a middle school or a senior high school mathematics class.

6. Prepare a collection of at least 10 applications of mathematics suitable for a mathematics class at a designated level.

7. Examine at least two junior or senior high school mathematics textbooks and report on the use of motivational techniques in each. In particular, report on any unusual approaches to motivation that are used.

8. Examine a textbook that has been specifically designed for a general mathematics class and report on any motivational techniques used.

9. Develop a one-period lesson plan for a mathematics class at a designated level that clearly indicates any procedures that are to be used to motivate the lesson.

10. Prepare a collection of at least 10 geometric challenges similar to those given in Section 2.4.

11. Prepare a collection of mathematical puzzles, placing each on an index card, with answers on the reverse side.

12. Prepare a collection of puzzles that are suitable for use on a bulletin board as the "Puzzle of the Week."

13. Select one of the topics listed on pages 60–61 and prepare a fifteen-minute oral presentation suitable for use in a mathematics class at a designated level.

14. Prepare a bulletin board display featuring the contributions of one or more of the mathematicians shown on the stamps illustrated in this chapter.

15. Read and report on one of the chapters of *Journey Through Genius* by William Dunham, New York: John Wiley & Sons, Inc., 1990.

3

MOTIVATING PROBLEM-SOLVING INSTRUCTION

At the start of the decade of the 1980s the National Council of Teachers of Mathematics published a document entitled *An Agenda for Action: Recommendations for School Mathematics of the 1980s.* Designed to serve as a blueprint for change, this document has served as a guide to both textbook authors and numerous communities and states throughout the country for revising the mathematics curriculum. Its first recommendation is the one that has received the widest attention and acclaim:

Problem solving must be the focus of school mathematics in the 1980s.

As a result of this NCTM recommendation, as well as widespread interest in problem solving by mathematics educators, the subject became the major topic of discussion throughout the decade at various professional meetings and a major theme of newly published textbooks. Then, in 1989, the NCTM produced a document entitled *Curriculum and Evaluation Standards for School Mathematics* that became the blueprint for curriculum change throughout the decade of the 1990s. Once again they wrote:

Problem solving should be the central focus of the mathematics curriculum.

Among the many recommendations made, they suggested that increased attention be given to:

- The active involvement of students in constructing and applying mathematical ideas
- Problem solving as a means as well as a goal of instruction
- The use of a variety of instructional formats (small groups, individual explorations, peer instruction, whole-class discussions, project work)

Some problems are just beautiful in their simplicity and yet reveal much about the solver through the solution offered. This problem was reported on in the Third International Mathematics and Science Study (TIMSS). It came up as part of an observation in an eighth-grade classroom in Japan, and reflects the kind of challenge we should be offering our students on a regular basis.

Notice that no computation is called for here. Below are two very interesting and different solutions that were among those received by the authors when giving this problem in class. Do you see how the students applied their knowledge in different ways in order to solve the problem? Try to describe each solution in writing.

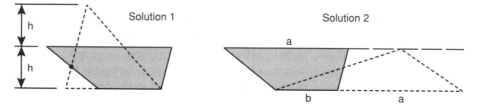

History offers a valuable source of interesting and challenging problems that, at the same time, help students appreciate the great diversity of our mathematical heritage. The ancient Babylonians were extremely advanced in their mathematical reckoning. This problem was found on a Babylonian tablet dating back well over one thousand years B.C. An exact translation is given in Example 4.

Example 4. A square, the side is 1.
Inside it 4 quadrants, 16 boat-shapes.
I have drawn 5 regular concave-sided
   tetragons.
This area, what is it?

Use this problem in a cooperative learning situation. Have small groups of students work independently on both its interpretation and its solution. Then let the students explain the different approaches that they used in solving the problem as they interpreted it. If the area referred to is that of a single tetragon, then the answer is

$$\frac{1}{4} - \frac{\pi}{16}$$

3.2 STRATEGY FOR PROBLEM SOLVING: TRIAL AND ERROR

Some problems are best solved by trial and error, with logical thinking accompanying the process. One suitable way to initiate students in this approach is to offer a famous historical problem, such as the following.

The Koenigsberg Bridge Problem

It is claimed that the inhabitants of the ancient town of Koenigsberg enjoyed taking walks over the seven bridges that connected the mainland to two islands in the river that ran through the town. The problem that they considered was this:

Is it possible to start a walk at any point and cross each bridge exactly once, without retracing your steps?

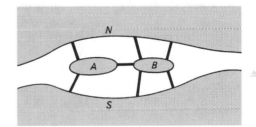

This is an interesting problem in discrete mathematics to give to junior high school students as a home assignment "just for fun." They will undoubtedly be extremely frustrated when you tell them the following day that such a walk is impossible! On the other hand, part of the strategy of trial and error is to try to find a solution by exhausting all possibilities. The solution to this particular problem is that there is no such path that crosses each bridge once and only once.

Traversable Networks

As a follow-up to the Koenigsberg Bridge problem, suggest that your students prepare a report on the work of the Swiss mathematician Leonhard Euler concerning networks. A network on a plane consists of points called *vertices*, paths connecting them called *arcs*, and *regions* bounded by them. Euler developed methods for determining whether such networks can or cannot be traced with a continuous path. For example, the two networks shown below on the left can be traversed without lifting your pencil from the paper or retracing any path more than once, whereas the two at the right are not traversable under these conditions.

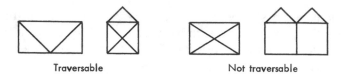

Traversable   Not traversable

An *odd vertex* is defined as one that has an odd number of arcs (line segments) that come to that point; an *even vertex* has an even number of arcs. Euler proved that networks, such as those shown above, can be traced if one of the following two conditions is met:

1. There are only even vertices in the figure.
2. There are exactly two odd vertices in the figure.

In the latter case, one must start at one of these odd vertices and the path will terminate at the other odd vertex. Encourage students to test Euler's conditions with figures of their own, and to draw a network that illustrates the Koenigsberg Bridge problem.

Regardless of whether a network can be traversed or not, Euler discovered an interesting relationship concerning such figures. He showed that the number of vertices plus the number of regions is always two more than the number of arcs.

$$V + R = A + 2$$

As a classroom experiment that leads students to discover this formula by themselves, provide them with a set of figures to use.

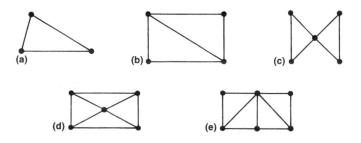

Have the students count the number of vertices, regions, and arcs for each of the networks shown and record the results in a table. In Figure (a), the three vertices and three arcs are obvious. The two regions are the interior and the exterior of the triangle.

Network	Number of		
	Vertices	Regions	Arcs
(a)	3	2	3
(b)			
(c)			
(d)			
(e)			

Now ask questions such as these:

1. For each of these networks is the number of arcs A ever less than the number of vertices V or the number of regions R? Is A less than the sum of V and R? Can you discover a relationship among the number of arcs A and the number of vertices and regions V and R? Try to express this relationship in symbols.
2. Now count V, R, and A for each of these networks. Do they support your formula from step 1?

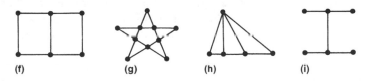

(f)   (g)   (h)   (i)

3. Can you construct a figure where your formula does not work?

Magic Triangles

Let us consider another example of a problem that can be approached by trial and error, or by combining that method with logical reasoning. The problem is to place the numerals 1 through 9 in a triangular array so that the sum of the numbers along each side of the triangle is the same. The solutions may not be unique, but here are illustrations of arrays that produce sums of 17 and 23 along each of the sides.

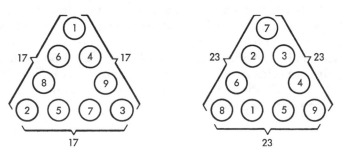

The problem now is to try to display such triangular arrays for all sums between 17 and 23 using the same numbers 1 through 9. Students can be asked to attempt a solution strictly by a trial-and-error approach. An alternative approach is to consider a logical development, noting that the sum of the corner numbers for the first triangle is 6 (1 + 2 + 3), and for the second triangle is 24 (7 + 8 + 9).

Sum of Numbers along the Sides	Sum of Corner Number	
17	6	
18	?	(9) If we consider the difference
19	?	(12) 24 − 6 = 18, and divide this
20	?	(15) into six equal intervals, we
21	?	(18) have a reasonable guess for
22	?	(21) the sums of corner numbers.
23	24	

Using the sums of corner numbers indicated in the table, and a trial-and-error strategy, it proves possible to find triangular arrays for sums of 19, 20, and 21. Unfortunately, no such triangular arrays are possible for sums of 18 and 22.

The very fact that the preceding problem is possible to solve for certain numbers, and not for others, usually motivates students to explore other solutions by using the valuable strategy of trial and error.

3.3 STRATEGY FOR PROBLEM SOLVING: USE AN AID, MODEL, OR SKETCH

Very often a problem can best be solved or at least understood by drawing a sketch, folding a piece of paper, cutting a piece of string, or making use of some other simple and readily available aid. The strategy of using an aid can make a situation real to a student, help to motivate her or him, and generate interest in the problem. Here are several problems that illustrate this strategy.

Example 1. You have five coins: a penny, a nickel, a dime, a quarter, and a half-dollar. You also have two identical boxes. How many different ways can these coins be distributed into the two boxes so that at least one coin is in each box?

This is a suitable problem for elementary or junior high school students to solve by actually drawing a sketch to show all logical possibilities. In the following, the five coins are designated by the numerals 1, 5, 10, 25, and 50. Note that the diagrams indicate a systematic way of enumeration so as to avoid omitting any possibilities.

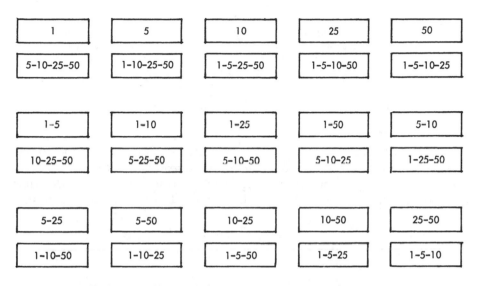

By actually listing all possibilities, we find the solution to be 15.

As another example, consider the following problem that is a standard in most elementary calculus textbooks.

Example 2. An open box, without a top, is to be formed from a 9 × 12-inch piece of cardboard by cutting off square corners of equal size and folding up the edges. What should be the size of the square corners cut off in order to obtain a box of maximum volume?

This problem, solved formally in calculus texts, can be solved informally and experimentally in a junior high school class. Make it a demonstration by the teacher or an experiment by groups of students in a laboratory setting. Use at least four pieces of cardboard of the same size and cut off square corners with dimensions of 1 inch, 2 inches, 3 inches, and 4 inches. Use tape to hold the sides together and allow students to guess which box appears to have the maximum volume before proceeding with any calculations. Many students will guess that all have the same volume.

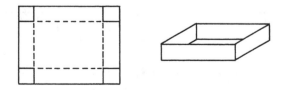

Now, by computation, we can find the volume of each box and summarize the data in a table such as the following:

Box	Size of Square Cut from Corner	Length-Width-Height in Inches	Volume in Cubic Inches
A	1"	$10 \times 7 \times 1$	70
B	2"	$8 \times 5 \times 2$	80
C	3"	$6 \times 3 \times 3$	54
D	4"	$4 \times 1 \times 4$	16

Graphing these volumes against the corresponding sizes of the corner squares provides further visualization of these results. Connecting the dots on the graph gives a general picture of the relationship involved, but does not indicate exactly what size squares will result in a box of maximum volume.

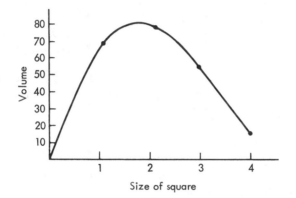

At this point, students should be ready to see that we can test corner squares of $1\frac{1}{2}$ inches and $2\frac{1}{2}$ inches for a better approximation. The respective volumes are then found to be 81 and 70 cubic inches. Thus square corners of $1\frac{1}{2}$ inches prove to be our best estimate for obtaining the maximum volume.

Other approaches will give better answers. Tracing along the curve drawn on a graphing calculator is one choice. For the function, $y = x(9 - 2x)(12 - 2x)$, the maximum volume appears at $x = 1.7021$. Zooming in gives a better estimate at $x = 1.6965$.

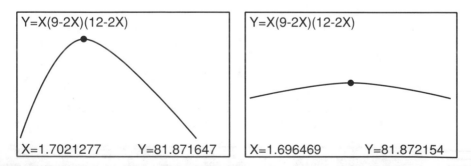

At best, these kinds of answers are always approximate. The exact answer can be found using the methods of calculus. It occurs at $\dfrac{(7 - \sqrt{13})}{2}$.

Example 3. Drawing a sketch sometimes sheds new light on a problem by exposing alternate approaches. Consider this problem dealing with successive slices in a cake.

One slice through a cake gives two pieces. Two slices can give as many as four pieces. What is the maximum number of pieces you can get with three successive slices? What about four successive slices?

Quick sketches verify the first two cases and offer a possible solution to the third.

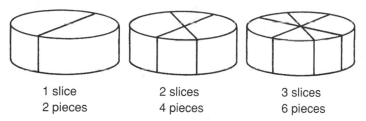

| 1 slice | 2 slices | 3 slices |
| 2 pieces | 4 pieces | 6 pieces |

If we assume there are no restrictions on the shape of the pieces, the third slice doesn't necessarily have to follow in the same fashion. Can a third slice through the cake be repositioned to yield more pieces? Here are two alternate choices that yield 7 and 8 pieces, respectively.

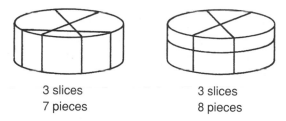

| 3 slices | 3 slices |
| 7 pieces | 8 pieces |

Starting with the sketch on the right above, where would you cut with the next slice to get the maximum number of pieces with four slices? Two possibilities immediately come to mind. How many pieces do you get in each of these cases?

| 4 slices | 4 slices |
| ? pieces | ? pieces |

The figure on the left gives 12 pieces while the one on the right gives 14. But there is a better choice for 4 cuts through the cake—one that gives even more pieces. Can you reposition the fourth slice for the maximum number of pieces possible? (See page 144 for further discussion on the number sequence generated by this problem. But don't turn there until you give this problem some more thought here by sketching other possibilities.)

Drawing a picture or using an aid not only serves as an effective strategy for problem solving in many situations, but also helps to motivate the student to pursue an otherwise vague problem. Many other examples of the use of aids are presented in the following chapters.

3.4 STRATEGY FOR PROBLEM SOLVING: SEARCH FOR A PATTERN

Searching for patterns and then forming generalizations is a very powerful problem-solving strategy that will be explored again in detail in later chapters. Once again, however, we need to search for suitable problems that will create interest on the part of students and thus motivate them to make use of this strategy. Here is one such problem:

* *Find the pattern in the following set of numbers:*

8, 5, 4, 9, 1, 7, 6, 3, 2

This is a good problem to give as the "Problem of the Week." Do not disclose the solution until sufficient time has elapsed for all students to try it. Many students may appear frustrated when they learn the answer: The numbers are arranged in alphabetical order according to their spellings!

A good teaching technique is to have students provide their own original sequences of numbers for others to discover. Challenge them to use their imagination. For example consider this sequence:

4   14   34   42   59   125

What's going on here? Students living in New York City would quickly recognize this as the first few numbered express stops northbound on the 8th Avenue subway!

Problems that involve searching for a pattern are plentiful, but selecting those that will stimulate the interest of students is a challenging task. The following problems have proved to be useful for motivating students to search for patterns.

Example 1. In the following decimal, how many 2's are there in all before the hundredth 3?

$$0.23223222322223\ldots$$

Here the student should note that there is one 2 before the first 3, two 2's before the second 3, and in general n 2's before the nth 3. Thus, before the hundredth 3, the total number of 2's is

$$1 + 2 + 3 + 4 + \ldots + 98 + 99 + 100$$

The total number is then found to be 5050, using the method of Gauss as described on page 5.

Example 2. What is the units digit in the power of 3 with an exponent corresponding to the current year? For example, what is the units digit in the expansion of 3^{2001}?

By expanding the first powers of 3 we can observe a pattern in successive units digits:

$$3^1 = \quad 3$$
$$3^2 = \quad 9$$
$$3^3 = \quad 27$$
$$3^4 = \quad 81$$
$$3^5 = \quad 243$$
$$3^6 = \quad 729$$
$$3^7 = 2187$$
$$3^8 = 6561$$
$$\ldots\ldots\ldots\ldots$$

The pattern formed by successive units digits is

$$3, 9, 7, 1, 3, 9, 7, 1, \ldots$$

Thus, when n is an integer, 3^{4n} will have a units digit of 1. The number 2000 is a multiple of 4.

$$3^{2000} = 3^{4(500)}$$

So 3^{2000} will have a units digit of 1. The number 3^{2001} is the next successive multiple of 3 and thus, by the pattern observed, will have a units digit of 3. Following this line of reasoning,

3^{2002} will have a units digit of 9,

3^{2003} will have a units digit of 7,

3^{2004} will have a units digit of 1 and so on.

A more difficult and challenging problem is to determine the tens digit in the expansion of 3^{2001}. (See Exercise 4 at the end of the chapter.)

Example 3. In all, how many squares of all sizes are there in a standard checkerboard?

Since this problem would be difficult to solve by actually counting, students should be urged to search for a pattern. Also, they should be reminded of the valuable strategy of attempting a similar, but less complex, problem. Thus, they might count the number of squares in smaller grids of $1 \times 1, 2 \times 2$, 3×3, and 4×4.

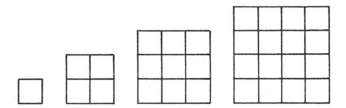

It is helpful to summarize the observed data in a table.

Size of Grid	Number of Squares of Different Size				Total
	1×1	2×2	3×3	4×4	
1×1	1	—	—	—	1
2×2	4	1	—	—	5
3×3	9	4	1	—	14
4×4	16	9	4	1	30

The pattern appears to involve the sums of squares. Thus for a checkerboard of size 8×8, the total number of squares is

$$1 + 4 + 9 + 16 + 25 + 36 + 49 + 64 = 204$$

The generalization for this and related problems can be found in Chapter 8.

Example 4. Consider the following array of fractions:

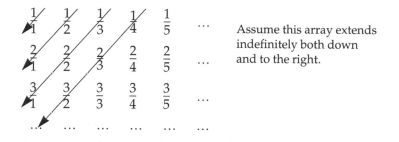

Assume this array extends
indefinitely both down
and to the right.

Now arrange the fractions along the indicated diagonals, and match each fraction with a counting number in this manner:

$$\frac{1}{1} \quad \frac{1}{2} \quad \frac{2}{1} \quad \frac{1}{3} \quad \frac{2}{2} \quad \frac{3}{1} \quad \frac{1}{4} \quad \frac{2}{3} \quad \frac{3}{2} \quad \frac{4}{1} \quad \cdots$$

$$\updownarrow \quad \updownarrow \quad \updownarrow \quad \updownarrow \quad \updownarrow \quad \updownarrow \quad \updownarrow \quad \updownarrow \quad \updownarrow \quad \updownarrow$$

$$1 \quad 2 \quad 3 \quad 4 \quad 5 \quad 6 \quad 7 \quad 8 \quad 9 \quad 10$$

If this array is continued, which counting number would be matched with the fraction $\frac{15}{21}$? Which number would be matched with the fraction $\frac{p}{q}$? (See Exercise 18.) As a hint, note the pattern of sums of the numerator and denominator of each fraction along each diagonal:

Diagonal	$\left(\frac{1}{1}\right)$	$\left(\frac{1}{2}, \frac{2}{1}\right)$	$\left(\frac{1}{3}, \frac{2}{2}, \frac{3}{1}\right)$	$\left(\frac{1}{4}, \frac{2}{3}, \frac{3}{2}, \frac{4}{1}\right)$	$\cdots$
Sum	2	3	4	5	$\cdots$

This particular problem is appropriate for a senior high school advanced mathematics class. It is related to the German mathematician Cantor's proof that the set of all rational numbers can be matched in a one-to-one correspondence with the set of counting numbers. (See Activity 10.)

3.5 STRATEGY FOR PROBLEM SOLVING: ACT IT OUT

Some problems are best solved by the strategy of acting out the situation involved. Such an approach allows students to become active participants rather than passive spectators, and helps them to see and understand the meaning of a problem. Many routine problems of elementary algebra dealing

This problem lends itself to an initial strategy of acting out so as to clarify details. Thereafter, a table of results should indicate the pattern and lead to a solution.

Ring Number	Number Who Enter	Total Number
1	1	1
2	3	4
3	5	9
4	7	16
5	9	25

It soon becomes evident that the total number at each stage is the square of the number of rings. That is, after the fourth ring the total number of guests will be

$$1 + 3 + 5 + 7 = 16 = 4^2$$

After the fifth ring the number of guests will be

$$1 + 3 + 5 + 7 + 9 = 25 = 5^2$$

By extending the pattern, we conclude that after the twentieth ring the total number will be

$$1 + 3 + 5 + 7 + \ldots + 39 = 20^2 \text{ or } 400$$

The mathematical generalization that comes from this activity is that the sum of the first n odd counting numbers is n^2.

Example 2. One hundred coins, all showing tails, are placed on a table of counting numbers from 1 to 100.

1	2	3	4	5	6	7	8	9	10
11	12	13	14	15	16	17	18	19	20
21	22	23	24	25	26	27	28	29	30
31	32	33	34	35	36	37	38	39	40
41	42	43	44	45	46	47	48	49	50
51	52	53	54	55	56	57	58	59	60
61	62	63	64	65	66	67	68	69	70
71	72	73	74	75	76	77	78	79	80
81	82	83	84	85	86	87	88	89	90
91	92	93	94	95	96	97	98	99	100

Now give the following instructions, in succession:

a. Change all the coins from tails to heads.
b. Change all the coins on squares that show multiples of 2 from heads to tails. These are the even-numbered squares.
c. Next change all the coins on squares that show multiples of 3. If the coin on that space shows heads, change it to tails; if it shows tails, change it to heads.
d. In a similar manner, change all coins on squares that show multiples of 4. Then repeat, changing all coins on multiples of 5.
e. Continue this process up through the multiples of 100.

At the end of the process described, which numbered squares will have coins that show heads?

This problem is best solved by forming an appropriate chart that describes the situation, and then searching for a pattern. For example, consider the first 10 counting numbers and the results obtained after five changes have taken place.

	1	2	3	4	5	6	7	8	9	10
Start	T	T	T	T	T	T	T	T	T	T
First Change	H	II	H	H	H	H	H	H	H	H
Second Change	H	T	H	T	H	T	H	T	H	T
Third Change	H	T	T	T	H	H	H	T	T	T
Fourth Change	H	T	T	H	H	H	H	H	T	T
Fifth Change	H	T	T	H	T	II	H	H	T	H

The reader is urged to extend the chart and continue until a pattern becomes evident. As an alternative approach, consider the number of factors for each counting number.

Example 3. Choose three numbers and challenge your class to guess them. Provide these clues:

> The product of the three numbers is 72.
> The sum of the three numbers is a multiple of 7.

To solve this problem, form a table that lists all possible sets of three factors of 72, together with the sums of these factors.

Factors			Sums		Factors			Sums
1	1	72	74		2	2	18	22
1	2	36	39		2	3	12	17
1	3	24	28		2	4	9	15
1	4	18	23		2	6	6	14
1	6	12	19		3	3	8	14
1	8	9	18		3	4	6	13

Students should recognize, from the table, that the solution is not unique with the information given. That is, there are three sets of factors whose sums are multiples of 7:

$$1, 3, 24 \qquad \text{Sum} = 28$$
$$2, 6, 6 \qquad \text{Sum} = 14$$
$$3, 3, 8 \qquad \text{Sum} = 14$$

Hopefully their response will be that there is inadequate information to solve the problem. Now you can provide the class with an additional clue so as to determine a single solution. For example, if you indicate that the three factors are unique (no duplications), then the only solution to the problem is the numbers 1, 3, and 24. Other clues can be given to obtain different sets of factors as the solution.

3.7 CONCLUSION

It is likely that the topic of problem solving will continue to dominate discussions about the mathematics curriculum well into the twenty-first century. Mathematicians, mathematics educators, psychologists, and teachers continue to strive for appropriate procedures that will help our students to become better problem solvers in real-world situations. Suitable methods to assess student abilities in this area are also the subject of study and research by various groups. As noted on page 209 in the NCTM *Standards:*

> *If problem solving is to be the focus of school mathematics, it must also be the focus of assessment. Students' ability to solve problems develops over time as a result of extended instruction, opportunities to solve many kinds of problems, and encounters with real-life situations.*

These words provide mathematics teachers with adequate challenges for the years ahead!

It should be noted that there are many lists of problem-solving strategies available in the literature, but no universal agreement on any single collection. Among the many strategies that can be found in textbooks are the following:

Obtain an answer by trial and error.
Use an aid, model, or sketch.
Search for a pattern.
Act out the problem.
Make a list, table, or chart.
Work backwards.
Start with a guess.
Solve an equivalent but simpler problem.
Relate a new problem to a familiar one.

As we enter the twenty-first century, we find that mathematics teachers and textbooks are stressing problem solving and strategies for problem solving to a greater extent than ever before. However, much remains to be done in developing standards for an appropriate balance between problem solving and basic computational skills, finding real-life problem-solving situations that are meaningful to our students, and finally, adequately assessing student knowledge in these areas.

EXERCISES

For each Exercise, identify one or more suitable problem-solving strategies and solve the problem.

1. How many games must be played in order to obtain a winner in a table tennis tournament of 20 players?

2. What is the units digit in the expansion of 7^{1999}?

3. What is the tens digit in the expansion of 7^{1999}?

4. What is the digit in the tens place in the expansion of 3^{2001}? (*Hint*: The tens digit repeats in cycles of 20.)

5. A number is formed by writing the counting numbers in order:

$$123456789101112131415\ldots$$

What is the one millionth digit in this number?

6. What is the sum of the first 100 odd counting numbers? the first 100 even counting numbers?

7. Consider the following charts of numbers. Place numbers in the second row so that each of the numbers in the first row appears as many times in the second row as is designated by the number placed beneath it. (Since the wording of this problem is complex, the first chart has been completed as an example.)

0	1	2	3
1	2	1	0

0	1	2	3	4

8. Repeat Exercise 7 for this chart:

0	1	2	3	4	5	6	7	8	9

9. Consider Exercises 7 and 8 and attempt to find solutions for charts that show numbers from 0 through 6, 7, and 8. Can you find a solution for a chart that shows numbers from 0 through 5?

10. Two mathematicians are each assigned a positive integer. Each knows his or her own integer, but neither one knows the other's. They are told that the product of the two integers is either 8 or 16. This is their conversation:

First mathematician: "I do not know your number."
Second mathematician: "I do not know your number."
First mathematician: "Give me a hint."
Second mathematician: "No, you give me a hint."

At this point one of the two mathematicians knows the other's number. Assuming both always tell the truth and do not guess, what is the number and who has it?

11. A penny and a quarter are on a table. You are told:

"If you tell me a true statement, I will give you one of the coins. If you tell me a false statement, you will get none."

What statement can you make that will guarantee that you will receive the quarter?

12. How many different tips are possible if you plan to use exactly three coins, and you have a penny, nickel, dime, quarter, and half-dollar available?

13. Two boats travel back and forth across a river at a constant rate of speed, without stopping. They start at the same time from opposite sides of the river and pass each other for the first time when they are 700 feet from one shore. After each makes one turn they pass again when they are 400 feet from the other shore. How wide is the river? (Draw a sketch and attempt to solve the problem without the use of algebra.)

14. Draw a network to illustrate the Koenigsberg Bridge problem. Then use Euler's conclusions about networks to show why the solution to this problem is impossible.

15. Use calculus to find the maximum volume possible for an open box formed from a 12 × 12-inch square piece of cardboard with squares of equal size cut off from each corner.

16. Consider the set of counting numbers from 1 through 1999. You are to remove any two of these numbers and replace them by their difference. Continue in this manner until there is just one number left in the set. Is that number odd or even? Justify your answer.

17. What is the greatest number of pieces of cake you can get with four successive slices through a cake?

18. Consider the matching of fractions (rational numbers) and counting numbers shown on page 79.
    a. Which counting number will be matched with the fraction $\frac{15}{21}$?
    b. Which counting number will be matched with the fraction $\frac{p}{q}$?

19. A book has one page missing. The sum of the digits of the remaining pages is equal to 10,000. How many pages are there in the book and which page is missing?

ACTIVITIES

1. Prepare a collection of nonstandard problems that are suitable for use in a junior or senior high school mathematics class.

2. Begin a collection of challenging problems that can be used with gifted mathematics students. One possible source is to review various competitive contests or examinations in mathematics.

3. Find a specific problem that can be used to illustrate each of the strategies listed in the conclusion to this chapter.

4. Write a report on the four-color problem that states the problem, describes some of the efforts made to solve the problem in the past, and states the current status of the problem.

5. Prepare a one-period lesson plan for a middle school or senior high school mathematics class that develops a particular problem-solving strategy.

6. Prepare a one-period lesson plan suitable for a high school geometry class that provides for student discovery of patterns.

7. Begin with a 12 × 12-inch piece of cardboard, and form a box without a top by cutting off squares of equal size and folding up the edges. Experiment to find the size of the square corners that should be cut off to obtain a box of maximum volume. Give your answer to the nearest half inch. Then use calculus to find the size of the corners that gives the maximum volume and find that volume.

8. Review several recently published high school algebra textbooks and report on the manner in which problem solving is treated. In particular, note any attention that may be given to strategies for problem solving.

9. Prepare a report on specific recommendations made by the NCTM concerning problem solving.

10. Read Chapter 2 in *Mathematics and the Imagination* by Edward Kasner and James Newman, New York: Simon and Schuster, 1967. Report on the proof developed there that the set of rational fractions is equivalent to the set of integers.

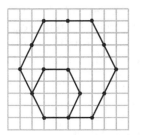

4

ACTIVITIES WITH
NUMERICAL CONCEPTS

This chapter deals with aids and activities that can be used to teach or to review fundamental arithmetic skills. Specific attention is given to fractions, decimals, and percents along with computational curiosities and number pattern experiments. Sample student worksheets are illustrated and simple classroom experiments described. Detailed construction steps appear as needed for the aids discussed in the chapter along with suggestions for their uses and possible extensions. Problem-solving experiences are emphasized throughout.

4.1 REVIEWING BASIC NUMERICAL CONCEPTS

Most students need practice in maintaining basic arithmetic skills throughout their mathematical training. However, always reviewing and drilling on skills in the same manner that they were first introduced can greatly reduce student interest. Thus it is essential that teachers search for a fresh approach to familiar topics.

Use Visual Aids

Visual aids can frequently serve as the vehicle to motivate review, disguising an otherwise unexciting but necessary topic. Here are several examples that can be used to review fundamental operations with whole numbers.

Example 1. Use a student's birthdate, or some specific date, such as the following:

31487 (3/14/87 for March 14, 1987)

Place these separate digits on five index cards. Have a student select one of these cards, such as 7, and challenge students to use the numerals on the four other cards, together with the fundamental operations of arithmetic, to obtain the selected number. Here are some possible answers assuming that 7 is selected as the objective card:

$$8 + 3 - (1 \times 4) = 7$$
$$3(8 \div 4) + 1 = 7$$
$$3 \times 1 + 8 - 4 = 7$$
$$(8 + 1) \div 3 + 4 = 7$$

$$\mathbf{3\ 1\ 4\ 8\ 7} \qquad \boxed{3}\,\boxed{1}\,\boxed{4}\,\boxed{8} \rightarrow \boxed{7}$$

Now let each student use his or her own birthday, or the day of the year, for more practice. Some will have 4 digits instead of 5 and others will have 6. Some will contain zeros and some will repeat digits. Some sets will be easy to work with while others will be hard or impossible. It is a simple idea, a simple aid, a simple activity—but far more motivating than a sheet of drill problems.

Example 2. Use ten 3×5 index cards and write the numbers 1 through 10 on them. Shuffle the cards and deal out five of them. The challenge is to use the values on these five cards, together with *any* mathematical operation with which students are familiar, to obtain the value on the next card turned over. Students can play individually or in teams, with points awarded to the first correct answer found or to all teams that find an answer within a specified period of time. Here are several examples of the use of five cards to obtain the number 7 found on the next card.

$$\boxed{6}\,\boxed{8}\,\boxed{1}\,\boxed{3}\,\boxed{4} \rightarrow \boxed{7}$$

$$(8 - 6 - 1)(3 + 4) = 7$$
$$(8 - 1)(3 + 4 - 6) = 7$$
$$\frac{1(8 + 34)}{6} = 7$$
$$3(6 - \sqrt{8 + 1}) - \sqrt{4} = 7$$

This game can give some good mental practice in problem solving by the strategy of trial and error. By having the students express the process algebraically, additional practice can be gained in the proper use of grouping symbols. This is an excellent game to help develop better number awareness.

Manipulate Geometric Models

Students need to see the connection as numerical equivalences emerge out of the manipulations of geometric models. Start with a square. Fold a pair of opposite vertices together and then fold them to the center point of the square. Starting with a unit square, what fractional parts remain at each step?

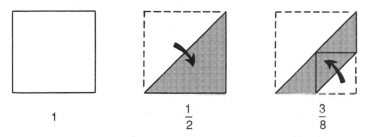

$$1 \qquad\qquad \frac{1}{2} \qquad\qquad \frac{3}{8}$$

- What fractional part results if the remaining two vertices of the square are now folded to the center point as well?

Pose Challenging Problems

Problems that reach beyond the routine often stimulate new interest in arithmetic computation.

A man was born in a year that was a perfect square. How old is he now?

Have your students guess first, and then use *trial and error* to find the last year that was a perfect square. Subtract from the current year to find the age.

For a more challenging adaptation of the same kind of problem, pose this question and discuss some of the possible answers.

In recording a woman's year of birth and death, one was a perfect square and the other was a perfect cube. How old was she when she died?

A calculator can be a handy tool here to show that the last two possible ages are 36 and 47.

4.2 FRACTIONS AND DECIMALS

Many students have difficulty understanding fractions and decimals and their related computational algorithms. Physical models and manipulative experiences often give these concepts and skills fuller meaning.

Recognizing Fractional Parts

The initial concept of a fraction is that of a fractional part of a whole, a geometric concept. If a student lacks this concept and yet is thrust into the algorithms of computation, success may be hard to come by. At all levels, take the time to connect fractions to geometry. This will allow for concrete experiences to bridge the gap to the abstractions inherent in the numerical symbols.

1. Fold a square piece of paper along its diagonals. Each small triangle formed is what fractional part of the square? Since 4 small congruent triangles result, each must represent $\frac{1}{4}$ of the original square.

2. The smaller square shown is what fractional part of the larger square? Ask first and then show that the answer must be $\frac{1}{2}$ by folding each corner of a large paper square to its center.

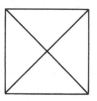

3. Use this arrangement of the seven *tangram* pieces. (See page 166.) The small square is what fractional part of the larger square? If your eye can see a possible geometric subdivision of the figure into 16 small congruent triangles, then you know the small square is clearly $\frac{1}{8}$ of the larger.

Forming Fractions

Write four different single-digit numbers on cards. Use them for the numerators and denominators of two fractions.

How many different fractions can be formed with single-digit numerators and denominators using these cards?

$$\frac{2}{5} \quad \frac{4}{3}$$

Can two equivalent fractions be formed? If not, which two are nearest in value?

Which fraction has the greatest value? the least? Which two have the greatest sum? the least?

Students all too often only see fractions as single entities and not as ratios of numbers that can change. By moving the cards around, the students have a physical model to recall mentally later when asked what happens to a fraction when the numerator or denominator increases or decreases.

Adding Fractions

Fold a long rectangular strip into thirds vertically. Fold another the same size into sixths. Fold another into halves.

Tear off $\frac{1}{3}$ of the first strip and $\frac{1}{6}$ of the next; show that they equal $\frac{1}{2}$.

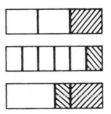

Use the same model to show these relationships:

$$\frac{1}{2}+\frac{1}{6}=\frac{2}{3} \qquad \frac{1}{2}-\frac{1}{6}=\frac{1}{3}$$

Multiplying Fractions

Take a rectangular piece of paper. Fold it in thirds one way and then fold it in half the other way. Each of the six resulting sections is $\frac{1}{3}\times\frac{1}{2}$ and hence the product must be $\frac{1}{6}$.

$$\frac{1}{3}\times\frac{1}{2}=\frac{1}{6} \qquad\qquad \frac{2}{3}\times\frac{3}{4}=\frac{6}{12}=\frac{1}{2}$$

Notice how a second similar folding can be used to show $\frac{2}{3}\times\frac{3}{4}$ geometrically.

Fractions in Ancient Egypt

Students need to know that fractions were not always written in the form we use today. This short example from ancient Egypt should create some interesting discussion. Begin by writing these characters on the chalkboard. Ask your students to offer possible interpretations based on what they see and know. At first, tell them only that it is a mathematical problem from ancient times written in Egyptian hieroglyphics.

After hearing a few of their thoughts, remind them that it is a computation problem involving numbers and operations. Later, try to lead them in the right direction. Offer the hint that fractions are involved. Finally, write down this literal translation.

$$\tfrac{1}{3} \text{ to be added} \qquad \tfrac{1}{5} \text{ to be subtracted}$$

Let them discover that the problem is read from right to left and that the inverse operations of addition and subtraction are represented as feet walking in opposite directions. Don't leave the problem until you ask them to write down the answer, and don't accept $\frac{2}{15}$. Keep them working until they give you the answer following the methods used in ancient Egyptian times where only unit fractions were used and where the same fraction was never repeated twice in a single answer.

$$\frac{2}{15} = \frac{4}{30} = \frac{3}{30} + \frac{1}{30} = \frac{1}{10} + \frac{1}{30}$$

Naming Decimals

Start with three cards on which you write the numbers 1, 2, and a decimal point. Name all the decimals that can be formed using all the cards in any order.

For a more challenging version, add another card with a different digit, use any or all of the cards, and list all the possible decimals in order.

$$\boxed{1}\,\boxed{2}\boxed{.}\,\boxed{3}$$

The length of the list may surprise you.

.1	.12	.123	.13	.132	.2
.21	.213	.23	.231	.3	.31
.312	.32	.321	1	1.2	1.23
1.3	1.32	2	2.1	2.13	2.3
2.31	3	3.1	3.12	3.2	3.21
12	12.3	13	13.2	21	21.3
23	23.1	31	31.2	32	32.1
123	132	213	231	312	321

There are many ways to use this idea in class. One method that the authors have used with good success goes like this:

- Start with some number in the set, say 2.
- Call on different students in rapid succession to give consecutively increasing decimal values that can be formed.
- Let the class react to each answer. As soon as a mistake is made, start over from the beginning again.

See if you can get through every student in class without any mistakes.

Another variation is to begin each day with this activity. Once a mistake occurs, try again the following day. Give the class just one try a day. See how many days it takes before the entire class can participate without a mistake by anyone. This activity can create a great deal of motivation and excitement in class. But be forewarned; it is not as easy as it appears, especially if you put your students under pressure with time constraints. The two common mistakes are giving a number that is not a possible choice and giving a number that is allowed but is not the next consecutive choice.

Ordering Decimals

Write a set of decimals on some strips of paper. Give students the decimals, one by one, and have them stand in the correct order, largest first, in front of the room. Choose the decimals at the appropriate level. Upper level students will find a set such as the following both interesting and challenging. Anticipate a great deal of discussion from the participating students.

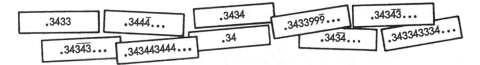

This activity can serve as a change of pace, but even more it can dramatically illustrate and emphasize problems and difficulties in ordering decimals. The activity is readily adaptable to the review of fractions, percents, and integers.

Multiplying Decimals

Start with four digits on cards. Which digits should go where to make the indicated products the largest possible?

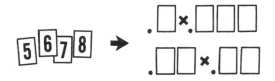

Moving the cards allows for visual reordering without repetitions, thus facilitating trial and error and analysis. For some, a calculator would be a useful tool. As a variation, do the same thing again but this time look for the smallest possible products.

Displaying Decimals

Keep a roll of paper tape and a marking pen available when teaching decimals. These aids can be used to make some dramatic and powerful impressions about the nature of infinite decimals, both repeating and nonrepeating.

Write a great many digits on the paper tape. Then, at just the right time in class, unroll the tape across the room or tack it on the bulletin board.

Here, as examples, are two infinite and repeating decimals:

$$\frac{1}{7} = 0.142857142857142857142857142857142857142857142857\ldots$$
$$\text{(repeats in blocks of 6 digits)}$$

$$\frac{1}{17} = 0.0588235294117647058823529411764705882352941176 47\ldots$$
$$\text{(repeats in blocks of 16 digits)}$$

Then ask such thought-provoking questions as these:

1. What is the one hundredth digit in the decimal for $\frac{1}{7}$; for $\frac{1}{17}$?   (8, 8)
2. How many digits precede the one hundredth 7 in the decimal for $\frac{1}{7}$? for $\frac{1}{17}$?   (599, 799)
3. What is the last digit in the decimal for $\frac{1}{7}$? for $\frac{1}{17}$?
   (There is none. No infinite decimal has a last digit.)

Nonrepeating decimals with properties such as the following can generate some interesting questions when a long sequence is displayed.

0.797797779777797777797777779777777797777777797777777779…

1. How many digits precede the one hundredth 9?
   (5050 sevens plus 99 nines, for 5149 digits)

2. Are there more 7's or 9's in the decimal?

(Particularly unsettling is the fact that the infinite decimal has no more 7's than 9's!)

When discussing the nonrepeating nature of the decimal representation for the irrational number π, many students nod in agreement but do not really believe that it *never* repeats. The message is much more impressive and lasting when the students can actually see and study 100 or so of the digits for repeating patterns. All the teacher needs is a strip of paper and the time to copy the digits down.

$\pi = 3.14159\ 26535\ 89793\ 23846\ 26433\ 83279\ 50288\ 41971$
$69399\ 37510\ 58209\ 74944\ 59230\ 78164\ 06286\ 20899$
$86280\ 34825\ 34211\ 70679\ 82148\ 08651\ 32823\ 06647$

Students may find it of interest to use the Internet to research the efforts that have been made by mathematicians throughout the ages to find ever greater representations of *pi*. From the ancient oriental value of π taken as 3, to the geometric approach used by Archimedes (ca. 240 B.C.) to locate the value of π between $\frac{223}{71}$ and $\frac{22}{7}$, to the use of modern high-speed computers, there has been a constant search to evaluate this fascinating number. According to a website located at the University of Tokyo, the record as of July, 1998 was found by Yasumasa Kanada and Daisuke Takahashi to be an expansion to 51,539,600,000 decimal digits, with the 50 billionth place being 2.

Many interesting sequences of numbers appear in this expansion. The sequence 01234565789 appears six times, whereas the sequence 9876543210 appears five times. Furthermore, there is a sequence of 12 successive 9's that appears beginning with the 12,479,021,132nd digit! Among other things, such listings are useful for those engaged in the art of cryptology, an increasingly important field concerned with maintaining secrecy in large computer-based systems such as those in banking, business, and the government.

Most students are fascinated by the concept of very large numbers, especially in this technological age. Some teachers have found it of interest to have a class collect examples of such numbers, and thus have brought a **googol** to class for display. A googol can be written as 1 followed by 100 zeros, or simply as 10^{100}. The number doesn't sound too big when you talk about it, but students can begin to appreciate just how large it is when the teacher pulls out a strip of paper and unrolls the 100 zeros clear across the classroom. By comparison, one million (1,000,000) looks trivial.

GOOGOL   10,000,000,000,000,000,000,000,000,000,000,
000,000,000,000,000,000,000,000,000,000,
000,000,000,000,000,000,000,000,000,000

4.3 PERCENT

Many students have trouble with percents both in the junior high and senior high schools. The National Assessment of Educational Progress tests clearly bear out this point. Perhaps part of the problem arises from the methods in which percents are usually taught. Heavy emphasis on computational algorithmic procedures often leaves the student without a solid understanding of the concept and with little skill in mental manipulation of percents. Many students cannot visually estimate percents because they seldom see the subject in a geometric light. Concrete aids, activities, and manipulative experiences related to percent often clarify and reinforce the concept, which to many is extremely abstract.

Presentation Techniques

Cut out two circular pieces of paper of the same size but different in color. Use a protractor to divide each into 10 equal sectors. Cut along one radius to the center of each circle. Insert one circle inside the other so that it can rotate exposing anything from 0% to 100% of that color. Using both marked sides, students can count off by 10% units to get a visual reinforcement of various percents. Using the unmarked sides, students gain valuable experience in visual estimation.

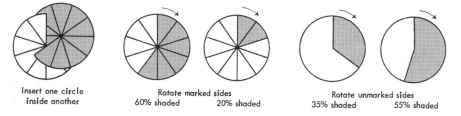

Insert one circle   Rotate marked sides   Rotate unmarked sides
inside another   60% shaded   20% shaded   35% shaded   55% shaded

A number line can serve as a valuable model in doing percent problems mentally. For problems involving 25%, 50%, and 75%, begin by dividing the number line into four equal parts. Then ask: What is 75% of 12?

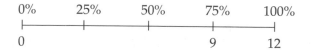

Place 0 under 0% and 12 under 100%. The number that would be under 75% is 9.

Note that the same picture can be used when mentally visualizing these problems as well.

9 is 75% of what number?

9 is what percent of 12?

Of course, the goal here is to encourage the students to think on the number line mentally. Time spent reviewing simple percent problems with models can significantly improve the students' understanding, comfort, and mental dexterity with percents later on.

Manipulative Experiences

Concrete activities in the hands of the students provide valuable experiences and afford the teacher an opportunity to show connections between geometric and arithmetic models. Here are several examples.

Example 1. Provide each student with a square piece of paper and directions to label the vertices in the order A, B, C, and D. Fold the square as indicated. What percent of the original square remains after each fold?

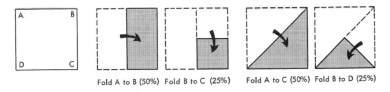

Fold A to B (50%)   Fold B to C (25%)   Fold A to C (50%)   Fold B to D (25%)

Now see how many students can give the correct percents of the original square remaining in these cases without actually folding the square. Use the folded square as a check.

Fold A to the midpoint of side AB.   (75%)
Fold A, B, C, and D to the center of the square.   (50%)
Fold A to C and then B to C.   ($37\frac{1}{2}$%)

Example 2. Start with a 2" × 8" strip of paper. Fold it in half and in half again to divide it into four squares.

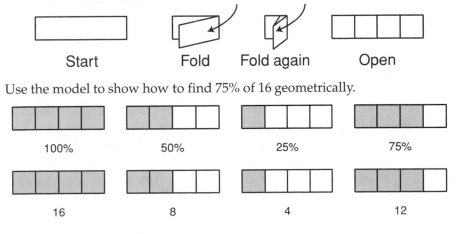

Use the model to show how to find 75% of 16 geometrically.

If 100% of the paper strip is defined as 16, then 75% of it is 12. It follows that 75% of 16 is 12. Of course, the strip can be defined by any numerical value and the same method will apply. Convenient choices are multiples of 4.

4.4 COMPUTATIONAL CURIOSITIES AND GAMES

Many interesting computational curiosities are available to motivate instruction in mathematics. These range from items that the teacher can use for classroom demonstration to those that can be given to students in the form of a puzzle. The collection that follows is representative of the many topics in the area of computation that can serve to motivate students in the mathematics classroom while providing a review of arithmetic fundamentals.

1. Digits in dates   One popular activity is to take the digits of a specific date and use these to generate various numbers. Usually the additional stipulation is stated that the digits must be used in the order in which they appear in the date under consideration. As an example, consider the date 1776. Here are two ways to use the digits of this date to obtain the number 4.

$$17 - 7 - 6 = 4 \qquad (17 + 7) \div 6 = 4$$

An interesting project is to attempt to represent as many numbers as possible from 0 through 100 using these four digits in order. Depending upon the level of ability of the class, various operations may be permitted.

0: $1^7 - 7 + 6$ 1: 1^{776}	with exponents
2: $1 + \sqrt{7 \times 7} - 6$ 3: $\sqrt{1 + 7 + 7 - 6}$	with square roots
4: $\lvert 1 + (7 \div 7) - 6 \rvert$ 5: $\lvert 1 - 7 \rvert - 7 + 6$	with absolute values
6: $1 \times (7 - 7)! \times 6$ 7: $1 \times 7 \times (7 - 6)!$	with factorials
8: $1 + (7 \div 7) + 6$ 9: $(1 + 7 + 7) - 6$	with fundamental operations only

This activity can be used in a variety of ways. For example, it can be given as an assignment, it can be used as the basis for a race between chosen teams, it can form the basis for a bulletin board display, and so forth. It is most appropriate to use near the start of a new year, using the digits of the forthcoming year. Try it for 1999. The first few years of the twenty-first century will be especially challenging!

2. Four fours Closely related to the preceding item is one that requires as many numbers as possible to be represented using four 4's and any available operation. Here, for example, are representations for the numbers 0 through 10.

$$0: 44 - 44$$
$$1: 44 \div 44$$
$$2: (4 \div 4) + (4 \div 4)$$
$$3: (4 + 4 + 4) \div 4$$
$$4: 4 \mid 4(4 \quad 4)$$
$$5: 4 + 4^{(4-4)}$$
$$6: \sqrt{4 \times 4} + 4 - \sqrt{4}$$
$$7: 44 \div 4 - 4$$
$$8: (4 \times 4) - 4 - 4$$
$$9: 4 + 4 + (4 \div 4)$$
$$10: (44 - 4) \div 4$$

3. One through nine A difficult but interesting project is to use all nine digits from 1 through 9 to represent 100. Challenge your class to find as many different ways as possible to do this, and make a collection of these on a bulletin board. Here are several examples.

$$1 + 2 + 3 + 4 + 5 + 6 + 7 + (8 \times 9) = 100$$
$$123 - 45 - 67 + 89 = 100$$
$$1 + 2 + 3 - 4 + 5 + 6 + 78 + 9 = 100$$
$$(56 + 34 + 8 + 2) \times (9 - 7 - 1) = 100$$
$$62 + 38 + [(1 + 7) \times (9 - 5 - 4)] = 100$$

To make it even more challenging the teacher may wish to restrict the use of the nine digits to their natural order, as in the first three illustrations above.

4.5 NUMBER-PATTERN EXPERIMENTS

One of the objectives in teaching mathematics is to develop number awareness. Experiments that offer physical situations leading to the recognition of number patterns and sequences meet this need. They involve the individual student with a hands-on activity, a direct instruction leading to a countable result, a chance to discover a pattern and offer educated guesses at successive results before actual verification, and a challenging opportunity to generalize algebraically where appropriate. These are valuable ingredients in a meaningful and motivating classroom experiment.

Some of the best classroom experiments involve student manipulatives made of the simplest materials and are based on straightforward directions and clear objectives. Such activities are all the better when they capture the imagination and contain unexpected surprises that lead to new observations, pose new questions, and force new strategies.

Consider the following classroom experiment that involves just a sheet of paper in each student's hands. By repeatedly folding the paper in half, some interesting number-pattern questions emerge.

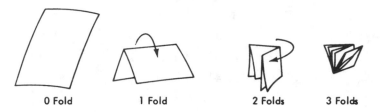

| 0 Fold | 1 Fold | 2 Folds | 3 Folds |

What is the relationship between the number of folds and the thickness?

Have the students fold and count. Encourage careful and systematic tabulation. Let the students make all the discoveries.

Number of folds	0 1 2 3 4 ...
Number of sheets thick	1 2 4 8 16 ...

Undoubtedly, many students will be able to visualize the results without actually folding the paper. The thickness doubles with each successive fold. Thus with n folds, the thickness is 2^n. Have the students compute the number of folds needed to get the number of sheets in a 500-page book. Recall that a 500-page book uses only 250 sheets. Give paper to some students and see if they can fold it to this thickness. They will probably get no more than 7 folds. Invariably, some student will suggest using a larger sheet of paper to get more folds. Be ready with some large pages from a newspaper. Let the students try. The results will undoubtedly surprise both them and the rest of the class.

The examples of experiments in number patterns that follow include some with detailed descriptions and analyses and brief suggestions for others. They are probably best used one or two at a time throughout the year rather than all at one time. Some are more suited for lower grades and slower classes; others can be challenging for the better secondary students. But in all cases, the student should take educated guesses and try to verify them with the material supplied. Students should be encouraged to discover and verbalize the pattern illustrated. However, many of the generalizations of the nth terms can be left for the better students.

EXPERIMENT 1   Folding Paper

Material
One sheet of paper per student.

Directions
1. Fold the paper once, open it up, and record the number of regions.
2. Fold again for the maximum number of regions possible.
3. Repeat the process again for 3 folds. Remember, open the paper flat before each new fold and always fold for the *maximum* number of regions possible.
4. Try to discover the number sequence and predict the result for 4 folds. Check your answer by folding again and counting regions.
5. Can you generalize the sequence for *n* folds?

Analysis
The maximum number of regions is always formed if the new fold cuts every existing fold without passing through any intersection or endpoint.

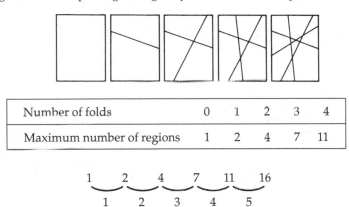

Number of folds	0	1	2	3	4
Maximum number of regions	1	2	4	7	11

$$\underbrace{1 \quad \underbrace{2 \quad \underbrace{4 \quad \underbrace{7 \quad \underbrace{11 \quad 16}}}}}$$
$$\quad 1 \quad\quad 2 \quad\quad 3 \quad\quad 4 \quad\quad 5$$

The differences of entries form the successive counting numbers. Hence for 5 folds, the answer is the sum of the first five counting numbers plus 1.

$$(1 + 2 + 3 + 4 + 5) + 1 = 16$$

For *n* folds the maximum number of regions is the sum of the first *n* counting numbers plus 1.

$$\frac{n(n + 1)}{2} + 1$$

EXPERIMENT 2 Cutting String

Material
Pieces of string and scissors.

Directions
1. If you know the number of cuts in a string, do you know the number of
    pieces? Try completing the table without cutting the string first.

number of cuts	0	1	2	3	4	5
number of pieces						

If there are *n* cuts in the string, how many pieces will there be?
If there are *n* pieces, how many cuts were made?

2. Fold the string as shown before you cut. Do you know the maximum number
    of pieces that will be formed this way from a given number of cuts? Again, try
    to complete the following table without cutting the string.

number of cuts	0	1	2	3	4	5
number of pieces						

If there are *n* cuts, how many pieces will there be?
If there are *n* pieces, how many cuts were made?

3. Loop the string through the scissors as shown. Find how many pieces you get
    for each number of loops.

0 Loop   1 Loop

number of loops	0	1	2	3	4	5
number of pieces						

If there are *n* loops, how many pieces will there be?
If there are *n* pieces, how many loops were cut?

Analysis
1. Each cut produces an extra new piece. Hence for *n* cuts there will be $n + 1$
    pieces. To get *n* pieces, $n - 1$ cuts are needed.
2. Here each cut produces 2 new pieces. Hence for *n* cuts there will be $2n + 1$
    pieces. Note that the number of pieces must always be odd. To get *n* pieces,
    with *n* odd, make $\frac{(n - 1)}{2}$ cuts.
3. In this case we are counting loops and pieces rather than cuts and pieces.
    Starting with 0 loops is the same as starting with 1 cut which gives 2 pieces.
    One loop is the same as 2 cuts and gives 3 pieces. Each additional loop means
    an additional piece when cut. For *n* loops, there are $n + 2$ pieces. To get *n*
    pieces, cut through $n - 2$ loops, but remember that *n* cannot be less than 2.

Material
Compasses, rulers, and paper.

Directions
Draw some circles on your paper and use them to try to discover the number patterns in each of these situations.

Find the maximum number of regions possible in a circle for various numbers of radii, diameters, chords, and tangents.

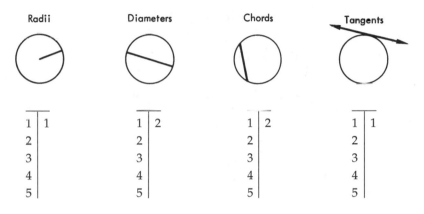

Radii		Diameters		Chords		Tangents	
1	1	1	2	1	2	1	1
2		2		2		2	
3		3		3		3	
4		4		4		4	
5		5		5		5	

Analysis
1. 1, 2, 3, 4, 5
   With 1 radius there is 1 region. Each additional radius, wherever it is drawn, increases the number of regions by 1. For n radii there must be n regions.
2. 2, 4, 6, 8, 10
   With 1 diameter there are 2 regions. Each additional diameter, wherever it is drawn, increases the number of regions by 2. For n diameters there must be $2n$ regions. It follows that the number of regions will always be even.
3. 2, 4, 7, 11, 16
   To produce the maximum number of regions, care must be taken as to where the successive chords are drawn. Each new chord must intersect all other chords drawn but not at any existing intersection or endpoint. For n chords, the maximum number of regions possible is $\frac{n(n+1)}{2} + 1$.
4. 1, 1, 1, 1, 1
   Since tangents to a circle contain points of the circle but never pass through its interior, the number of regions inside the circle remains 1 for any number of tangents. However, an interesting counting pattern emerges when all regions inside and outside the circle are counted. In this case these would be the tabled values:
   3, 6, 10, 15, 21
   For n tangents to a circle the maximum number of regions possible in the plane is $\frac{(n+1)(n+2)}{2}$, which is the sum of the first $n+1$ counting numbers.

Another challenging version of this last experiment counts the maximum number of regions possible in the plane using increasing numbers of secants. The results are 4, 8, 13, 19 for 1, 2, 3, 4 secants. Successive second differences increase by 1 each time. For n secants, a maximum of $\dfrac{(n+2)(n+3)}{2} - 2$ regions are possible in the plane. (See Exercise 18.)

EXPERIMENT 4   Figurate Numbers

Materials
Graph paper to facilitate drawing the similar figures.

Directions
1. Copy the figures shown. Then sketch the next one.
2. Count the dots in each figure.
3. Find the first differences. What pattern do you get?
4. Find the second differences. What pattern do you get?
5. What is the nth figurate number in the set?

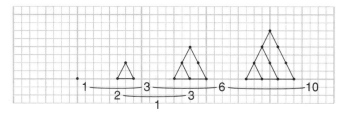

Triangular numbers

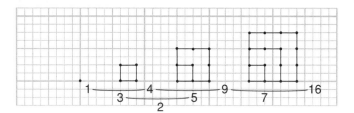

Square numbers

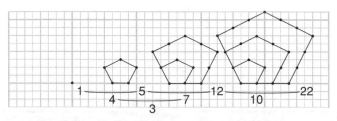

Pentagonal numbers

Analysis

Triangular numbers	1,	3,	6,	10,	15,	21,	28,	36, ...
first differences		2	3	4	5	6	7	8 ...
second differences			1	1	1	1	1	1 ...

The nth triangular number is $\dfrac{n(n+1)}{2}$.

Square numbers	1,	4,	9,	16,	25,	36,	49,	64, ...
first differences		3	5	7	9	11	13	15 ...
second differences			2	2	2	2	2	2 ...

The nth square number is n^2.

Pentagonal numbers	1,	5,	12,	22,	35,	51,	70,	92, ...
first differences		4	7	10	13	16	19	22 ...
second differences			3	3	3	3	3	3 ...

The nth pentagonal number is $\dfrac{n(3n-1)}{2}$.

Note that the second differences are especially interesting. For each of the given sets the second differences are constant and take on the value of two less than the number of sides in the figurate number.

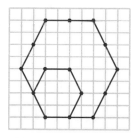

Hexagonal numbers

Students might be interested in also exploring hexagonal figurate numbers. The first three are shown in the figure as 1, 6, 15. Others can be computed quickly using the fact that all second differences must be 4.

Tables can be set up on a graphing calculator to display successive figurate numbers of any type, given the appropriate formulas. On these screens, Y_1 lists triangular numbers while Y_2 lists hexagonal numbers.

X	Y₁	Y₂
1	1	1
2	3	6
3	6	15
4	10	28
5	15	45
6	21	66
7	28	91

$Y_2=91$

X	Y₁	Y₂
8	36	120
9	45	153
10	55	190
11	66	231
12	78	276
13	91	325
14	105	378

$Y_2=378$

X	Y₁	Y₂
15	120	435
16	136	496
17	153	561
18	171	630
19	190	703
20	210	780
21	231	861

$Y_2=861$

The seventh hexagonal number is 91.

The fourteenth hexagonal number is 378.

The twenty-first hexagonal number is 861.

The following experiment focuses on discovering number patterns using geometric figures and manipulatives. Such activities provide valuable geometric as well as numerical experiences.

EXPERIMENT 5   Counting Triangles

Material
A triangular piece of paper.

Directions
Repeatedly fold a triangle through one of its vertices. Count the total number of triangles formed after each fold. Try to discover the pattern.

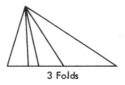

3 Folds

Analysis

number of folds	0	1	2	3	4	5
number of triangles	1	3	6	10	15	21

4.6 MAGIC SQUARES ACTIVITIES

Many interesting activities involving arithmetic review can be presented within the format of magic squares. A magic square is a square array of numbers where the sums of the entries in each row, each column, and each diagonal are all the same.

This 3 × 3 magic square has a magic constant of 201.

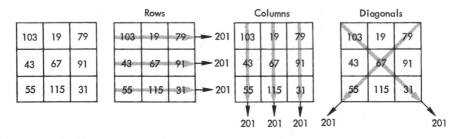

Every magic square has eight different rotations and reflections. Can you find the other seven positions for the nine numbers in the magic square above?

New magic squares can be formed from existing ones by using one or more of the four fundamental operations. Notice that the simple 3×3 magic square using the numbers 1 through 9 can be transformed into the one shown above by changing every entry x to $12x + 7$.

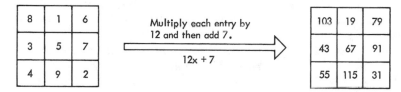

8	1	6
3	5	7
4	9	2

Multiply each entry by 12 and then add 7.

$12x + 7$

103	19	79
43	67	91
55	115	31

What algebraic transformation will change the above magic square on the right, back to the one on the left?

Magic squares can involve decimals, fractions, integers, and variables as well as whole numbers. Verify that each of these is a magic square.

1.75	0.5	4	2.25
3	3.25	0.75	1.5
0.25	2	2.5	3.75
3.5	2.75	1.25	1

2/3	1/12	1/2
1/4	5/12	7/12
1/3	3/4	1/6

-1	-8	15	8	1
-7	11	9	2	0
12	10	3	-4	-6
6	4	-3	-5	13
5	-2	-9	14	7

N+2	N+3	N-2
N-3	N+1	N+5
N+4	N-1	N

Here is a method that can be used to construct odd-ordered magic squares, those with an odd number of rows and columns.

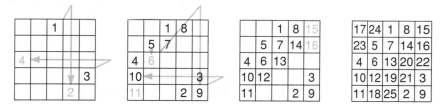

Step 1: Write the first number, 1, in the middle of the top row. Fill in successive counting numbers moving diagonally upward and to the right. When the next position is off the square, enter the number at the opposite end of the next row or column. Note how this has been done for the entries 2 and 4.

Step 2: Continue working diagonally upward and to the right. When you come to a position already occupied, enter the number in the space immediately below the last one filled. Note how this has been followed for the numbers 6 and 11.

Step 3: The space that follows the upper right-hand corner is the lower left-hand corner. Since this space is occupied by 11, the 16 is placed below 15 following the rule from step 2.

Step 4: Continue the process until the 5 × 5 magic square is finished. A 5 × 5 magic square has 5 × 5, or 25, entries. Since 1 was the first number, 25 is the last.

Check to see that the completed array is indeed a magic square.

Using this method, construct a 7 × 7 magic square starting with a 1 in the middle of the first row. How would you construct a 7 × 7 magic square starting with a 100 in the middle of the first column?

			100			

The following pages illustrate how individual worksheets can be prepared for exploring properties of magic squares. The suggestions can be readily modified and extended to fit other needs. Worksheet 1 deals with rotations and reflections of a given magic square and involves visualization skills. Worksheet 2 calls for the completing of magic squares using problem-solving strategies. Worksheet 3 reviews computational skills and leads to a generalization concerning transforming one magic square into another. Worksheet 4 ties the topic to algebraic symbolism and proof.

Worksheet 1

Rearranging Entries in a Magic Square

Many different numbers can be used in forming a 3 × 3 magic square. Likewise, many arrangements can be made from the same set of numbers in a magic square.

8	1	6
3	5	7
4	9	2

This simple 3 × 3 magic square uses the numbers 1 through 9. The numbers in each row, column, and diagonal add to 15.

See if you can complete these magic squares using the same set of numbers, 1 through 9. Remember, the numbers in each row, column, and diagonal still must add to 15.

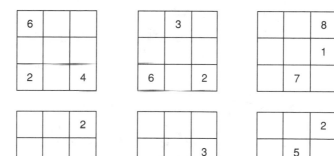

6		
2		4

3		
6		2

		8
		1
7		

		2
8	3	

		3
	1	8

		2
	5	
	1	

Cut out a square piece of paper and mark it with the original magic square. Turn the paper over and mark it on the back so that each number is in exactly the same square as in the front. Now see if you can get the magic squares above by simply rotating and flipping over this cutout. For example, if you flip over the original magic square about its vertical axis, you get the square in the upper left-hand corner. Find the one remaining arrangement possible with the numbers 1 through 9 that still forms a magic square.

Worksheet 2

Completing Magic Squares

Study these incomplete square arrays. Then try your problem-solving skills in completing them so that they become magic squares.

16	2	12
	18	

8		14	3
15	2	9	4
	11		13

13	12	6	25	
	14	8	7	
		15		3
4			16	
11	5	24		17

		53	10
13		4	7
	9	11	
51	12		

1		
$\frac{3}{8}$		
$\frac{1}{2}$		$\frac{1}{4}$

$1\frac{1}{6}$		
	$\frac{11}{12}$	
1		$\frac{2}{3}$

An odd-ordered magic square has an odd number of rows and columns. Each one also has a special relationship between its magic sum and its center value. See if you can discover this property and use it to complete these magic squares.

32		24
	20	

		7
		21
		11

12		4
		8

Worksheet 3

Operating on Magic Squares

What happens when you add to or multiply each entry in a magic square with a constant? Will you get another magic square?

Start with the magic square shown. In each case add the constant given to each entry to form a new array. Then check to see if it, too, is a magic square.

5	6	1
0	4	8
7	2	3

Add 25

Add $1\frac{1}{4}$

Add 1.5

Does it appear that when you add the same number to each entry in a magic square, another magic square is formed?

Now multiply each entry in this magic square by the numbers given.

21	0	15
6	12	18
9	24	3

Multiply by 9

Multiply by $\frac{3}{4}$

Multiply by 1.3

Does it appear that when you multiply each entry in a magic square by the same number, another magic square is formed?

The entries in this magic square are integers. Show that the numbers in each row, column, and diagonal add to 0. Then perform the operations indicated. In each case, see if the resulting array is also a magic square.

–3	2	1
4	0	–4
–1	–2	3

Subtract –2

Multiply by –3

Add $-\frac{3}{4}$ then multiply by $-\frac{1}{2}$

Choosing Your Own Magic Sum

Here is a very special 4 × 4 magic square that you can build with any magic sum. First select any number for the magic sum. When you complete the square below using this value for S, all ten rows, columns, and diagonals will have this sum S.

Let $S =$ _____. Then compute the values given and enter them in the positions shown. (For all cells to be positive, S must be 22 or more.)

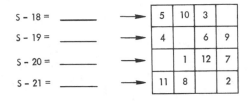

$S - 18 =$ _____	⟶
$S - 19 =$ _____	⟶
$S - 20 =$ _____	⟶
$S - 21 =$ _____	⟶

5	10	3	
4		6	9
	1	12	7
11	8		2

Check your work with these values. Add along each row, each column, and each diagonal. Each sum should equal the magic sum S that you chose.

Here is why this will always work. Enter the algebraic expressions for the missing values using the variable S.

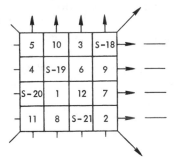

5	10	3	S–18
4	S–19	6	9
S–20	1	12	7
11	8	S–21	2

Find the sum for each row, each column, and each diagonal and write it in the space provided. What is each sum?

Try the same process for this 5 × 5 magic square.

Let $S =$ _____. Then compute the values given and enter them in the positions shown. (For all cells to be positive, S must be 45 or more.)

$S - 40 =$ _____	⟶
$S - 41 =$ _____	⟶
$S - 42 =$ _____	⟶
$S - 43 =$ _____	⟶
$S - 44 =$ _____	⟶

11	18		2	9
17		1	8	15
	5	7	14	16
4	6	13	20	
10	12	19		3

Show algebraically why this method must yield a magic square with the magic sum S.

4.7 MORE NUMERICAL AIDS AND ACTIVITIES

Napier's Rods

Invented by the Scottish nobleman John Napier (1550–1617), these simple computing devices were in common use during much of the 1600s. They were designed to simplify the burdensome task of multiplication by the very man who later invented logarithms—which, in effect, translated multiplication problems into addition problems. The original rods were made from strips of wood or bone and small enough to carry in the pocket. Each rod had four sides with a scale on each side. By placing the appropriate rods side by side, you had a convenient computing device for multiplying quickly.

Despite the speed with which computations can be completed with modern electronic calculators, Napier's Rods can be an interesting and exciting topic for students at most levels of ability, especially when placed in their proper historical perspective. This activity also offers an excellent opportunity for individual involvement in which students construct and manipulate their own personal set of Napier's Rods made from paper.

Index	1	2	3	4	5	6	7	8	9	0
1	0/1	0/2	0/3	0/4	0/5	0/6	0/7	0/8	0/9	0/0
2	0/2	0/4	0/6	0/8	1/0	1/2	1/4	1/6	1/8	0/0
3	0/3	0/6	0/9	1/2	1/5	1/8	2/1	2/4	2/7	0/0
4	0/4	0/8	1/2	1/6	2/0	2/4	2/8	3/2	3/6	0/0
5	0/5	1/0	1/5	2/0	2/5	3/0	3/5	4/0	4/5	0/0
6	0/6	1/2	1/8	2/4	3/0	3/6	4/2	4/8	5/4	0/0
7	0/7	1/4	2/1	2/8	3/5	4/2	4/9	5/6	6/3	0/0
8	0/8	1/6	2/4	3/2	4/0	4/8	5/6	6/4	7/2	0/0
9	0/9	1/8	2/7	3/6	4/5	5/4	6/3	7/2	8/1	0/0

Construction

For the chalkboard, mark a large sheet of poster paper as shown, using a special color for the index numbers. Cut it into strips and set them on the chalk ledge or attach them to the board for demonstration.

For the overhead projector, copy the strips on a sheet of acetate, cut them out, and project them on the screen or board.

For individual use, supply students with copies as shown. Once they cut off the strips, they can then proceed at their own pace in exploring and using the activity. Loose strips can be kept in an envelope for future use.

Uses

1. Place the index rod alongside one of the others and show how the corresponding multiples are given. For example, with the 8-rod and the index, ask for such products as 7×8.

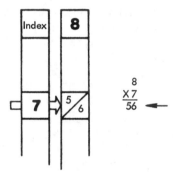

2. Repeat using two- and three-digit factors. For example, show 7×86 and 7×862. Explain how "carrying" works when adding along the diagonals. Let students read other products involving 8, 86, and 862 from the same settings.

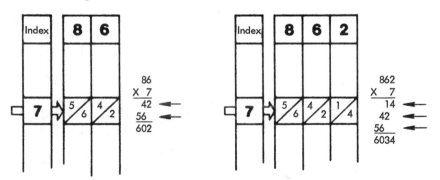

3. Allow students to suggest other multiplication problems, still with one-digit multipliers, and let others illustrate them at the board. See that some include the 0-rod.

4. Relate the results shown on the rods to the common computing algorithm now used for multiplying.
5. Let students discover how the rods can be used with two- and three-digit multipliers.

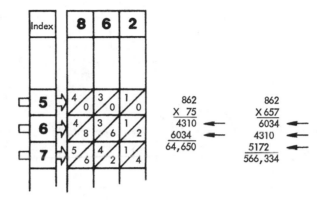

Binary Cards

Here is an interesting classroom experiment that can be used to reinforce the concept of the binary system.

Materials
Index cards, paper punch, scissors.

Directions
As a first step, write the numbers from 0 through 15 in binary notation. Prefix zeros so as to have a four-digit numeral for each number.

BASE 10	BASE 2	BASE 10	BASE 2
0	0000	8	1000
1	0001	9	1001
2	0010	10	1010
3	0011	11	1011
4	0100	12	1100
5	0101	13	1101
6	0110	14	1110
7	0111	15	1111

Next have each student prepare a set of 16 index cards, with four holes punched in each and with one of the corners cut off for purposes of identifying the face of the card. Now the numbers from 0 through 15 are represented as in the following figures. In each case a hole alone represents 0, while a slot cut above the hole to the edge of the card represents 1. The number that each card represents should be written on the face of the card, as shown.

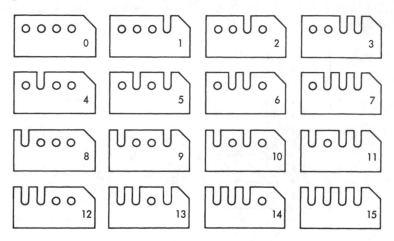

Follow the construction with these activities:

1. Place the cards in a stack and shuffle them well. How can all even-numbered cards be located? The even-numbered cards have 0's in the units place, the first hole on the right. Therefore, use a pencil or paper clip to push through this first hole. The cards lifted out will be the even-numbered ones. How can you sort out all the multiples of 4?
2. With only four sorts, any number from 0 through 15 can be located. Explain how to locate card 13 in just four sorts.
3. With only four sorts, put the shuffled cards back into numerical order from 0 through 15.

Analysis
1. Sort to remove those cards with 0's in the first two places from the right. These will be 0, 4, 8, and 12. How can the number 0 be sorted out?
2. Working from right to left,
   discard those pulled in the units place,
   keep only those pulled in the twos place,
   discard those pulled in the fours place,
   discard those pulled in the eights place.

3. Start with the first hole from the right. Place all the cards that lift up in front of the other cards. Then repeat this procedure for each of the three remaining positions in order. When finished, the cards will appear in numerical order.

Suggested Extensions
Have students write instructions for locating a particular card. Let other members in class follow the instructions to find the card in question.

Ask how many cards and holes are needed to sort out 32 pieces of data. How many cards can be sorted using 10 holes?

The Game of Nim

Although the game of Nim may be used purely as recreation at any time, it is best presented after the student has some knowledge of the binary system of numeration, thus providing an interesting application of that topic. The game is played by two students at a time and is probably best introduced by having the teacher challenge a student to a match.

Rules for playing

Many versions of the game can be played. Probably the easiest one to start with consists of three piles of chips. Pile A contains 3 chips, pile B contains 4 chips, and pile C contains 5 chips. At your turn, you select one pile of chips and remove as many chips as you wish from that one pile. You must, however, remove at least 1 chip. Players alternate, and the player who picks up the last chip on the board is the winner.

Strategy

Students may develop informal strategies for winning. The formal winning strategy is quite complex and consists of writing the number of chips in each pile in binary notation. In order to win, one must be certain that the sum of the digits in each binary place is even after the move. To illustrate this principle, here is an example of a game where the first player wins:

1.	A	XXX	In binary notation:	11	First player takes 2
	B	XXXX		100	chips from pile A,
	C	XXXXX		101	as shown next.
2.	A	X	In binary notation:	1	Second player takes 3
	B	XXXX		100	chips from pile C.
	C	XXXXX		101	
3.	A	X	In binary notation:	1	First player takes 1
	B	XXXX		100	chip from pile B.
	C	XX		10	
4.	A	X	In binary notation:	1	Second player takes
	B	XXX		11	both chips in pile C.
	C	XX		10	
5.	A	X	In binary notation:	1	First player takes 2 chips
	B	XXX		11	from pile B.
6.	A	X	In binary notation:	1	Second player takes 1 of
	B	X		1	the chips, and the first
					player wins on the seventh
					move by taking the
					remaining chip.

Note in the preceding game that the first player always made a move that left the second player with an array of chips whose number in binary notation had an even number of 1's in each column.

Extensions

The game can be played using the rule that the one who is forced to take the last chip is the loser. It can also be played with an indefinite number of chips in each of the original three piles, although the strategy for winning remains the same.

Nomographs

The word *nomograph*, which comes from the Greek and means a written law, applies in mathematics to a graphic technique for computing and for the solution of specific equations. Nomographs can serve as the source of many experiments that lead to discoveries and reviewing skills. Students gain valuable experience in constructing these graphs and in reading their scales as well as in verifying the results of computational problems.

The simplest example is the parallel scales nomograph. Better students can construct one from scratch using a ruler. With slower students you may prefer that it be constructed on graph paper.

Each of these examples of nomographs involves addition in the form $a + b = c$. The scales are parallel with equal spaces between them. Outer scales are calibrated alike while the middle scale is reduced to half-size.

This nomograph may be used to

1. find the sum of two integers
2. illustrate that each integer and its opposite add to 0
3. illustrate the commutative property for addition
4. relate subtraction of integers to addition

- Use geometry to explain why this nomograph works as it does.

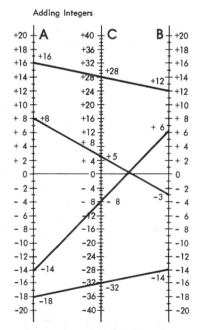

Adding Integers

Overhead Projector Ideas

The overhead projector can be an extremely effective teaching tool, especially when the transparencies are designed to capture the attention of the students. Make use of overlays, masks, color, and motion wherever possible. The two ideas shown here can be used to present familiar computational review in a new format and can easily be modified for other related skills.

Use a flowchart format to review addition, subtraction, multiplication, and division with whole numbers, integers, and rational numbers expressed as fractions, decimals, or percents. Slide the strips right or left to vary the problems and change the strips as needed.

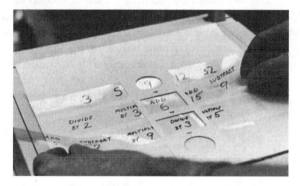

The dynamics of motion and change can be captured using acetate dials mounted on a mask with common sewing snaps. Cut small triangular holes at the points where the snaps are attached. The circles can be turned easily to vary the problem. This illustration shows how the idea can be applied to a review of exponents and powers.

This illustration allows for exponents of 0, 1, 2, 3, 4, or 5 to be applied to any one of the same set of base values. Use it with your students for computational practice or for exploring patterns in the units digits of successive powers of different bases, or modify it for fractional and negative exponents and bases.

4.8 CALCULATOR APPLICATIONS

The current age of technology has made the computer available to virtually every school and the calculator to essentially every interested student. These electronic marvels are certain to have a long-term effect on the mathematics curriculum. We need to reevaluate certain extensively taught computational algorithms in light of their current practical value. Calculators should be readily available and their use encouraged. Students need experience in recognizing when a problem is most appropriately done mentally, with pencil and paper, or with a calculator. Problem-solving situations once avoided because of the tediousness of the necessary computations can now be explored with a calculator and computer. Problem-solving strategies such as guess-and-test are now more accessible, and numerical tables for discovering patterns and critical values are now more easily generated.

The ideas that follow are but a brief sampling of the many possibilities that exist for classroom use of technology. They relate to the arithmetic aspects of the curriculum but have objectives that extend well beyond those of just computing the correct answer.

Prime Numbers

To test to see if a number is prime, check for possible prime divisors up to the square root of the number. Try 677. Its square root is just over 26, so it is only necessary to test those primes less than 26 for prime factors.

$$\sqrt{677} = 26.01922366\ldots$$

These graphing calculator displays show the tests on 2, 3, 5, 7, 11, 13, 17, 19, and 23. The results show that 677 must be prime.

```
677/2
            338.5
677/3
      225.6666667
677/5
            135.4
```

```
677/7
      96.71428571
677/11
      61.54545455
677/13
      52.07692308
```

```
677/17
      39.82352941
677/19
      35.63157895
677/23
      29.43478261
```

What is the next prime number after 677?

Repeating Decimals

Repeating decimals offer a rich source of activities for calculator use in the classroom.

Divide the numbers 1 through 3 by 9. Look for a pattern. Guess the results for dividends of 4 through 8. What about 9?

1/9	.1111111111
2/9	.2222222222
3/9	.3333333333

Now have each student guess these results as decimals, using the calculator as a check.

100 divided by 9

2000 divided by 9

3,000,000 divided by 9

Use a calculator to explore the repeating decimals formed by dividing 13 by 99, 999, and 9999. One set of examples is shown here.

13/99	.1313131313
13/999	.013013013
13/9999	.00130013

What patterns can you discover for dividing successive counting numbers by 11?

The following worksheet uses the calculator to explore an interesting convergence problem involving fractions. Start with a fraction $\frac{a}{b}$ between 0 and 1. Add the numerator and denominator to form a new denominator and add this sum to the original denominator to form a new numerator.

$$\frac{a}{b} \longrightarrow \frac{(a+b)+b}{a+b}$$

As the process is repeated, each time starting with the newly formed fraction, one discovers that the decimal equivalences appear to converge to the decimal for $\sqrt{2}$.

Worksheet

Converging Ratios

Start with a fraction between 0 and 1.
Follow these steps to form a new fraction.

1. New denominator—Add the numerator and denominator of the original fraction.
   New numerator—Add this new denominator to the original one.
2. Write the new fraction and use a calculator to find a decimal equivalent to four decimal places.
3. Repeat the steps again, this time starting with the new fraction. Continue the process until you make a discovery about the decimal equivalent.

Starting Fraction _____

New Denominator	New Numerator	New Fraction	Decimal Equivalent

4. Now try the same process with another fraction between 0 and 1.

EXERCISES

1. The four digits 5, 6, 7, and 8 are placed on separate cards. How many counting numbers can be formed using one or more of the cards?

2. The four digits 6, 7, 8, and 9 are used to form two two-digit numbers. Which two have the greatest difference? the greatest product?

3. The four numbers 4, 5, 6, and 7 are used as numerators and denominators for two fractions. Which two have the greatest sum? the greatest difference?

4. Represent the numbers from 10 through 20 using the digits of the year 1776. Any familiar mathematical operation may be used. Try to use the digits in the order in which they appear in the year.

5. Extend the list using four 4's on page 101 to represent as many of the numbers from 11 through 20 as possible.

6. Find several ways to represent 1000 using all nine digits from 1 through 9. (For example, $291 + 678 + 35 - 4 = 1000$)

7. Is a 10% raise followed by a 10% cut in pay better, worse, or the same as a 10% cut followed by a 10% raise? Explain why neither yields the original salary.

8. Order the three decimals $0.2\overline{332}$, $0.2\overline{332}$, and $0.\overline{2332}$. Then write a decimal for a rational number that lies between the smaller two and an irrational number that lies between the larger two.

9. What is the one millionth digit in the decimal expansion of $\frac{1}{7}$?

10. What is the last digit in the decimal expansion of $\frac{1}{6}$?

11. How many digits are there before the one hundredth 3 in the nonrepeating decimal 0.43443444344443444443...?

12. Write any three-digit number and then repeat the same digits again to form a six-digit number. Now divide by 7, then divide the quotient by 11, and finally divide the resulting quotient by 13. Repeat the same procedure, starting with another three-digit number. State your discovery, and then provide a mathematical explanation as to why the trick works as it does.

13. Write the first eight hexagonal figurate numbers. What is the nth hexagonal number?

14. Construct a 7×7 magic square using consecutive integers starting with 5.

15. Construct a 5×5 magic square using multiples of 3 starting with 3. What is the sum of each row, column, and diagonal? What is the middle entry?

16. Show that the sum of each row, column, and diagonal in an nth-order magic square formed from successive integers starting with 1 is $\frac{n(n^2 + 1)}{2}$. Explain why it follows that the middle entry must be $\frac{n^2 + 1}{2}$.

17. What is the sum of all entries in an nth-order magic square formed from consecutive integers starting with 5?

18. Show that the maximum number of regions that can be formed in a plane by a circle with n secants is $\dfrac{(n+2)(n+3)}{2} - 2$.

19. Prove that the sum of the first n odd counting numbers is n^2.

ACTIVITIES

1. Mark twenty cards with the numbers 1 through 20. Shuffle them and deal out the top five cards. Use each of the selected values once, with any of the four fundamental operations to give the value on the sixth card. Practice by playing the game with a friend.

2. Start with a rectangular sheet of paper. Fold the left edge over to the right edge and then reopen. Refold repeatedly, each time folding the left edge to the crease just made and then reopen. Set up a table of values relating the total number of rectangles formed to the total number of folds made. Generalize the number pattern for n folds.

3. Fold a paper square in half vertically and horizontally. Without unfolding, fold it in half again vertically and horizontally. Guess at the total number of rectangles of all sizes before you open up the square and count. Describe how you might lead a class to discover the answer by looking for a pattern using some simpler cases.

4. Make up a variety of games on mathematical skills that can be played with a simple deck of ten 3×5 file cards numbered 0 through 9.

5. Describe how you would explain the difference between "200% of 24" and "200% more than 24" to an eighth-grade class.

6. Prepare a set of 16 punched cards that can be sorted in just four operations. Then describe how, once shuffled, they can be sorted to spell out the message MATHEMATICAL FUN.

7. Construct a laboratory worksheet that can be used to lead a student to discover that the sum of each row, column, and diagonal in an nth-order magic square formed from the integers 1 through n is $\dfrac{n(n^2+1)}{2}$.

8. Prepare a short lesson plan on how you would show an eighth-grade class how to construct various 3×3 magic squares. Include three examples, one with fractions, one with decimals, and one with integers.

9. Prepare a flow chart transparency that can be used to review skills in percent. List various inputs and operations on movable strips of acetate.

10. Construct a transparency for reviewing powers. Place the different values of the exponent and base on movable acetate dials as shown on page 121.

11. Complete the calculator activity on converging ratios described on the worksheet on page 124.

12. Construct a nomograph similar to the one on page 120 such that a line drawn through points on scales A and B will cross scale C at a point such that the corresponding numbers show that C = A + 2B. Explain, geometrically, why your construction works.

13. Prepare a report on very large numbers. Be certain that you include research on the largest prime number known as of this date.

14. Read Chapter 3, "Beyond the Googol," from *Mathematics and the Imagination* by Edward Kasner and James Newman, New York: Simon and Schuster, 1967. Summarize how several of the topics presented could be incorporated into lessons for the mathematics classroom.

15. Refer to a history of mathematics book and read about the gelosia algorithm for multiplication popular in the late 15th and 16th centuries. Compare this method to that used with Napier's Rods.

16. Examine two different mathematics textbook series at a designated level and report on the ways that they use calculator activities to illustrate numerical patterns and computational procedures.

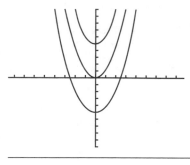

5

ACTIVITIES IN ALGEBRA

One often thinks of concrete models and aids as being most appropriate for the early stages of learning mathematics at the elementary level. While their roles may change somewhat, these same experiences remain equally important in the middle, junior high, and senior high school years. The abstract nature of algebra makes manipulative experiments, visualization activities, and motivational introductions, reviews, and extensions all the more valuable. This chapter looks at the use of aids and activities in the algebra class.

5.1 MOTIVATION IN ALGEBRA

Variety is a key element in the effective teaching of algebra. Not only does it offer a change of pace, but it also provides opportunities for bringing aids and activities into the classroom.

Geometric Models

Geometric models often give a much needed concrete stepping-off point into an algebraic generalization as illustrated here in developing a formula for the first n counting numbers.

Each set of stairs shown next can be used to represent the sum of the numbers 1 through 6. Put two together and you get a rectangle measuring 6 by 7.

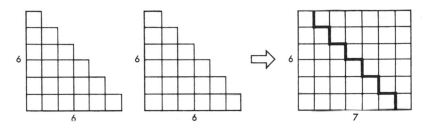

The rectangle has 6×7 or 42 squares, but it was made from two sums of 1 through 6. Thus,

$$1 + 2 + 3 + 4 + 5 + 6 = \frac{6 \times 7}{2} = \frac{42}{2} = 21$$

Now imagine each set of stairs as having n steps. Two such sets joined together this way would form a rectangle measuring n by $n + 1$ with $n(n + 1)$ squares. It quickly follows that

$$1 + 2 + 3 + \cdots + n = \frac{n(n + 1)}{2}$$

The initial geometric model sets the stage for the transition to the general case for the variable n.

Proof without Words

Algebraic proofs without words can be fun in the classroom. What algebraic idea can be discovered from these figures?

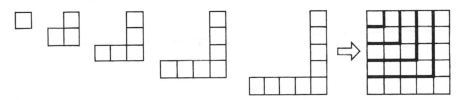

The figures illustrate a specific example of the generalization that the sum of the first n odd counting numbers is n^2.

Varied Format

For many, the notational manipulations of algebra need to be explained in more than one way. In this next figure, a common approach to multiplying binomials is shown on the left, but another method, given on the right, may be easier for some to understand.

$$(2x + 3)(4x - 5) = 8x^2 + 2x - 15$$

These are just two different formats for the same process. They both give the same trinomial result, $8x^2 + 2x - 15$, but one more clearly shows that four partial products are needed.

It also helps to compare this process with the algorithm used for multiplying two-digit numbers in arithmetic. This example shows the connection to the product 27×36.

$$27 \times 36 = 972$$

	30	6
20	600	120
7	210	42

Historical Connections

This ancient Chinese problem incorporates some interesting algebraic analysis.

A door uses a rod as a diagonal brace. The width of the door is 4 units less than the rod and the height is 2 units less. What are the dimensions of the door?

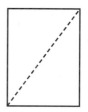

Application of the Pythagorean theorem, using variables, produces a quadratic equation that, when simplified and factored, leads to the correct dimensions.

Algebraic Analysis

Many of the familiar numerical curiosities and puzzles designed to create, motivate, and maintain interest have algebraic analyses that help to show the student just how useful the tools of algebra can be. Consider this mathematical trick involving the number 1089.

STEPS	EXAMPLE
Write any three-digit number such that the hundreds digit is at least two more than the units digit.	Choose 783.

Reverse the digits and subtract.

$$\begin{array}{r} 783 \\ -\ 387 \\ \hline 396 \end{array}$$

Reverse the digits again and add.

$$\begin{array}{r} 396 \\ +\ 693 \\ \hline 1089 \end{array}$$

The surprising result is that the answer will always be 1089! Imaginative teachers can make this property work for them in many ways. Here is one way to extend this trick.

Express your birth date as a four-digit number. Use the first two digits for the month and the last two for the day. Add it to the number you found in the last step above.

To guess the date, the teacher simply subtracts 1089. Every final result has a unique birth date. Here are some examples.

Final result	1206	1800	2106	2196
	$-\ 1089$	$-\ 1089$	$-\ 1089$	$-\ 1089$
	0117	0711	1017	1107
Birth date	Jan. 17	July 11	Oct. 17	Nov. 7

To the teacher, the number 1089 is special. But why does it always arise when you follow this process? An algebraic analysis gives the answer.

Let a be the hundreds digit,
    b be the tens digit, and
    c be the units digit, with $a > c + 1$

Original number	$100a + 10b + c$
Reverse digits	$100c + 10b + a$
Subtract	$100(a - c) + (c - a)$

$$= 100(a - c - 1)\ +\ 90 + (10 + c - a)$$

Reverse digits $\underline{100(10 + c - a) +\ \ 90 + (a - c - 1)}$
Add $100(\ 9\ )\qquad\quad + 180 + 9$
              $= 1089$

Tying this numerical curiosity to algebra makes it a valuable topic for discussion in the classroom.

5.2 SOLVING EQUATIONS

A substantial proportion of the algebra curriculum centers around the solving of equations of various types. The solution of two-step linear equations can be especially troublesome for those who lack a meaningful model with which to associate the algorithmic procedures. This section is designed to offer some suggestions.

Flow Chart Format

Many students have difficulty solving an equation in algebra because they do not know how to find the particular sequence of steps needed to solve it. A simple, yet surprisingly effective technique for introducing this topic makes use of flow charts. The obvious step-by-step sequencing built into a flow chart is used to analyze the correct sequence needed to solve the corresponding equation.

Cut out a series of circular and rectangular pieces of paper for input/output and operations. Attach them to the board to form a flow chart. As an alternative, draw them on pieces of acetate and arrange them on an overhead projector. Those shown here will be used in the illustrations that follow, but they can obviously be varied and expanded. For each operation given, the corresponding inverse operation is needed.

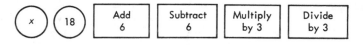

Form some flow charts using two of the available operation pieces. Have the students write the corresponding equations.

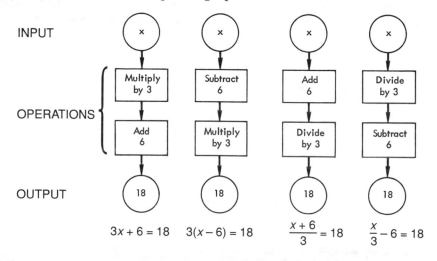

$$3x + 6 = 18 \qquad 3(x - 6) = 18 \qquad \frac{x + 6}{3} = 18 \qquad \frac{x}{3} - 6 = 18$$

In all, 12 different two-step equations are possible from the operations shown using x as input. Which pairs of equations will have the same solutions and why?

Now write out some of the possible equations, such as these, and have the students correctly select and arrange the corresponding pieces for the flow chart.

$$3(x + 6) = 18 \qquad \frac{x - 6}{3} = 18$$

This activity gives the students a physical format in which to associate abstract equations. Substantial drill at this level can produce significantly better performance in the writing and understanding of equations and word problems later on. Once the students have this experience in putting equations together, ask how they can be taken apart. It is this basic idea, easily shown with flow charts, that leads to a concrete model for solving equations.

To show the steps for the solution, start with a flowchart and the corresponding equation. Then, beginning with the output, reverse the sequence, and perform the inverse operations as you go.

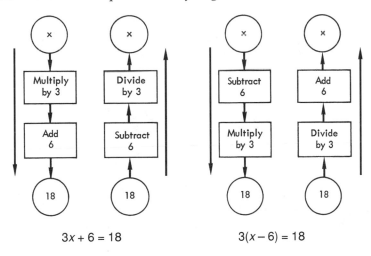

$3x + 6 = 18$ $\qquad$ $3(x - 6) = 18$

Rule of False Position

Showing ancient methods of computation can be an effective motivational technique. Long before algebra as we know it was invented, the ancient Egyptians were solving equations using a strange "guess, test, adjust" process called the *rule of false position*.

As an example, consider solving this equation. $x + \dfrac{x}{7} = 24$
First, choose a convenient guess, say 7.
Next, use 7 in place of x on the left. $7 + \dfrac{7}{7} = 8$

Our guess gives a value of 8, but we wanted 24. Since 24 is 3 times 8, the solution must be 3 times the guess of 7. Check to see that 21 is the solution.

Here are two problems from the Rhind Papyrus, an ancient Egyptian scroll dating back to 1650 BC. Use the method of false position to solve each problem.

A quantity and its $\frac{1}{7}$ added together become 19. What is the quantity?

A quantity and its $\frac{1}{2}$ added together become 16. What is the quantity?

The *rule of double false position* is more complicated, but it can be used very effectively during a unit on the solution of pairs of linear equations. Here one begins by taking two guesses, x_1 and x_2. These guesses are then substituted in the given equation and the results are noted as r_1 and r_2. The correct solution is then found by substitution in the following formula:

$$x = \frac{r_1 x_2 - r_2 x_1}{r_1 - r_2}$$

Consider the equation $3x - 13 = 0$ with guesses $x_1 = 2$ and $x_2 = 5$.

For $x_1 = 2$: $r_1 = 3(2) - 13 = -7$
For $x_2 = 5$: $r_2 = 3(5) - 13 = 2$

By substitution in the formula we have

$$x = \frac{(-7)(5) - (2)(2)}{-7 - 2} = \frac{-39}{-9} = 4\frac{1}{3}$$

After applying the formula to several problems to be assured that it works, the class can be asked to justify it and can be led to do so by considering the general linear equation $ax + b = 0$.

$$\text{For } x = x_1: \quad \begin{cases} ax_1 + b = r_1 \\ ax_2 + b = r_2 \end{cases}$$
$$\text{For } x = x_2:$$

Now we also know that the solution of the general equation $ax + b = 0$ is $x = -\dfrac{b}{a}$.
Thus all that is needed to verify the given formula for the rule of false position is to use the linear equations given and find $-\dfrac{b}{a}$ in terms of x_1, x_2, r_1, and r_2.

5.3 GRAPHING AND THE GRAPHING CALCULATOR

René Descartes' contribution to mathematics was immense. In laying out the elements of coordinate geometry, he brought together algebra and geometry. Abstract algebraic expressions were given visual geometric counterparts that could be seen. Now an equation such as $y = 3x - 4$ appears as a specific straight line on a rectangular coordinate plane. Its graph can be drawn by the student. But not all students see the more general linear equation $y = ax + b$ as clearly.

Using the Graphing Calculator

The graphing calculator is an excellent device to use in class to have students develop important concepts about graphing lines and curves in a plane. For example, ask your students to graph each of the following on the same screen.

$y = x + 2$

$y = 3x + 2$

$y = -x + 2$

$y = -3x + 2$

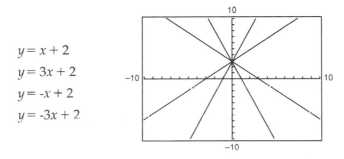

After studying the four graphs they should be ready to form a generalization about the graph for any linear function of the form $f(x) = ax + 2$. Next use the calculator to graph the following equations, leading students to form a generalization for graphs of a linear function of the form $f(x) = 3x + b$:

$y = 3x$

$y = 3x - 5$

$y = 3x + 10$

$y = 3x - 10$

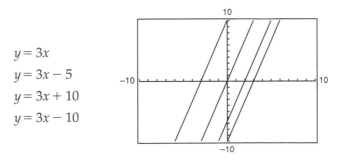

Through this means of visualization the students should now be able to describe the role of a and b when graphing equations in the form $y = ax + b$, thus providing a more meaningful approach to graphing than just the plotting of points.

Paper Folding a Sequence

Here is a simple paper-folding activity that can generate some interest and lead into a discussion of infinite sequences and series.

Start with a unit square cut from a piece of paper.   Its area is 1 square unit.

Fold the four corners to the center.   The area is $\frac{1}{2}$ sq. unit.

Fold the four corners in again.   The area is $\frac{1}{4}$ sq. unit.

Repeat the process another time.   The area is $\frac{1}{8}$ sq. unit.

Imagine that the process is repeated again.   The area is $\frac{1}{16}$ sq. unit.

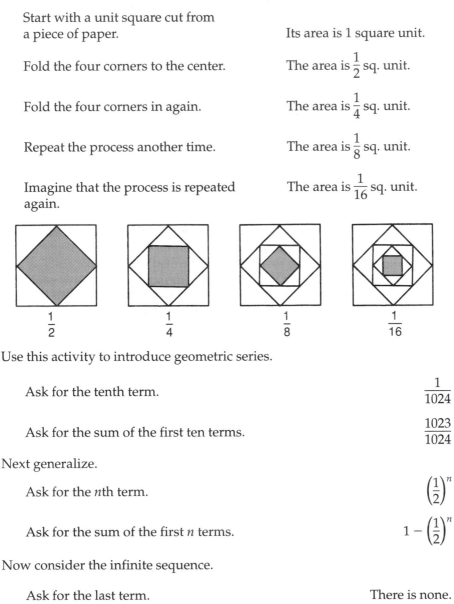

$$\frac{1}{2} \qquad \frac{1}{4} \qquad \frac{1}{8} \qquad \frac{1}{16}$$

Use this activity to introduce geometric series.

Ask for the tenth term. $\dfrac{1}{1024}$

Ask for the sum of the first ten terms. $\dfrac{1023}{1024}$

Next generalize.

Ask for the nth term. $\left(\dfrac{1}{2}\right)^{n}$

Ask for the sum of the first n terms. $1 - \left(\dfrac{1}{2}\right)^{n}$

Now consider the infinite sequence.

Ask for the last term.   There is none.

Ask for the sum of all of the terms.   1

Fibonacci Sequence

In the Fibonacci sequence, each term after the second is the sum of the two preceding terms.

$$1, 1, 2, 3, 5, 8, 13, 21, 34, 55, 89, 144, \ldots$$

The chart illustrates, in a visual format, the process used in generating successive terms. The repeating steps are shown in a loop.

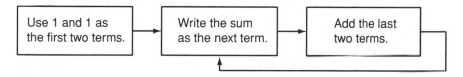

The Fibonacci sequence continues without end, but interesting questions can be asked about specific terms. Here are some examples.

What is the fifteenth term in this Fibonacci sequence?	(610)
What is the first term greater than 10,000?	(10,949)
What is the eighth even number in the sequence?	(46,368)

A Fibonacci sequence can be formed by starting with any two numbers for the first two terms. Do you see why these are also called Fibonacci sequences?

$$1, 3, 4, 7, 11, 18, 29, 47, 76, 123, 199, 322, \ldots$$
$$2, 5, 7, 12, 19, 31, 50, 81, 131, 212, 343, 555, \ldots$$

The sum of the first 10 terms in any Fibonacci sequence can be used to illustrate an interesting property. Start by encouraging students to try to discover a connection between the seventh term and the sum of the first 10 terms. Have them test their conjectures with some additional Fibonacci sequences. Then let them try to prove algebraically that the property must hold. Try the process yourself before continuing.

This relationship affords the opportunity for an interesting classroom demonstration and a worthwhile lesson in discovering and establishing a generalization. The teacher plays the role of "magician" along the way, but it is the tools of algebra that yield the proof.

A student is asked to write any two numbers on the board. Assume they are 4 and 9. The class then helps to list the first 10 terms of a Fibonacci sequence that starts with these two numbers. When the class reaches the seventh term, 92, the teacher mentally multiplies this by 11 and writes 1012 on the side of the board. The class continues through the tenth term, and the students are then asked to find the sum. They are amazed to find that the sum is a number that the teacher had written down before they ever completed writing the sequence!

First	4
Second	9
Third	13
Fourth	22
Fifth	35
Sixth	57
Seventh	92 ⟹ 11 × 92 = 1012
Eighth	149
Ninth	241
Tenth	390
	1012 Sum of first 10 terms

Note that the sum of the first 10 terms is 1012, the same as 11 times the seventh term.

Finally the class is asked to try to discover the teacher's method. A hint may be given, if necessary, that the sum is a function of the seventh term. Possibly the class may need to be guided to represent the first 10 terms of a Fibonacci sequence in general form, but this should be all the hint that is necessary.

First	a
Second	b
Third	$a + b$
Fourth	$a + 2b$
Fifth	$2a + 3b$
Sixth	$3a + 5b$
Seventh	$5a + 8b$ ⟹ $11 \times (5a + 8b) = 55a + 88b$
Eighth	$8a + 13b$
Ninth	$13a + 21b$
Tenth	$21a + 34b$
	$55a + 88b$ Sum of first 10 terms

Note that the sum of the first 10 terms is $55a + 88b$. By factoring, this is equivalent to $11(5a + 8b)$, which proves to be 11 times the seventh term.

Finite Differences

Some of the best classroom activities are the ones that start out with something concrete or geometric and lead into a number pattern, a conjecture, and a generalization established algebraically. When they also introduce new mathematics of significant importance, they are all the better. This activity illustrates the point by offering at the end a discussion of finite differences and a procedure for finding an nth-degree polynomial from $n + 1$ or more given data points.

What is the greatest number of regions into which a circle can be divided by x chords?

Begin by experimenting with some simple cases.

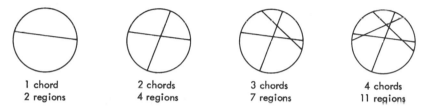

| 1 chord
2 regions | 2 chords
4 regions | 3 chords
7 regions | 4 chords
11 regions |

Close investigation reveals a connection between the number of regions

$$2, 4, 7, 11, 16, \ldots$$

and the successive sums of the counting numbers

$$1, 3, 6, 10, 15, \ldots$$

A generalization follows quickly.

Consider here another approach. Collect these data in a table and find the first and second differences.

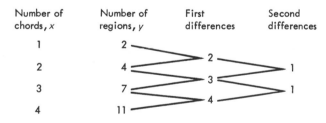

Number of chords, x	Number of regions, y	First differences	Second differences
1	2		
		2	
2	4		1
		3	
3	7		1
		4	
4	11		

Inasmuch as the second differences are constant, we assume that the formula relating the number of regions (y) as a function of the number of chords (x) is given by the second-degree function $y = ax^2 + bx + c$. To solve for the constants $a, b,$ and c we proceed to substitute the values given in the table and solve the three linear equations thus obtained.

$$\text{For } x = 1: \quad ax^2 + bx + c = a + b + c = 2$$
$$\text{For } x = 2: \quad ax^2 + bx + c = 4a + 2b + c = 4$$
$$\text{For } x = 3: \quad ax^2 + bx + c = 9a + 3b + c = 7$$

EXPERIMENT 3   Factoring a Trinomial

Material
A set of large squares measuring x by x, each representing x^2.
A set of small squares measuring 1 by 1, each representing 1.
A set of rectangles measuring x by 1, each representing x.

Directions
Monomials, binomials, and trinomials in x can now be represented by the appropriate geometric figures.

In factoring a trinomial, the various monomial parts are arranged in a rectangular shape. The two dimensions of the rectangle give the two factors.

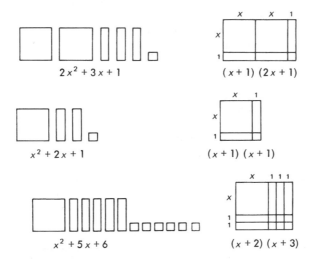

$2x^2 + 3x + 1$ $(x+1)(2x+1)$

$x^2 + 2x + 1$ $(x+1)(x+1)$

$x^2 + 5x + 6$ $(x+2)(x+3)$

1. Show how to factor $3x^2 + 4x + 1$ using a model.
2. Show how to factor $4x^2 + 8x + 3$ using a model.
3. Show some other trinomials that can be factored using a model. Show some that cannot be factored.
4. Imagine a rectangular array of these pieces measuring $5x + 1$ by $2x + 3$. How many pieces are in it? How many of each size are there? What trinomial factorization does it represent?

Analysis
Consider the trinomial $ax^2 + bx + c$. See if a of the larger squares, b of the rectangles, and c of the smaller squares can be arranged to form a rectangle. If they can, then the dimensions of the rectangle give the two factors.

For $3x^2 + 4x + 1$, use 3 large squares, 4 rectangles, and 1 small square to get the factored form $(3x + 1)(x + 1)$.

For $4x^2 + 8x + 3$, use 4 large squares, 8 rectangles, and 1 small square to get a factored form of $(2x + 1)(2x + 3)$.

A rectangular array of $5x + 1$ by $2x + 3$ would require 30 pieces from the trinomial $10x^2 + 17x + 3$.

While the multiplication of two binomials usually does not present the difficulties that factoring does, it, too, can be introduced by a similar method. Draw a rectangle with dimensions equal to those of the two binomial factors given. Then subdivide the rectangle into x^2's, x's, and 1's to find the product.

$$(x + 1)(x + 2) = x^2 + 3x + 2$$

$$(x + 2)(x + 2) = x^2 + 4x + 4$$

Small colored acetate figures on an overhead projector can be used instead of paper figures. Students can also try drawing the appropriate figures on graph paper at their seats.

The experiments thus far have dealt with second-degree expressions and two-dimensional models. Experiment 4 presents a third-degree expression using a three-dimensional model that can easily be constructed in a school woodworking shop.

EXPERIMENT 4   A Model for
$$(a + b)^3 = a^3 + 3a^2b + 3ab^2 + b^3$$

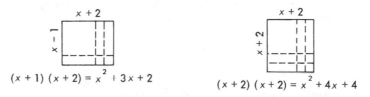

Material
Eight blocks of wood cut to these dimensions, where a and b are any convenient lengths.

one	$a \times a \times a$
three	$a \times a \times b$
three	$a \times b \times b$
one	$b \times b \times b$

Directions
Arrange the eight pieces to form a cube. How does the resulting model illustrate this algebraic identity?

$$(a + b)^3 = a^3 + 3a^2b + 3ab^2 + b^3$$

Analysis
The cube measures $a + b$ on each edge so its volume is $(a + b)^3$. But it was made from eight pieces with this collected value.

$$a^3 + a^2b + a^2b + a^2b + ab^2 + ab^2 + ab^2 + b^3$$

Since the volumes of the original cube and the eight pieces combined are the same, we have

$$(a + b)^3 = a^3 + 3a^2b + 3ab^2 + b^3$$

5.6 MORE AIDS AND ACTIVITIES

Many believe that motivation is the very key to learning. An enthusiastic teacher can do much to stimulate, maintain, and increase interest in the subject by varying the things that are done in the classroom. This section contains more motivational ideas for the algebra classroom.

Number Line Model

Students have little trouble recognizing that the whole numbers form an infinite set that goes on without end. Correspondingly, the number line extends without bound. But it is more difficult to accept the fact that there are just as many real numbers on the entire number line as there are within a specific interval, say from 0 to 1. Yet every time students draw a continuous graph through selected points, they are using the completeness property of the real numbers and the corresponding concept of continuity of points on a line. Here is an activity to help clarify the concept of continuity:

Have each student code his or her initials by replacing each letter with the appropriate digit or digits.

A	0	J	9	S	18
B	1	K	10	T	19
C	2	L	11	U	20
D	3	M	12	V	21
E	4	N	13	W	22
F	5	O	14	X	23
G	6	P	15	Y	24
H	7	Q	16	Z	25
I	8	R	17		

The resulting numbers will range up to six digits, to the hundred thousands. By placing a decimal point in front, they all become less than 1. Here are some examples.

L.P.M.	111512	0.111512
G.R.N.	61713	0.61713
C.A.F.	205	0.205
I.K.H.	8107	0.8107

Ask some questions at this point.

1. What three initials will code into the largest whole number possible?   ZZZ

2. What three initials will, when preceded by a decimal point, code into the largest decimal?   JJJ
3. What three initials will code into
      the smallest decimal greater than one-tenth?   KAB
      the largest decimal less than one-tenth?   AJJ
4. Is there a one-to-one correspondence between
      the initials and their coded whole numbers?   no
      the coded whole numbers and their decimals?   yes

Next, hold up a piece of string horizontally in front of the class as a model of the number line with your fingers locating the points 0 and 1. Have students come up and locate where the decimal codes for some familiar words such as these can be found.

algebra   geometry   mathematics

Then try the name of your town or state. Finally, try something like the Gettysburg address or the pledge of allegiance. Everything said and yet to be said—it is all there coded in that short interval from 0 to 1!

Babylonian Mathematics

A rich collection of interesting algebraic tidbits can be found in the annals of the history of mathematics. This Babylonian clay table (1650 BC) can be discussed when studying radicals or the Pythagorean theorem. The original cuneiform writing, in base 60, is shown on the left. The deciphered translation is shown on the right.

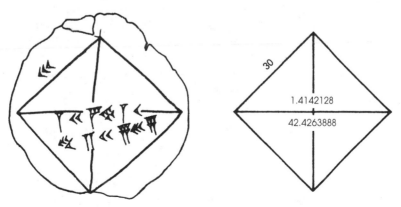

One quickly sees from this example both their method and their precision in computing the length of the diagonal of a square.

To find the diagonal of a square, multiply by length of a side by $\sqrt{2}$.

$$30\sqrt{2} = 30(1.4142135\ldots) = 42.426405\ldots$$

Their results were amazingly close considering all this happened more than 1000 years before the great Pythagoras lived!

Guessing a Quadratic

Here is a little mathemagical trick with an interesting algebraic analysis based on values of a quadratic equation. Its solution depends upon the mathematics of finite differences and, as such, is an excellent application for most students in their study of algebra.

EXAMPLE

Think of a quadratic function of the type $f(x) = ax^2 + bx + c$.	$f(x) = 3x^2 - 5x + 2$
Substitute 0, 1, and 2 for x in that order, and give the corresponding values for $f(x)$.	For $x = 0$, $f(0) = 2$ $x = 1$, $f(1) = 0$ $x = 2$, $f(2) = 4$

To determine the original expression, find the first and second differences.

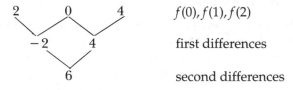

$f(0), f(1), f(2)$

first differences

second differences

The coefficient of the x^2 term is one half of the number at the bottom; $\frac{1}{2} \times 6 = 3$. The coefficient of the x term is the first number of the middle row minus one half of the number at the bottom; $-2 - 3 = -5$. The first number of the top row is the constant, 2. Thus, the original expression is $3x^2 - 5x + 2$.

The explanation for these rules can be found by considering the general case, $f(x) = ax^2 + bx + c$. For this we have:

$$f(0) = c$$
$$f(1) = a + b + c$$
$$f(2) = 4a + 2b + c$$

Finding first and second differences we have the following:

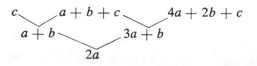

From this array it is clear that one-half of the bottom number is a, the coefficient of x^2. The first number of the middle row minus one half of the bottom number gives $a + b - a = b$, the coefficient of x. The first number of the top row is c, the constant term.

5.7 OVERHEAD PROJECTOR IDEAS

The overhead projector can be used in a variety of ways in the algebra classroom. It can serve as a very powerful instructional tool when teaching graphing. It can be used to motivate a discovery which is then proved algebraically. Examples are illustrated here; many other applications are possible as well.

Teaching Graphing

Concepts in graphing can be dramatically and vividly illustrated with the overhead projector by using the graph of a function and the corresponding set of axes on different sheets of acetate. Here is an illustration in which absolute values are used. Begin by constructing two acetate sheets.

Sheet 1: A conventional set of axes in one color.

Sheet 2: The graph of the function $y = |x|$ in another color.

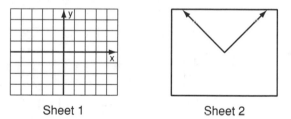

Sheet 1   Sheet 2

When sheet 2 is placed on top of sheet 1, the basic graph is projected. Displacing sheet 2 one unit up from its original position illustrates another graph. Displacing it two units down gives another.

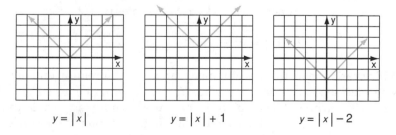

$y = |x|$ $\qquad$ $y = |x| + 1$ $\qquad$ $y = |x| - 2$

At this point other positions of vertical translation should be illustrated, with the class giving the proper equations. This first concept can then be further reinforced by offering the equation and having the student position the graph properly. The effect of vertical translation and the constant a in $y = |x| + a$ is thus illustrated.

Sheet 2 is now moved one unit to the right of its original position and the corresponding equation developed. Then it is moved two units left for another equation.

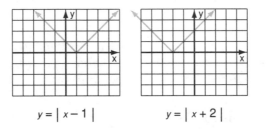

$$y = |x - 1|$$ $$y = |x + 2|$$

Again the horizontal translation is reviewed with additional examples by giving new equations and by giving new positions. The role of the constant b in $y = |x + b|$ is thus developed.

Now the two translations are combined for still other graphs.

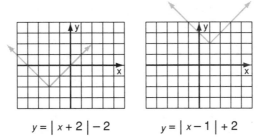

$$y = |x + 2| - 2$$ $$y = |x - 1| + 2$$

These concepts can be reviewed with more positions and more equations until the student grasps the concepts involved in graphing equations of the form $y = |x + b| + a$.

When sheet 2 is flipped about the horizontal axis, a new graph is projected. Rotating 90° clockwise or counterclockwise illustrates two other graphs.

$$|y| = -x \quad \text{and} \quad |y| = x$$

A nice variation on this development can follow for reinforcement of concepts by placing sheet 1 on top of sheet 2 and moving the axes rather than the graph. The whole development is, of course, readily adaptable to other functions. Furthermore, as illustrated earlier in this chapter, these concepts of rotations and translations can also be developed through the use of a graphing calculator in connection with the overhead projector. This allows students to perform these operations at their seats while the teacher works at the projector.

Motivating Discovery

In this illustration, a mask is used to isolate a selected square array of numbers from a given set. Students try to discover how to find the sum of the numbers in each array without adding them all. Then they try to prove their conjecture algebraically.

Step 1: The calendar for the month is copied on a sheet of acetate. Since accurate spacing is needed, use a piece of graph paper under the acetate for horizontal and vertical alignment of the numbers.

Step 2: With a razor blade a square is cut from a sheet of heavy paper or tagboard large enough to just expose a 3 × 3 array of numbers.

Step 3: By placing this mask over the number grid of the calendar, only a 3 × 3 array will be projected. Repositioning the mask simply exposes a new array.

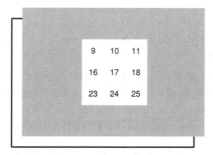

Students are asked to add the numbers in various arrays and then try to discover the relationship between each sum and the particular numbers exposed. Various suggestions should be encouraged and tested. The discovery hopefully will come from the students, aided, if necessary, with helpful hints. The sum of the numbers in each 3×3 array will always be 9 times the center number.

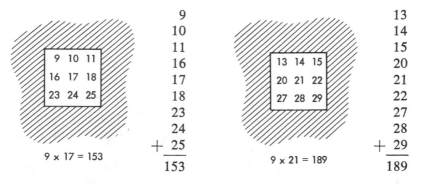

Encourage the students to verify the discovery algebraically. If the middle number is a, then the nine numbers can always be expressed as shown below regardless of where the mask is placed on the calendar. Illustrate this display with another transparency.

The sum of these numbers is obviously $9a$.

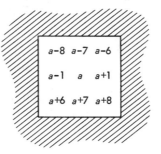

Drill and Practice

Many algebraic skills call for frequent review and practice. If this can occur in a novel, unusual fashion, it will stimulate more interest. The following aid can be used to review binomial products. Factors can be easily changed so the speed in which the drill takes place can be controlled by the teacher. The level of difficulty can easily be adjusted by the proper selection of factors from among those available. And a wide choice of exercises is immediately available at your fingertips. This can be especially important when doing rapid-fire oral drill.

Mark two acetate disks with selected and varied binomial factors. Mount the two disks on the solid mask, with an appropriate window, using sewing snaps so they can rotate easily. The teacher can see all the factors all the time but the class sees only one product projected at a time through the opening in the mask.

5.8 CALCULATOR APPLICATIONS

There are many possible uses of the calculator in the algebra classroom. The study of convergent sequences and series offers many applications as does finding approximate roots of higher-degree equations.

Golden Ratio

The first 12 terms in the Fibonacci sequence are listed here.

$$1, 1, 2, 3, 5, 8, 13, 21, 34, 55, 89, 144$$

Have your students use a calculator to study the ratios of successive terms, larger to smaller. These results are from an 8-digit calculator.

1 to 1	1.0000000
2 to 1	2.0000000
3 to 2	1.5000000
5 to 3	1.6666666
8 to 5	1.6000000
13 to 8	1.6250000
21 to 13	1.6153846
34 to 21	1.6190476
55 to 34	1.6176470
89 to 55	1.6181818
144 to 89	1.6179775

The sequence of ratios is converging by oscillating below and above this limiting value called the *golden ratio*.

$$\frac{1 + \sqrt{5}}{2} = 1.6180339\ldots$$

With even the greatest of patience and perseverance and the best calculator available, the exact value can never be reached on a calculator. But interesting questions can still be asked and valuable experience gained on the concept of convergence.

The Number Pi

Many infinite series have a value of π. This one, given by Leibniz, is especially interesting because of the simplicity of the pattern in the terms.

$$\pi = 4\left(1 - \frac{1}{3} + \frac{1}{5} - \frac{1}{7} + \frac{1}{9} - \cdots\right)$$

Have students extend the pattern and evaluate the expression using the first 10 terms. Check to see how they use the calculator. Ask the class if the sequence is converging rapidly. The answer is an emphatic no! The fact is, most students would doubt the genius of Leibniz entirely were it based on this one example.

Continued Fractions

Continued fractions give students a good opportunity to plan out the best sequence of steps to follow in solving a problem using the calculator. Encourage students to do all their work without writing down intermediate results.

$$1 + \cfrac{1}{1 + \cfrac{1}{1 + \cfrac{1}{1 + \cfrac{1}{1 + \ldots}}}}$$

The simplicity of this continued fraction belies the fact that its limiting value is the golden ratio, $\frac{1 + \sqrt{5}}{2}$ or $1.6180339\ldots$

As a follow-up, let students explore the following continued fraction using their calculators. The elegant tie displayed between the two integers 1 and 2 and the irrational $\sqrt{2}$ is another example of the striking beauty of mathematics.

$$\sqrt{2} = 1 + \cfrac{1}{2 + \cfrac{1}{2 + \cfrac{1}{2 + \cfrac{1}{2 + \dots}}}}$$

The Number e

What happens to $\left(1 + \frac{1}{n}\right)^n$ as n increases without bound? Get some reactions from your students on this question before continuing. It can be shown that the limit is the irrational, transcendental number e.

$$\lim_{n \to \infty} \left(1 + \frac{1}{n}\right)^n = e = 2.7182818\dots$$

Have your students investigate this interesting number using a calculator and this series:

$$e = 1 + \frac{1}{1} + \frac{1}{2 \cdot 1} + \frac{1}{3 \cdot 2 \cdot 1} + \frac{1}{4 \cdot 3 \cdot 2 \cdot 1} + \frac{1}{5 \cdot 4 \cdot 3 \cdot 2 \cdot 1} + \dots$$

Evaluate the first 8 terms of this series and find the sum. Compare the results with the value of e given above.

Euler, who invented the symbol e, also provided this interesting continued fraction which has a value of e.

$$e = 2 + \cfrac{1}{1 + \cfrac{1}{2 + \cfrac{2}{3 + \cfrac{3}{4 + \cfrac{4}{5 + \dots}}}}}$$

Graphical Iteration

One of the reasons mathematical thinking is so powerful is because it offers such a wide variety of different tools that can be used for analysis. Consider graphical iteration, where the dynamics of change are shown visually. These graphing calculator displays show the different effects that can arise through graphical iteration on linear functions. Have your students investigate iteration behaviors of this type. See if they can find what it is about the linear function that determines a particular behavior.

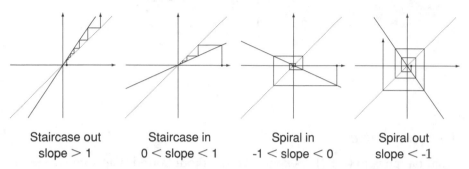

Staircase out	Staircase in	Spiral in	Spiral out
slope > 1	0 < slope < 1	-1 < slope < 0	slope < -1

Once investigated carefully, graphical iteration on a linear function becomes very predictable. It is the slope that determines the characteristic behavior.

Positive slopes produce staircases, out if greater than 1 and in if less than 1.

Negative slopes produce spirals, out if less than -1 and in if greater than -1.

Iteration on a quadratic function can produce widely different behaviors. Have students explore the quadratic $f(x) = ax(1 - x)$ that crosses the x-axis at 0 and 1. Start with an initial iterate in the interval between 0 and 1 and all successive iterates will be trapped in this same interval as long as the parameter a stays in the interval, $1 < a \leq 4$. However, the different behaviors that can appear are very striking!

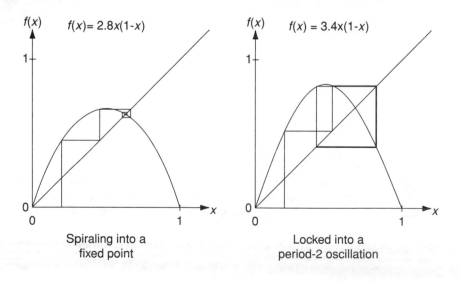

Spiraling into a
fixed point

Locked into a
period-2 oscillation

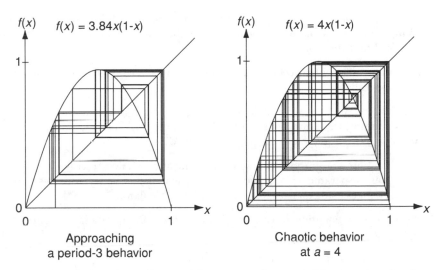

Approaching
a period-3 behavior

Chaotic behavior
at $a = 4$

Graphical iteration offers a rich source of material for cooperative learning activities in upper-level mathematics classrooms that make use of the graphing calculator. Students can use sequence graphing and the web format already built into most machines or write their own programs. Note how these calculator displays show a behavior leading to period-2 both numerically and graphically.

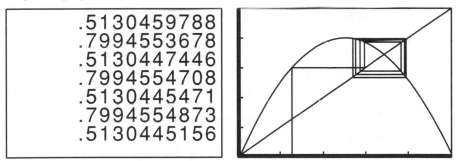

.5130459788
.7994553678
.5130447446
.7994554708
.5130445471
.7994554873
.5130445156

graphical iteration under $f(x) = 3.2x(1 - x)$

In chapter 8 you will find a wide variety of other iteration activities in arithmetic, algebra, and geometry.

EXERCISES

1. The sum of the first n counting numbers is $\dfrac{n(n + 1)}{2}$. What is the sum of their squares and the sum of their cubes?

2. Start with the first n counting numbers. Find formulas for the sums of the first half and the second half of these numbers. Assume n is even.

3. Write and solve the 12 equations that can be represented in flowchart form using an input of x, an output of 24, and any two of the operations *add 4, subtract 6, multiply by 8,* and *divide by 10.*

4. How many different flowcharts can be formed in Exercise 3 using any three of the given operations.

5. Points are located for a parabola by starting at the origin and then moving two units at a time right and left successively, then moving down 1, 3, 5, 7, and so on. What is the equation of the parabola formed?

6. Describe how the graph of the general quadratic function, $f(x) = a(x - h)^2 + b$ change as the parameters a, b, and h all increase in value. Verify your description of the changes using an example on a graphing calculator.

7. Write the new equation for $y = (x - 2)^2 + 3$ when the parabola is rotated $180°$ about the origin.

8. Find the two complex roots for $y = (x - 2)^2 + 3$.

9. Graph $y = |x - 2| + 3$. Then give the new equation for the graph when rotated $90°$ clockwise about the origin.

10. Imagine the ends of a piece of string tied together to form a 20-inch loop and the loop stretched open to form a rectangle. As the length of the rectangle changes, the height changes accordingly. Sketch three graphs showing how the width, perimeter, and area change as the length changes. Find the corresponding algebraic equations defined over the interval 0 through 10.

11. Solve this problem from the Rhind papyrus using the method of false position: *A quantity and its $\frac{1}{7}$ added together become 19. What is the quantity?*

12. Verify the rule of double false position. Assume the two guesses x_1 and x_2, when substituted into the linear equation $ax + b = 0$, give results of r_1 and r_2 and show that $x = \dfrac{r_1 x_2 - r_2 x_1}{r_1 - r_2}$.

13. Find the tenth term in the Fibonacci sequence that starts with 3 and 7. Is the sum of the first 10 terms the same as 11 times the seventh term?

14. Start with a four-digit number with all digits different. Prove algebraically that the sum of all possible three-digit numbers that can be formed from these digits divided by the sum of the digits of the original number must equal 666.

15. The ancient Babylonians used a place-value system base 60 for writing their numbers. Within each place, the symbol V was used for 1 and < for 10. Write $100, 1000$, and $1,000,000$ in this cuneiform notation.

16. Show how the base-60 place values of the Babylonians system of numeration can yield the values of 30, 1.4142128, and 42.4263888 from the three numbers on the tablet shown on page 149.

17. Find the function $f(x) = ax^2 + bx + c$ given that $f(1) = 0, f(2) = 1$, and $f(3) = 8$.

18. Use successive differences to establish a polynomial that can be used to generate these terms: $f(0) = -4$, $f(1) = -2$, $f(2) = 2$, $f(3) = 14$, and $f(4) = 40$.

19. Use your calculator and the first eight terms in this series to approximate the value of e.

$$1 + \frac{1}{1} + \frac{1}{2 \cdot 1} + \frac{1}{3 \cdot 2 \cdot 1} + \frac{1}{4 \cdot 3 \cdot 2 \cdot 1} + \frac{1}{5 \cdot 4 \cdot 3 \cdot 2 \cdot 1} + \cdots$$

20. Use your calculator and this continued fraction to approximate the value of $\sqrt{2}$.

$$1 + \cfrac{1}{2 + \cfrac{1}{2 + \cfrac{1}{2 + \cfrac{1}{2 + \cdots}}}}$$

21. Graphical iteration is applied to the function $f(x) = -\frac{x}{2}$ starting with $x_0 = 8$. Is the iteration graph a spiral or a staircase? Find the eighth value, x_8. Are these iteration values diverging or converging.

22. Describe the long term iteration behavior for the quadratic $f(x) = ax(1 - x)$ for $a = 2.5, a = 3.2, a = 3.5$, and $a = 3.9$.

ACTIVITIES

1. Describe two different formats that can be used in teaching the six partial products that are formed when multiplying the binomial $a + b$ and the trinomial $c + d + e$.

2. Illustrate with an appropriate drawing how the trinomial $3x^2 + 7x + 2$ can be factored geometrically.

3. Start with a large equilateral triangle cut from paper. Fold each vertex to the midpoint of the opposite side. Repeat the process with each new equilateral triangle formed. If it could be folded, what fractional part of the original triangle would be represented by the tenth such triangle formed?

4. Plan a short lesson on squaring the trinomial $a + b + c$ that makes use of a geometric model cut from a paper square.

5. Plan a short lesson on squaring the trinomial $a + b + c$ that makes use of a geometric model cut from a square paper.

6. Discuss the advantages in having an aid to demonstrate the algebraic concept of factoring.

7. Develop a lesson centered around translating, rotating, and reflecting a transparency overlay of the parabola $y = x^2$ on a grid base.

8. Construct a transparency that can be used to illustrate the family of lines with (0, -6) as their y-intercepts. Contrast its potential effectiveness with a similar demonstration using a projected image from a graphing calculator.

9. Plan a lesson on teaching inequalities using a projected image from a graphing calculator.

10. Construct a model showing all complex points, both real and imaginary, in $y = x^2 + 2$ using the method shown on page 139. Be sure to locate and identify the two complex roots.

11. Prepare a report on the apparent relationship between the Fibonacci sequence and certain aspects of nature.

12. Collect information on the ancient Babylonian tablet called Plimpton 322 and its connection to trigonometry. Describe its potential value to an upper-level secondary mathematics teacher.

13. Read about Omar Khayyam, his writings, and his contributions in the field of mathematics. How might this knowledge be useful in teaching?

14. Identify a series expansion for π that converges more rapidly than Leibniz's series expansion as given on page 156.

15. Summarize the beautiful connection among π, i, and e as discovered by Euler.

16. Use a graphing calculator to create graphical iteration displays for $f(x) = ax(1 - x)$ such as those shown on pages 158–159. Make use of sequence graphing and the web format or write your own program. Explore the different iteration behaviors for values of a from 1 through 4.

17. A major source of information on the mathematics of the ancient Egyptians is the Rhind Papyrus. Problem 48 in the collected set of arithmetical problems in the third part of the papyrus compares the area of a circle with that of the circumscribed square. Read a translation of the problem, describe the procedure, and the resulting approximation used for π. An excellent reference is *The Rhind Papyrus* by A. B. Chance reprinted by the National Council of Teachers of Mathematics in 1979.

18. Read about graphical iteration in *Fractals for the Classroom: Strategic Activities Volume Two* by Peitgen, Jurgens, Saupe, Maletsky, Perciante, and Yunker, published jointly by the National Council of Teachers of Mathematics and Springer-Verlag, 1992.

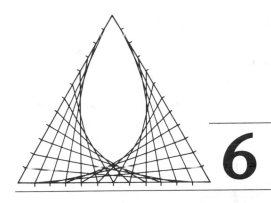

6

ACTIVITIES
IN GEOMETRY

Geometry is a subject rich in motivational material that can capture the attention and imagination of students from the earliest grades on through the advanced secondary level and beyond. Activities in informal geometry in the middle and junior high school can be used to introduce new ideas and reinforce old ones. Theorems from high school geometry can have their beginnings with concrete, manipulative experiences that give meaningful insight and understanding before structured proof. Visualization activities can help stretch students' minds and make them more flexible and creative. Equally important, geometric thinking and analysis give students powerful problem-solving tools, often offering a fresh new outlook to a challenging situation.

This chapter begins with some short motivational activities for geometry and then examines material related to the teaching of polygons, polyhedrons, and the conic sections. Visualization, measurement, and construction activities and experiments follow along with some ideas for applications of the overhead projector, calculator and computer.

6.1 MOTIVATION IN GEOMETRY

This section lists some strategies for teaching geometry with illustrations of simple classroom activities and experiences.

Encourage Students to See Things from a Geometric Vantage Point

This classification of digits with the letters A, B, and C focuses on one of their properties that students may not have noticed before. How would you classify the digit 9?

A	1	4	7	
B	2	5		
C	0	3	6	8

Use Geometry as a Vehicle for Problem-Solving Activities

Have every student divide a 2-inch by 8-inch strip of paper into quarters as shown, labeling the four parts on both sides as 1, 2, 3, and 4. Think of all the four-digit numbers possible using all four digits.

- Which numbers can be formed by folding the strip into a stack of squares, reading the digits from the top down? Which cannot be formed?

1 2 3 4   3 4 2 1

Illustrate Applications of Geometric Properties

It's one thing to know the converse of the Pythagorean theorem, but it's quite another thing to show it in action. Take a rope and put knots in it at every foot. Then see if your students can figure out how to use it to form a right angle. The ancient Egyptians used this very method in marking off the right-angled corners of their fields each year after the annual flooding of the Nile River. All it takes is knowledge of a 3–4–5 right triangle.

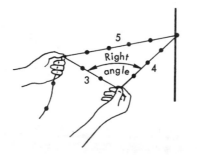

Use Models for Illustration and Comparison

When teaching about cylinders, take an 8½-inch × 11-inch sheet of paper. Roll it end-to-end lengthwise and then widthwise, as shown. Which cylinder has the greater volume? Estimate what percent more. Does the smaller have the same percent less?

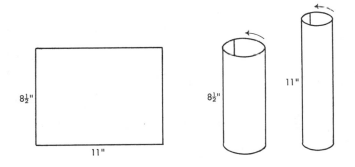

Put Things in Your Students' Hands

Consider metric units of volume. If students can see, touch, and manipulate models of a cubic meter, centimeter, and millimeter, they are far more likely to remember them. Students are always impressed with the size of a model of a cubic meter (m^3). Even a cubic centimeter carries little real meaning unless students get a visual impression of it by holding some centimeter cubes in their hands. Pass some out and let the class see how many different solids they can form by joining centimeter cubes together face-to-face. Use 2 cubes, 3 cubes, and then 4 cubes. Watch for mirror images that are identical and look for those that are not.

To dramatize just how small a cubic millimeter cube is, cut some from the square ends of flat toothpicks. Use a razor blade. You can get two or three good models off each toothpick. Drop one of them in each student's hand. Don't tell them where they came from. Just let them react to their size. Students will not soon forget just how small a millimeter cube really is.

Get the Most You Can Out of Your Classroom Demonstrations

When using a classroom demonstration, stay with it long enough to realize its full potential. Here is an example.

Fold a square piece of paper in half vertically as shown. Ask how many pieces you will get if you cut the results in half again. If your students say 2, cut vertically. If they say 3, cut horizontally. Students need these surprises once in a while.

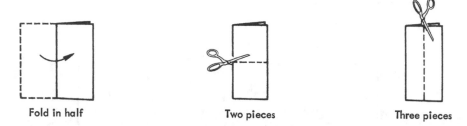

Fold in half   Two pieces   Three pieces

The original visualization problem is done. But don't stop. Suppose the cut is made vertically down the middle of the folded square. Three rectangles are formed, two small and one large. Without first showing the pieces, ask how their areas compare. Follow that easy question with one about how their perimeters compare, smaller to larger. It's a nice little arithmetic or algebra exercise to show that the ratio of perimeters is 5 to 6, smaller to larger. This is much higher than the 1 to 2 ratio for their areas.

Now stretch the activity into the problem-solving stage.

- Can you cut the original folded square vertically so that the ratio of perimeters of the rectangular pieces, smaller to larger, is 1 to 2?

6.2 POLYGONS

Much time is spent in the classification of polygons at the elementary and middle school levels. Once definitions have been given, students need to see polygons in a wide variety of situations so they can recognize them and become familiar with their properties and applications. These activities can take the form of motivational puzzles, basic concept review and extension, and challenging problem-solving experiments. Several illustrations are given here that involve hands-on materials for student use.

Tangrams

One of the oldest known puzzles in mathematics is the ancient Chinese game of tangrams. Having amused and challenged people for thousands of years, it is certain to capture the interest of many students as well.

Tangram sets can be purchased commercially, but they are easy to make. Draw this figure on a square piece of heavy paper or cardboard. The points are lettered here for construction purposes and are not needed in the puzzle itself.

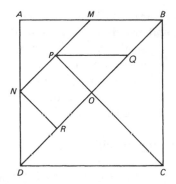

First locate points M and N as midpoints of sides AB and AD. Draw MN. Then draw diagonal BD and PC, which is part of the other diagonal. Finally, draw PQ parallel to AB and NR parallel to PC. Cut the figure along the lines drawn to get 7 separate pieces consisting of 5 triangles, 1 square, and 1 parallelogram. The original tangram puzzle consists of arranging these 7 separate pieces into a square.

A particularly appropriate adaptation for the middle school is to arrange the seven tangram pieces into convex polygons. There are 13 different possibilities including 1 triangle, 6 quadrilaterals, 2 pentagons, and 4 hexagons. Challenge your students to find all 13 solutions. The complex set makes an attractive bulletin board display.

One of each set is shown here. Note that different arrangements of pieces within each polygon are also possible but are not counted separately.

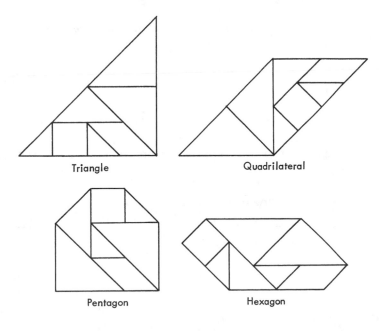

Triangle

Quadrilateral

Pentagon

Hexagon

The tangram activity described above involves certain problem-solving skills such as trial and error. It also involves visualization skills since the final polygons cannot be seen physically until the pieces are properly arranged. Once assembled, be sure your students can see all the different polygons within the arrangement, not just the entire figure.

Consider again the lettered square arrangement of the seven tangram pieces, as shown on the preceding page.

- Name all the convex polygons within the square.

Triangles	BCO, CDO, AMN, DNR, OPQ, ABD, BCD
Quadrilaterals	
squares	ABCD, NPOR
parallelograms	BQPM
trapezoids	BOPM, BRNM, QRNP, ODNP, BDNM, PQDN
others	BCPM, CDNP, ABRN
Pentagons	BCDNM

See if your students can recognize that quadrilaterals BCPM, CDNP, and ABRN are all congruent. What other sets of congruent polygons can you find?

Take advantage of geometric activities such as these to review arithmetic and measurement skills.

- Assuming the original square is a unit square, find the perimeter of each of these polygons.

triangle BCO	$(1 + \sqrt{2})$
square NPOR	$(\sqrt{2})$
quadrilateral BCPM	$(1\frac{1}{2} + \sqrt{2})$

- What percent of the original square is represented by the area of each of these polygons?

triangle BCO	(25%)
square NPOR	$\left(12\frac{1}{2}\%\right)$
quadrilateral BCPM	$\left(43\frac{3}{4}\%\right)$

Of course, the perimeter can also be found for every polygon that can be formed by rearranging the original 7 pieces of the tangram puzzle. For example, assuming the original square has sides of 1 unit, this hexagon has a perimeter of $2 + 2\sqrt{2}$ units.

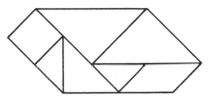

Congruency

Many believe congruency is an easy concept, quickly mastered. In general, this is true but the orientation of the figures can have much to do with successful recognition. This activity is designed to reinforce this aspect of the concept of congruency.

Cut some 4×4 squares from graph paper. Then find how many different ways you can cut them into congruent halves along the grid lines. Six different polygonal shapes are possible from the halves.

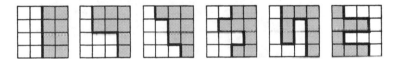

Students can explore the same problem by drawing on graph paper. However, the advantage to cutting out the pieces is that they can physically reorient the pieces and immediately check for congruence by placing one on top of the other to see if they coincide.

Several interesting extensions are possible. The two halves, of course, have the same areas. But what about their perimeters? Compute them starting with the 4×4 square. Students may be surprised to find that two pairs of halves have perimeters greater than that of the original whole square!

Classifying Triangles

Make this a cooperative learning activity. Each group of students starts with 12 toothpicks. Their task is to arrange any number of toothpicks, end-to-end, to form a triangle. Identify each different solution as a number triple. For example, use 3,3,4 for an isosceles triangle with two congruent sides 3 toothpicks long and a base 4 long. Don't count 3,4,3 or 4,3,3 separately as they give the same triangle as 3,3,4.

Each group makes a list of all possible triangles that can be formed with any number up to 12 toothpicks. Be sure they classify each triangle as equilateral, isosceles, or scalene.

Equilateral Triangles	Isosceles Triangles	Scalene Triangles
1,1,1	1,2,2	2,3,4
2,2,2	1,3,3	2,4,5
3,3,3	1,4,4	3,4,5
4,4,4	1,5,5	
	2,3,3	
	2,4,4	
	2,5,5	
	3,4,4	

Geoboards

The geoboard can serve as an excellent aid for individual exploration and experimentation. It is so easy to use that students can become actively involved at a concrete level in the creative, imaginative aspects of geometric discovery. Classroom sets of geoboards are readily available commercially or they can be constructed by the school's shop classes with little difficulty.

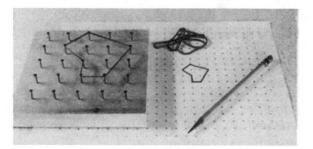

Dot paper is a useful supplement for the geoboard and should be readily available to students so that they can easily record specific figures when needed. A geoboard made of clear plastic can serve as a very effective and dynamic aid for the teacher when used with an overhead projector.

Many geometric concepts of the early elementary grades through the secondary years can be developed through geoboard activities and experiments. Some applications are suggested here in the format of student worksheets. The first deals with finding squares of various sizes on a square dot grid. The second offers a discovery experience leading to Pick's formula.

Pick's Formula $\qquad A = \dfrac{b}{2} + i - 1$

This is an interesting algebraic formula relating the area A of a polygon to the number of points on the boundary b and in the interior i. It can be applied to all polygons drawn with vertices on the points of a square grid.

Worksheet 1

Squares
Use your geoboard.

1. Form squares using the segments shown as sides.

2. Find all the squares of different sizes that you can form on the geoboard. In all there are eight possibilities. Draw the eight squares here, arranging them in order, smallest to largest.

A   B   C   D

E   F   G   H

3. Using the total area of the geoboard grid as 16 square units, give the area of each square drawn in question 2.

   A __ B __ C __ D __ E __ F __ G __ H __

4. Now find the perimeter of each square using 1 unit as the distance between adjacent points on the geoboard.

   A __ B __ C __ D __ E __ F __ G __ H __

5. Connect all 25 points with line segments such that the polygon formed has the greatest possible perimeter.

Worksheet 2

Pick's Formula

Construct each polygon described using the geoboard. Enter the required values for b and i for that polygon in the table. Then complete its area.

Let b be the number of points on the boundary of the polygon.
Let i be the number of points in its interior.

Polygon	b	i	Area
1			
2			
3			
4			
5			
6			
7			
8			

1. A 1×1 square
2. A 1×3 rectangle

3. A right triangle with legs 1 and 4
4. A right triangle with legs 1 and 3

Study the entries in the table thus far.
Can you discover how to get A from b and i?

5. A 2×2 square
6. A 3×4 rectangle

7. A right triangle with legs 2 and 3
8. An isosceles triangle with two equal sides of 4

Study the entries in the table now.
Can you discover how to get A from b and i?

9. Is b always greater than A?

10. Is $\dfrac{b}{2}$ always greater than A?

11. Is $\dfrac{b}{2} + 1$ always greater than A?

12. How is A related to b and i?

$$A = \underline{\hspace{2cm}}$$

Test your final formula using another figure of your own choice.

6.3 POLYHEDRONS

Students need to know the definitions of prisms and pyramids along with their properties and formulas. They also need problem-solving experiences and applications involving these and other solids formed with flat faces bounded by polygons. This section covers some activities with various polyhedrons while the next section covers some methods of constructing appropriate models.

Sketching

Models play an important role in the study of polyhedrons but students also need to be able to "see" these 3-dimensional solids and their properties from 2 dimensional representations. With that in mind, take time to share with your class some procedures for sketching prisms and pyramids. One of the most useful makes use of graph paper.

By copying figures drawn on a grid, students can quickly and accurately sketch their own while preserving parallelism and aspects of congruency. Prisms have congruent bases and parallel and congruent lateral edges and these are clearly evident in the sketch as well. Have your students copy these figures first and then create some others of their own.

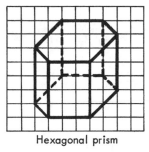
Hexagonal prism

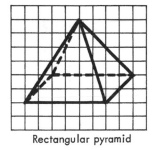
Rectangular pyramid

Prisms and Pyramids

Some students can look at 2- and 3-dimensional representations of prisms and pyramids and clearly see the separate faces that make up the solid. Others cannot. For them, this particular activity would be especially valuable.

Cut the indicated number of pieces for each polygon from construction paper of a different color.

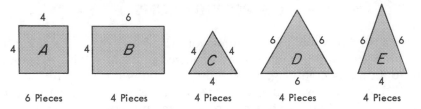

| 6 Pieces | 4 Pieces | 4 Pieces | 4 Pieces | 4 Pieces |

Divide the class into teams. Take turns having a member of a team come up and demonstrate how particular prisms and pyramids can be formed from selected sets of pieces. Use only one piece per face. Use the appropriate letters to keep record of those formed. Keep the score for each team. Require proper identification of each solid formed.

A surprising number of possibilities exist, some easier to find than others. All can be readily verified by assembling the pieces correctly.

Rectangular Prisms	**Rectangular Pyramids**
AAAAAA	ACCCC
AABBBB	AEEEE
	BDDEE
	BCEEE
Triangular Prisms	**Triangular Pyramids**
AAACC	CCCC
ABBEE	DDDD
BBBCC	CEEE
BBBDD	DDEE
	EEEE

It may well be that the triangular prism EEEE is the most surprising and the hardest to find. For a simpler version of this activity, delete the four D pieces (6-6-6 equilateral triangles). For a more difficult version, add four new F pieces (4-4-6 isosceles triangles). In this latter case, watch for those who then add FFFF as a triangular prism. While EEEE does work, FFFF does not. Can you explain why?

Euler's Formula

Although known to Descartes more than 100 years earlier, this simple relationship among the number of vertices, faces, and edges of a polyhedron was independently discovered by Euler and now bears his name.

If V is the number of vertices, E the number of edges, and F the number of faces of a simple polyhedron, then

$$V + F = E + 2$$

Worksheet 1

Euler's Formula
A polyhedron is a figure in space that has flat faces bounded by polygons. The prisms and pyramids shown here are examples of polyhedrons.

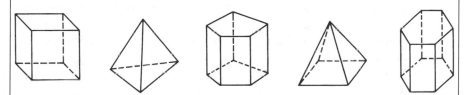

1. Count the number of vertices, faces, and edges for each prism and pyramid shown. Then record the numbers in the table.

| | Number of | | |
Polyhedron	Vertices	Faces	Edges
cube			
tetrahedron			
pentagonal prism			
square pyramid			
hexagonal prism			

2. Study the values in the table. For each of these polyhedrons is the number of edges E greater than the number of vertices V and greater than the number of faces F? Is E always less than the sum of V and F? Can you discover a relationship among the number of edges E and the number of vertices and faces V and F? Try to express this relationship in symbols.

3. Support your formula from step 2 using the V, F, and E from each of these polyhedrons.

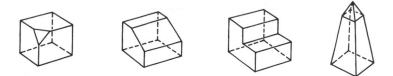

4. Now imagine a small piece cut off each of the eight corners of a cube. Mentally count the number of vertices, faces, and edges of the resulting polyhedron. Do V, F, and E support Euler's formula?

5. Consider a prism with n-gons as bases. Express V, F, and E in terms of n and see if you can support Euler's formula algebraically.

6. Try the same with a pyramid with an n-gon as its base.

Regular Polyhedrons

The literature in the history of mathematics is rich with stories about regular polyhedrons. Their unique special beauty and symmetry has been of intrigue in all ages of time. Some of the solids were probably known to the ancient Egyptians, and the Pythagoreans (ca. 500 B.C.) discovered others. They were later known as the Platonic solids when Plato (ca. 400 B.C.), wrote of their role in the design of matter with this mystical association to the four so-called "elements" of the Universe:

tetrahedron   fire
hexahedron (cube)   earth
octahedron   air
icosahedron   water
dodecahedron   universe

Euclid (ca. 300 B.C.) devoted the last of the 13 books in his famous *Elements* almost entirely to these solids. He included a proof that only five such solids exist.

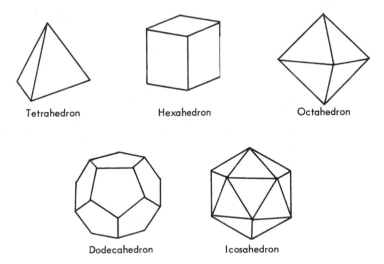

Tetrahedron   Hexahedron   Octahedron

Dodecahedron   Icosahedron

Not many students, looking at solids such as these, are aware of their various parts. Ask the students to count vertices, faces, and edges. See who can come up with a simple counting technique.

Edges are joined at vertices and faces joined at edges. A dodecahedron has 12 pentagonal faces. The separate edges of the individual faces

$(12 \times 5 = 60)$ are paired to form the edges $\left(\frac{60}{2} = 30\right)$ of the solid. The separate vertices $(12 \times 5 = 60)$ are joined three at a time for the $\left(\frac{60}{3} = 20\right)$ vertices of the solid.

Regular Polyhedron	Shape of Faces	Number of		
		Vertices	Faces	Edges
Tetrahedron	equilateral triangles	4	4	6
Hexahedron	squares	8	6	12
Octahedron	equilateral triangles	6	8	12
Dodecahedron	regular pentagons	20	12	30
Icosahedron	equilateral triangles	12	20	30

Each of these number triples satisfies Euler's formula, $V + F = E + 2$.

An interesting and challenging question related to the regular polyhedrons involves coloring. Faces of each solid are painted individually, each with a single color. What is the least number of colors needed to paint each solid such that no two adjacent faces have the same color? The answers are surprising!

Students who show interest in regular polyhedrons may well want to do some research on the 13 semiregular polyhedrons as well. These are known as the Archimedean solids after the famous Greek mathematician Archimedes (c. 287–212 B.C.).

- This semiregular polyhedron has 6 squares and 8 equilateral triangles as faces, with two of each alternating at each of its 12 vertices. How many edges does it have?

Magic Cubes

Don't hesitate to use polyhedrons in a geometry unit as the basis for problem-solving activities. This next worksheet has the students explore the special properties of a $3 \times 3 \times 3$ magic cube.

Worksheet 2

What Is Magic about This Cube?

Here is a pattern for a model of a 3 × 3 × 3 magic cube. When assembled, it appears to be formed from 27 smaller cubes bearing a single number from 1 through 27.

			10	24	8						
			23	7	12						
			9	11	22						
10	23	9	9	11	22	22	12	8	8	24	10
26	3	13	13	27	2	2	25	15	15	1	26
6	16	20	20	4	18	18	5	19	19	17	6
			20	4	18						
			16	21	5						
			6	17	19						

1. Cut out, fold, and assemble the cube.
2. Find the face with 1 on it. Write the three numbers in each of the two rows that contain the 1. Add each set of numbers. Are both sums the same? Now add the three numbers in each of the four other rows on the same face. Do you always get the same sum?
3. Find the face with 27 on it. Add each of the six rows of three numbers on this face. What do you find?
4. There are 24 different rows of three numbers on the six faces of the cube. Can you find them all? Are all their sums the same?
5. One of the numbers from 1 through 27 is not marked on any face. What number is it? Where is the cube located with this number on it?
6. The missing cube is numbered 14 and it is in the very middle of the 3 × 3 × 3 cube. There are 13 different rows and diagonals in the cube that contain this small middle cube numbered 14. Can you find them all? Are all their sums the same?
7. Why do you think this 3 × 3 × 3 cube is called a magic cube?

6.4 CONSTRUCTING MODELS

Students enjoy making their own models from the simplest prism or pyramid to the most complex semiregular or stellated polyhedron. This section illustrates a variety of possible techniques, some more suitable at one level with one kind of figure than at another with a different figure.

Paper Strips

Cut some paper strips 6 cm wide and 12 cm long. Fold them in different ways to form simple models of a variety of prisms.

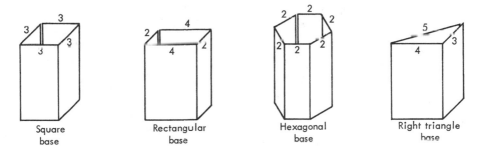

| Square base | Rectangular base | Hexagonal base | Right triangle base |

Toothpicks and Straws

Glue some toothpicks together to form the edges of a pyramid or cut straws and connect them with twist-ties.

Regular tetrahedron   Pentagonal pyramid

Nets

Complicated figures are often formed by first constructing a *net* showing the layout of adjacent faces on card stock. Cut around the boundary and score along the interior edges to facilitate accurate folding. Then fold together and tape.

Here are nets for the five regular polyhedrons. One way to copy them is to cut a template in the shape of each of the basic faces from a file card. The net can then be laid out accurately by marking each vertex of each face.

One set of possible patterns for construction is shown here.

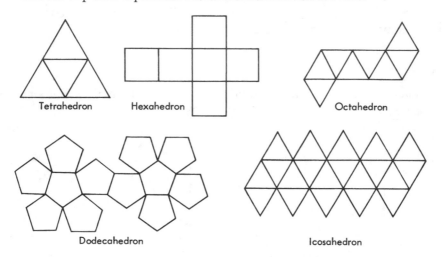

Tetrahedron   Hexahedron   Octahedron

Dodecahedron   Icosahedron

The skills involved in the careful and accurate construction of these solids are often neglected in the mathematics class. As an activity, it can be justified for this reason alone. However, work with these solids can help develop still another important, often neglected, skill, that of three-dimensional visualization.

Folding Paper Hexagons

Cut some regular hexagons from heavy paper. Fold each on its three main diagonals and cut along one to the center. As you curl up the hexagon, models of a pentagonal, square, and triangular pyramid are formed. A paper clip can be used to hold the pyramid in place.

Use the three pyramids formed to help the students discover and generalize the relationship between the number of vertices in the base and the total number of vertices and of edges. A pyramid with an n-gon as a base has $n + 1$ vertices and $2n$ edges.

Folding a Paper Circle

Teachers often associate a model with a particular grade-level topic. However, most geometric models have a wide variety of applications from the simple to the challenging, elementary through secondary. Consider this folding of a paper circle into a model of a truncated tetrahedron.

1. Start with an 8-inch circle cut from a sheet of paper

2. Fold two diameters to locate the center of the circle.

3. Take the edge of the circle and fold it back onto the center three times in such a way as to form an equilateral triangle.

4. Fold one vertex to the midpoint of the opposite side for an isosceles trapezoid, two for a rhombus, and all three for a small equilateral triangle.

5. Open the model up so that the four equilateral triangles form the faces of a regular tetrahedron.

6. When you fold each vertex of the large triangle into the center, a regular hexagon is formed.

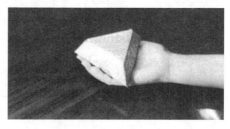

7. Now rest the folded paper loosely in the palm of your hand.

8. Tuck the three upper flaps together to form a model of a truncated tetrahedron.

When the process is demonstrated by the teacher, students at most levels can follow the steps and construct their own model. But where and how can it be used in the classroom? The following possibilities illustrate just how widely applicable this activity can be.

1. *Classifying polygons* By the time step 6 is reached in the construction, these different polygons have been formed:

equilateral triangle   isosceles trapezoid
rhombus   regular hexagon

By refolding along various existing folds, quite a collection of polygons can be formed. Supply triangular grid paper as shown and have students copy each polygon they find. The complete set of 10 is shown here.

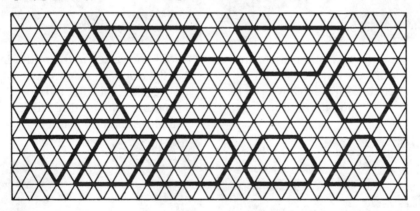

By changing the process just slightly to allow folds under as well as over, a whole new set of concave polygons is added to those convex ones given above.

- Can you find all 10 concave polygons?

2. *Fractions* Call the area of the original equilateral triangle 1. Then the isosceles trapezoids have areas of $\frac{3}{4}$ and $\frac{8}{9}$, the rhombus $\frac{1}{2}$, and the small equilateral triangle $\frac{1}{4}$.

- Can you show by the way the hexagon was folded that it must have an area of $\frac{2}{3}$?

Every one of the 20 polygons mentioned above has a corresponding fraction that can be used to describe its area. The area of the pentagon shown here can be found by subtracting $\frac{1}{4}$ and $\frac{1}{9}$ from 1.

$$1 - \frac{1}{4} - \frac{1}{9} = \frac{23}{36}$$

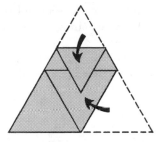

3. *Measurement* In comparing the small tetrahedron cut off the top to that of the original tetrahedron,
    the ratio of heights is 2 to 3.
    the ratio of surface areas is 4 to 9.
    the ratio of volumes is 8 to 27.

4. *Algebra* If the original circle has a diameter of 8 inches, find each of these lengths:
    An altitude of the original equilateral triangle
    A side of the original equilateral triangle
    The height of the original tetrahedron
    The height of the truncated tetrahedron

5. *Advanced Algebra* What are the surface area and volume of the truncated tetrahedron? Careful analysis of the problem can lead to an interesting plan of attack.

If you study the last two steps of the construction, it is apparent that the area of the truncated tetrahedron is exactly $\frac{7}{9}$ that of the original tetrahedron, which is nothing more than the area of the original equilateral triangle.

When considering the volume of the original large tetrahedron, note that the height of the small tetrahedron cut off the top is $\frac{2}{3}$ that of the large tetrahedron. Since the two tetrahedrons are similar in shape, it follows that the ratio of their volumes must be $\left(\frac{2}{3}\right)^3$ or 8 to 27. The remaining portion, that of the truncated tetrahedron, must therefore be $\frac{19}{27}$ of the original volume.

6.5 CONIC SECTIONS

One of the most important sets of curves in mathematics is the conics. The ancient Greek Apollonius (225 B.C.) wrote a treatise entitled *Conic Sections* in which he described how the ellipse, parabola, and hyperbola can be formed by passing a plane through a cone at various angles. Later, with the introduction of coordinate geometry, the conic sections were expressed algebraically as well. Several of the many methods for constructing these curves are given here.

Most mathematics teachers are familiar with the wooden models of cones that can be taken apart to show cuts in the shape of circles, ellipses, parabolas, and hyperbolas.

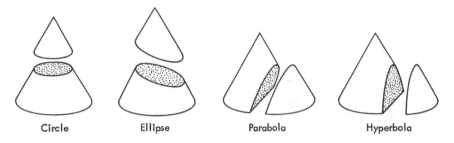

| Circle | Ellipse | Parabola | Hyperbola |

While these models offer vivid illustrations, they are by no means unique since many examples of each curve can be found on the very same cone. Every plane that cuts a cone forms a conic section of one kind or another.

Start with a cutting plane through some point P on the cone. If it is perpendicular to the axis, a circle is formed. At the exact position where it is parallel to an element of the cone, a parabola occurs. All other positions produce ellipses or hyperbolas. These positions are illustrated in this head-on cross-section view.

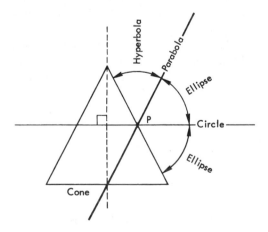

A simple flashlight can be a useful aid when teaching conics. Held at different angles, the circular reflector can project on the wall a circle, ellipse, parabola, and hyperbola. As you move it through the different angles, you can see the curves change much as illustrated above with the cone.

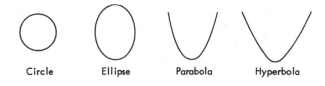

| Circle | Ellipse | Parabola | Hyperbola |

Use a loop of string to show the construction of an ellipse. If the string loop is 18 inches long and the tacks are 8 inches apart, the distance from any point on the curve to the two tacks, which are the foci, is fixed at 10 inches. The semimajor axis is 5, the semiminor axis is 3, and the equation of the ellipse is

$$\frac{x^2}{25} + \frac{y^2}{9} = 1$$

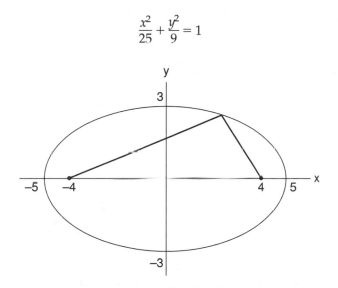

As the tacks get closer together, the curve, while remaining elliptical, approach a circle with radius 9 inches. Only when the two points coincide will a circle be formed.

To illustrate this transition in reverse, consider a plane slicing a can. A cut perpendicular to the axis of the can forms a circle with the center at the axis. But tip the cutting plane and an ellipse is formed with the axis located midway between the two foci. Try making a model from an empty frozen juice can cut with a band saw in the school shop.

Although most algebra courses include some treatment of the conic sections from an analytic approach, little is usually done with them at a more informal level. The following experiments illustrate some simple methods for constructing the conics. They offer interesting and valuable activities for students at both the junior and senior high levels.

EXPERIMENT 1   Conics from Circles and Lines

Material
Worksheets with sets of equally spaced concentric circles and parallel lines as shown.

Directions
1. PARABOLA: Locate and mark the intersection of circle 1 and line 1. Next mark the two intersections of circle 2 and line 2. Then repeat for circle 3 and line 3, circle 4 and line 4, and so on. All these points are the same distance from line 0 and the center of the circle. Connect these points with a smooth curve, a parabola.

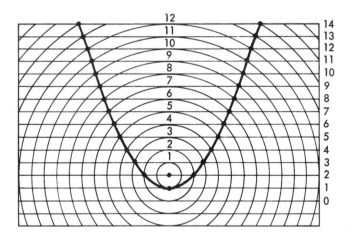

2. ELLIPSE: Locate and mark the points where circles numbered 4 and 8 intersect. Each of these four points is 4 units from one center and 8 units from the other. The sum of the distances from the two centers is 4 + 8, or 12. Next mark the four intersection points of circles 5 and 7. They, too, are located such that the sum of their distances from the two centers is 12. Now mark all other sets of points where the sum of the distances from the two centers is 12. For example, 3 and 9 and 2 and 10. Connect the points with a smooth curve, an ellipse.

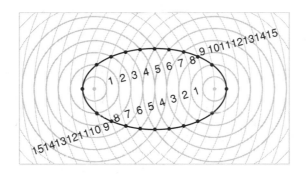

3. HYPERBOLA: Locate and mark points in a similar fashion, but this time with those that always have a difference of 6. For example, 8 and 2, 9 and 3, 10 and 4, and so on. The two smooth curves formed by connecting these sets of points are branches of a hyperbola.

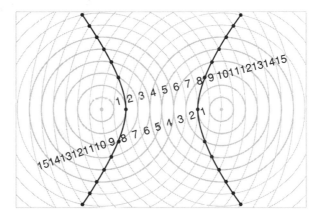

Analysis

These constructions yield the desired conics because they are based on the following loci definitions:

> *Parabola*—the set of points such that each is equidistant from a fixed point and a fixed line.
>
> *Ellipse*—the set of points such that the sum of the distances of each from two fixed points is constant.
>
> *Hyperbola*—the set of points such that the differences of the distances of each from two fixed points is constant.

Try drawing an entire family of conics on each worksheet. Just measure from a different line than zero for more parabolas. Let the sum and difference be some values other than 12 and 6 for more ellipses and hyperbolas.

EXPERIMENT 2   Paper Folding the Conics

Material
A sheet of paper with a line on it and two sheets with circles.

Directions
On a sheet of paper mark a point as shown. Repeatedly fold so the point coincides with the line or circle. The more creases made, the more apparent the conic becomes and the smoother the curve.

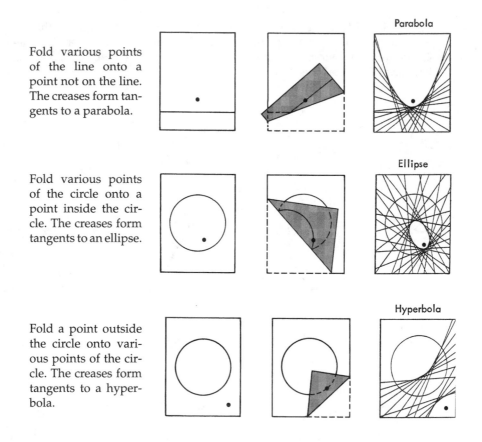

Fold various points of the line onto a point not on the line. The creases form tangents to a parabola.

Parabola

Fold various points of the circle onto a point inside the circle. The creases form tangents to an ellipse.

Ellipse

Fold a point outside the circle onto various points of the circle. The creases form tangents to a hyperbola.

Hyperbola

Excellent examples of these curves can be formed using waxed paper where the creases are more vivid. These can then be easily projected on the overhead projector.

Analysis
Geometry students should be able to prove that these constructions give the conics.

PARABOLA

1. PARABOLA. Point *P* is folded onto the line at *P'*. The crease is tangent to the parabola at point *A*. The focal point of the parabola is *P*.

The crease is the perpendicular bisector of segment *PP'*, so *PA* and *P'A* are equal in length. Since *P'A* is perpendicular to the given line, it measures the distance from *A* to that line. Therefore, point *A* is equidistant from point *P* and the line must lie on the parabola.

ELLIPSE

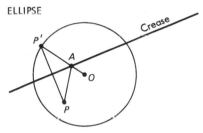

2. ELLIPSE. Point *P* is folded onto circle *O* at *P'*. The crease is tangent to the ellipse at point *A*. The foci of the ellipse are at *P* and *O*.

The crease is the perpendicular bisector of segment *PP'*, so *PA* and *P'A* are equal in length. Hence *PA* plus *AO* are equal in length to *P'A* plus *AO*, which is the radius. Since the radius is constant in length, the sum of the distances of *A* from *P* and *O* is constant. Thus point *A* must be on the ellipse.

HYPERBOLA

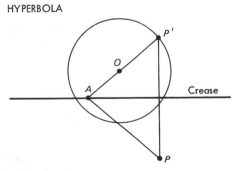

3. HYPERBOLA. Point *P* is folded onto circle *O* at *P'*. The crease is tangent to the hyperbola at *A*. The foci of the hyperbola are at *P* and *O*.

The crease is the perpendicular bisector of segment *PP'*, so *PA* and *P'A* are equal in length. Hence *PA* less *AO* is equal in length to *P'A* less *AO*, or simply *OP'*. But *OP'* is a radius and constant in length. Therefore, the difference of the distances of *A* from *P* and *O* is constant. Thus point *A* must be on the hyperbola.

Curve Stitching

Curve stitching is an enrichment topic of particular interest because it seems to capture the attention of students of varying levels of ability. It is an effective topic to use before a holiday, and can serve as the basis for very dramatic bulletin board displays.

Classroom Procedures

Before allowing students to complete designs of their own, it is well to first have everyone construct one together under the teacher's guidance. A basic one with which to start begins by drawing an angle and marking off the same number of equally spaced units on each side of the angle. In the figure, 12 units are located and marked as shown. Next connect point A to point A', B to B', C to C', and so on. The line segments drawn will appear to form a parabola.

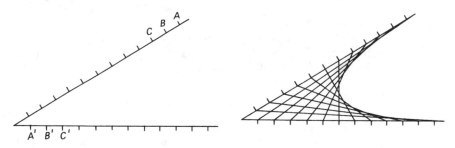

Many different variations are possible merely by changing the angle between the line segments, the distance between points, and by combining several curves. Here is an example of one possible variation.

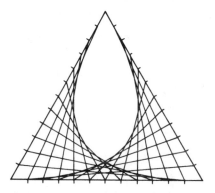

This enrichment topic is entitled "curve stitching" because the figures can be made by using colored thread and stitching through cardboard. Push up through each point from the back, and then stitch between points in the same manner as you would draw line segments.

Extensions

It is worthwhile to prepare a school exhibit consisting of a variety of curve-stitching designs made by individual students. A contest can be held with viewers asked to vote for the most attractive as well as the most original design created.

6.6 VISUALIZATION ACTIVITIES

One valuable problem-solving skill is the ability to think geometrically—to visualize a geometric interpretation or result mentally without having the physical model to hold, position, or otherwise analyze. The activities in this section are directed toward that goal. They may still involve models, but these serve now as a method of check or support following a conjecture arrived at through mental visualization.

Folding Paper Squares

This activity is excellent for both classroom demonstration and individual student involvement. It calls for mental observations that at the same time review basic geometric definitions and numerical relationships which, when needed, can immediately be reinforced with the physical model.

Imagine a paper square with vertices labeled in order as *A*, *B*, *C*, and *D*. Visualize the figure that will result from each of these folds.

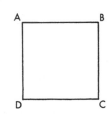

Single Folds

1. Fold vertex *A* to vertex *B*.
2. Fold vertex *A* to vertex *C*.
3. Fold vertex *A* to the center of the square.
4. Fold vertex *A* to the midpoint of side *AD*.

Successive Folds

5. Fold *A* to *B* and then *B* to *C*.
6. Fold *A* to *C* and then *B* to *D*.
7. Fold *A* to *C* and then *B* to *C*.
8. Fold *A* and *C* to the center of the square.

As a follow-up, tie these same visualization questions to arithmetic and algebra.

- If the original square has an area of 1, what percent of it is represented by each folded result?
- If the original square measures $n \times n$, what algebraic expressions represent the area and perimeter of each folded result?

At a more challenging level, use a regular hexagon or regular pentagon.

- Fold a pair of opposite vertices of a regular hexagon to the center of the hexagon. What figure results? What fractional part of the area of the original hexagon remains?

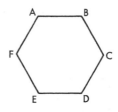

- In this regular pentagon fold A to C and then fold B to D. What percent of the area of the original pentagon remains?

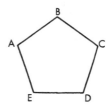

Truncating a Cube

To truncate a solid means to cut off corners. Truncating the regular polyhedrons can produce some of the most impressive and beautiful of the semiregular solids. In general, these have faces of more than one shape but identical corners.

The value of such models in the mathematics class is inherent in their special shapes and properties. But indeed, of even more value is the skill in space perception that comes from imagining certain of these solids formed from truncating others. This activity is suggested with that in mind. Designed for the better student, it can serve as an exciting, challenging exercise in visualization which culminates, rather than begins, with the model. Use a model of a cube only as a final verification of the initial answer.

- Imagine cutting off each corner of a cube by passing a plane through the midpoints of the three adjacent edges. Describe the resulting figure.

The result is a *cuboctahedron*. Here is a net that can be used in constructing a model of a cuboctahedron.

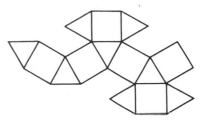

If you cut off the corners of a cube in stages, moving in from each vertex, step-by-step, this sequence of solids is formed. The construction of a complete set of these models would make an interesting special project.

Stage 1:	cube	6 square faces
Stage 2:	truncated cube	6 octagonal and 8 triangular faces
Stage 3:	cuboctahedron	6 square and 8 triangular faces
Stage 4:	truncated octahedron	6 square and 8 hexagonal faces
Stage 5:	octahedron	8 triangular faces

Stage 1   Stage 2   Stage 3   Stage 4   Stage 5

The original 6 faces of the cube become octagonal, then square again, and finally disappear. The original 8 corners become triangular, then hexagonal, and finally triangular again. Surprisingly, if you start with the regular octahedron and begin truncating corners, the reverse sequence is formed, and the final solid is again a cube. This explains why the solid in the middle is given the combined name cuboctahedron.

A thorough discussion of this successive truncation of a cube yields a vast amount of visualization experience, some challenging problems to solve, and a glimpse into the subject of semiregular polyhedrons. The mere fact that the equilateral triangle, regular hexagon, and regular octagon are part of this process that starts with the squares on a cube illustrates again the beauty of mathematical relationships!

The two visualization activities given thus far were discussed in some detail and each can serve as the source of a classroom lesson on the subject. Similar experiences are noted elsewhere in this chapter. But visualization activities can take the form of short questions to start off the class, to end the week, or as an extra-credit challenge. Here are a few of the many possibilities.

1. Take a long, narrow strip of paper. Carefully tie an overhand knot in it, pull together, and then crease it flat. What regular polygon is formed?

2. Show how a solid regular tetrahedron can be cut with one slice into two congruent halves. What shape is the intersecting cut?

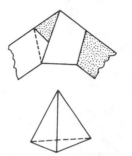

3. Describe the shape of a single solid that will snuggly fit through each of these openings.

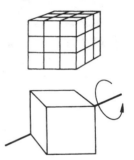

4. How many $1 \times 1 \times 1$, $2 \times 2 \times 2$, and $3 \times 3 \times 3$ cubes can be found in this solid?

5. Describe the shape of the surface formed by spinning a cube using a major diagonal as an axis. Conjecture first, and then actually spin a model of a cube. The results may surprise you.

6. Name the polygon formed when each cube is cut by a plane passing through the midpoints of the three sides shown.

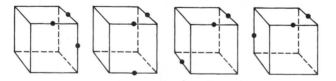

These problems, while easily stated and assigned, can lead to some very creative visual experiences. Remember, encourage students to share and discuss their intuitive ideas, their plans of attack, their diagrams and listings, their models, and their experiments, whether they led them to the correct and complete solution or not.

The two worksheets that follow illustrate yet another possible format for visualization experiences. Students should try these first without any models or aids.

Worksheet 1

Can You Spot the Cubes?
Many different patterns can be used to form models of cubes. Each pattern must have six squares for faces arranged so that, when assembled, no faces overlap.

1. Study the patterns given here and circle those that you think can be used for a cube. Be careful!
2. Check your answers by cutting out the patterns you are not sure of and trying to assemble them.
3. Copy those that work onto a sheet of graph paper. Then draw as many more as you can find. Remember, count only those that are different patterns, not those that are different positions of the same pattern.

Worksheet 2

What Do You See?

Imagine that a $3 \times 3 \times 3$ cube is painted red and then cut into 27 small 1-inch cubes.

1. Complete the table describing how the 27 small cubes are painted.

Number of Faces Painted	Number of Small Cubes
0	
1	
2	
3	
4	
total	27

2. Suppose that a $4 \times 4 \times 4$ cube was cut into 1-inch cubes the same way. How would the 64 small cubes be painted?

Number of Faces Painted	Number of Small Cubes
0	
1	
2	
3	
4	
total	64

3. If you had no trouble with these, try the same with an $n \times n \times n$ cube. Be sure that the sum of your answers here add to n^3.

Using the Overhead Projector

Given all the audiovisual equipment available for the classroom, the overhead projector remains a valuable teaching tool. With some imagination and creativity, many striking effects are possible, especially in geometry where motion and change are important elements.

Use a copy machine to reproduce a protractor on a sheet of acetate. Cut two acetate strips with rays drawn on them and attach them to the center point of the protractor with a sewing snap as shown.

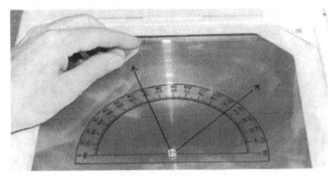

Practice reading the angle size on the correct scale when the initial side is to the right. Then place the initial side to the left and practice reading the other scale. Finally, move both rays off the base line and have students discuss some methods that can be used to find the measure of the angle between them.

Students need to see triangles, not as rigid and static, but as flexible and dynamic. They should be able to see in their minds how a triangle might change were its vertices allowed to move around. Cut the pieces shown from an old file folder. Motion is created by using a movable mask attached to a base with a sewing snap. As the small rectangular mask is moved, the projected triangle changes in shape and size and through various classifications. The visual effect is vivid and striking!

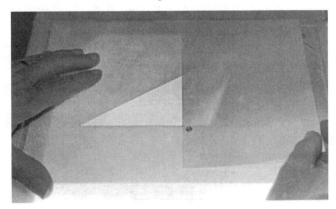

Begin with the moveable mask in the upright position projecting a right triangle. Students will be surprised to see the triangle change shape as the mask is rotated counterclockwise until the triangle disappears entirely. Ask at that point if any other right triangles were formed in the process. Then, as you gradually open up the triangle by rotating the mask clockwise, have the students classify the projected triangle as acute, right, or obtuse. The projected triangle is acute between the two positions of the right triangles. Otherwise, it is obtuse. Now close the figure again. Ask the students to imagine its opening up and count the number of different places where an isosceles triangle is formed. Many students will not see all three positions until the triangles are actually projected.

6.7 MEASUREMENT EXPERIMENTS

Hands-on experiences are a common part of most measurement units taught in the classroom. However, it is still surprising just how many interesting experiments are possible involving measurement and estimation.

Estimation should be an important part of teaching measurement. Try some of these with your class. Bring out the objects and measuring tools only after the students make their initial estimates.

1. What is the length of a dollar bill in inches?
   (a) 5   (b) 6   (c) 7   (d) 8   (e) 9
2. What is the ratio of the length of a dollar bill to its width?
   (a) $\frac{5}{3}$ (b) $\frac{6}{3}$ (c) $\frac{7}{3}$ (d) $\frac{8}{3}$ (e) $\frac{9}{3}$
3. How many pennies can be placed on a dollar bill without overlapping the edges of the bill or the other pennies?
   (a) 18   (b) 21   (c) 24   (d) 27   (e) 30

The experiments that follow illustrate the wide diversity of measurement applications over various age and ability levels.

EXPERIMENT 1   Angles of a Triangle

Directions

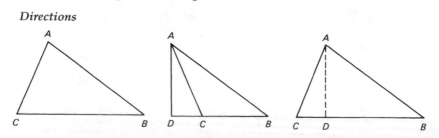

1. Begin with a triangular piece of paper with vertices labeled *A, B,* and *C.*

2. Fold vertex *C* onto side *BC* so that the crease passes through vertex *A.*

3. The crease *AD* is the altitude through vertex *A.*

4. Fold vertex *A* onto point *D.*
   Fold vertex *C* onto point *D.*
   Fold vertex *B* onto point *D.*

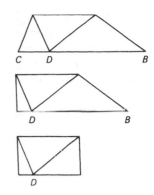

Show that the sum of the measures of the angles *A, B,* and *C* is 180.

Analysis
The three angles of the triangle have been folded onto a straight line. Hence the sum of their measures must be 180.

EXPERIMENT 2   Area of a Triangle

1. Use the folded triangle from Experiment 1. Note that twice the area of the rectangle is the area of the triangle.

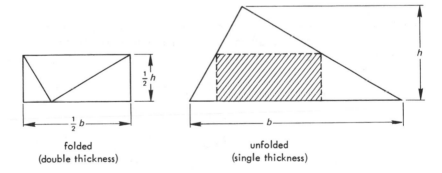

| folded | unfolded |
| (double thickness) | (single thickness) |

2. The length of the rectangle is half the base of the triangle. The width of the rectangle is half the height of the triangle. Show that the area of the triangle is $\frac{1}{2}bh$.

Analysis
Area of triangle = 2(Area of rectangle)

$$= 2(l \times w)$$

$$= 2\left(\frac{1}{2}b \times \frac{1}{2}h\right) = 2\left(\frac{1}{4}bh\right) = \frac{1}{2}bh$$

Many students enjoy field activities in the mathematics class. The *hypsometer* is a simple, useful instrument designed to help determine the height of an object by indirect measurement. It can be made and used by the students themselves with results that can be surprisingly accurate. Adaptable to a variety of levels, it can be effectively used as a supplement to units on measurement, scale drawing, and ratios, or even as an introduction to numerical trigonometry.

The principle of the hypsometer is based on similar figures.

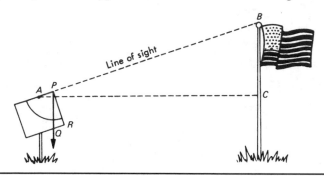

EXPERIMENT 3   Hypsometer

Materials
The scale shown, a plumb line, and a pole

Directions
Students can draw the scales themselves or attach a copy supplied by the teacher on a rectangular piece of cardboard. Suspend a plumb line from the upper right-hand corner of the grid as shown and attach it to a pole of convenient height so that it will pivot freely.

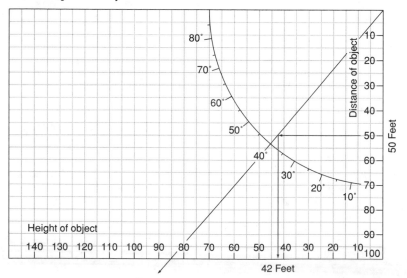

Analysis

With the hypsometer, the height can be read directly from the grid, given the distance to the object. Note how similar triangles are involved in the use of the scales. For the setting shown, the distance to the object is 50 feet. The corresponding height of the object is 42 feet plus the height of the instrument.

Pythagorean Property

Many different aids can be used in teaching the Pythagorean property. Some serve best for initial investigation and discovery while others are best in review. Some are very formal and exact while others are informal and approximate. Several are illustrated here.

This first model offers convincing support for the property but only for the 3–4–5 right triangle. Similar models can be made for other Pythagorean triples. A modification, drawn on graph paper, allows any positive integers for the legs. The square on the hypotenuse can always be subdivided by this method and its area easily found.

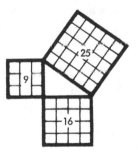

$$3^2 + 4^2 = 9 + 16$$
$$= 25$$
The legs are 3 and 4 and
the hypotenuse is 5.

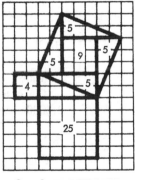

$$2^2 + 5^2 = 4 + 25 = 29$$
$$29 = 9 + 4(5)$$
The legs are 2 and 5
and the hypotenuse is $\sqrt{29}$.

This puzzle offers a challenging hands-on activity for your students. Cut out the squares on the two legs, and subdivide the larger one as shown. The task is to arrange these five separate pieces so that they just fill the square on the hypotenuse.

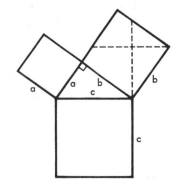

Angles of a Polygon

Most students know the number of degrees in each of the interior angles of an equilateral triangle and a square. Those for a regular pentagon, hexagon, and octagon can easily be found.

equilateral triangle	60° angles
square	90° angles
regular pentagon	108° angles
regular hexagon	120° angles
regular octagon	135° angles

For any regular polygon, first subdivide into triangles. Take the number of triangles, multiply by 180, and then divide by the number of sides in the regular polygon. In general, for a regular *n*-gon, the number of degrees per angle is

$$\frac{(n-2)180}{n}$$

But to explore what happens to the size of the angles of a regular polygon as the number of sides increases focuses not on the computation but on the pattern or trend in the results. A calculator facilitates the computation.

- Find the number of degrees in the angles of these regular polygons.

10 sided	(144°)
100 sided	(176.4°)
1000 sided	(179.64°)
10,000 sided	(179.964°)

- How many sides does a regular polygon have with angles of these sizes?

179°   179.9°   179.99°   179.999°

Maximum Volume

Give to each student a circular piece of paper with radius 8 cm and cut once through to the center. Let them curl the paper up to form cones. As students curl the paper tighter and tighter, their cones change in radii and heights. But in all cases, the slant height remains fixed at 8 cm.

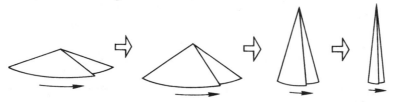

The elements of the limit concept should become part of the students' thinking long before they see it in the context of the calculus. Use this model to encourage some informal thinking along these lines.

As the height approaches 0,
    what length does the radius approach?   (slant height)
    what does the volume approach?   (0)
    what does the surface area approach?   (twice area of original circle)
As the length of the radius approaches 0,
    what does the height approach?   (slant height)
    what does the volume approach?   (0)
    what does the surface area approach?   (0)

Now have every student do this estimation activity.

> Curl up the cone to the place where it appears to have maximum volume and fasten it with a paper clip at that point.

Have the students hold up their cones so the whole class can see the choices. There are sure to be many, but which has the maximum volume?

Use a graphing calculator, construct a table of increasing radii and decreasing heights along with the corresponding volumes. Then search for the maximum volume.

X = radius   Y₁ = height   Y₂ = volume   X = radius   Y₁ = height   Y₂ = volume

X	Y₁	Y₂
1.5	7.8581	18.515
2	7.746	32.446
2.5	7.5993	49.738
3	7.4162	69.896
3.5	7.1937	92.283
4	6.9282	116.08
4.5	6.6144	140.26

Y₂=116.083159311

X	Y₁	Y₂
5	6.245	163.49
5.5	5.8095	184.03
6	5.2915	199.48
6.5	4.6637	206.34
7	3.873	198.73
7.5	2.7839	163.98
8	0	0

Y₂=206.340729636

The volume of the cone when the radius is 4 cm is about 116 cm³.

The maximum volume of about 206 cm³ occurs when the radius is 6.5 cm.

Another approach is to graph the volume as a function of the radius with the slant height fixed at 8 cm.

Using the Pythagorean theorem, define the volume, y, in terms of the radius, x, for the cone. Enter the function, draw the graph, and then trace along the curve to find the maximum volume and the corresponding radius. Both the shape of the curve and the numerical answer will surprise most students.

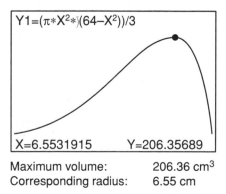

Y1=(π*X²*)(64–X²))/3

X=6.5531915   Y=206.35689

Maximum volume: 206.36 cm³
Corresponding radius: 6.55 cm

Geometry Software

Software packages now exist for use by students in learning geometry. They can use length and angle measurement to explore and discover geometric relationships, both simple and complex, and see dynamic action and change in figures displayed on the computer screen. These software materials now offer powerful options in teaching geometry and should be explored by the reader.

EXERCISES

1. Square and rectangular pieces of paper measuring 2×2, 2×4, 2×6, 4×4, 4×6, and 6×6 are available in quantity for building models of rectangular prisms. How many different-sized rectangular prisms can be constructed from them using only one piece per face?

2. Multiple copies of rectangles and triangles are cut from paper. The rectangles measure 3×3 and 3×5. The triangles have sides measuring 3, 3, and 5 and 3, 5, and 5. How many different prisms and pyramids can be constructed using only one piece per face?

3. A circular piece of paper has a 5-cm radius. It is cut once through to the center and curled up to form a model of a cone with a height of 4 inches. Find the volume and total surface area of the cone.

4. A cone is formed from a circular piece of paper cut through to the center. When curled up in different ways, different cones are formed, all with the same slant height. Draw graphs to show the relationship between the radius and the height, the radius and the volume, and the radius and the total surface area.

5. A 9×12-inch sheet of paper is curled up edge-to-edge in two different ways to form models of two different cylinders. Find the volume and total surface area of each cylinder.

6. Archimedes proved that the volume relationship among a cone, sphere, and cylinder of the same radius and height is 1 to 2 to 3. Prove this relationship algebraically.

7. Twelve congruent square pieces of paper are cut out, six red and six green. How many different-colored models of a cube can be made using any six of the squares?

8. Show how Euler's formula $V + F = E + 2$ applies to a prism and a pyramid with an n-gon as bases.

9. Find the number of vertices, faces, and edges in each of the five regular polyhedrons. Look for shortcuts in doing the counting.

10. A soccer ball has the general shape of a truncated icosahedron. This is a semiregular polyhedron with 20 hexagons and 12 pentagons as faces that has two hexagons and a pentagon coming together at each vertex. How many vertices and edges are on this polyhedron?

11. Five 1-cm cubes are joined face-to-face in all possible ways. How many different figures are possible?

12. A triangle is cut from a piece of paper and the midpoints of its sides connected by three folds. What condition must be imposed on the original triangle such that the folded model can be used to form a tetrahedron?

13. A 32-inch string loop is used to draw an ellipse around two thumbtacks that are 12 inches apart. Write the equation of the ellipse formed if the origin is at the midpoint of the segment connecting the thumbtacks and the axes are marked in inches.

14. A 3 × 3 grid of squares can be divided into two congruent halves along polygonal paths joining intersection points on the grid. Show the thirteen different-shaped congruent halves that are possible.

15. Find the volume and surface area of the cuboctahedron formed from a 4-inch cube by cutting off its eight corners with planes passing through the midpoints of the adjacent sides.

16. Pyramids are built using four triangular pieces for their faces. The triangles available for this construction measure 4–4–5, 4–5–5, and 5–5–5, all in inches, and an unlimited number are available in each size. How many different pyramids can be built?

ACTIVITIES

1. Use a string knotted at 1-foot intervals to lay out a 10-foot square as the ancient Egyptians might have done.

2. Describe in detail an experiment involving rulers, string, and some circular objects that students might follow in establishing an approximate value for *pi*.

3. Develop a classroom demonstration that could be used to show that there can only be five regular polyhedrons.

4. Develop a paper-folding experiment that can be used to illustrate how to find the area of a parallelogram.

5. Cut out two congruent regular hexagons from paper. Fold, cut, and assemble them into a triangular and a square pyramid, as shown on page 180. Then compute and compare their volumes, assuming each edge to have a length *e*.

6. Fold a parabola, ellipse, and hyperbola on paper using the method shown on page 188.

7. Find the ten concave polygons that can be formed from the paper-folding activity on classifying polygons described on page 182.

8. Develop an experiment that students can follow in discovering the pattern relating the number of diagonals to the number of vertices on a polygon.

9. Prepare a lesson plan on Euler's formula for a middle school class. Pay specific attention to the motivation of the lesson, the use of classroom models, individual student involvement, and an appropriate assignment.

10. Start with some squares cut from paper. It's easy to cut one into triangular pieces but see if you can make all the triangles acute. This problem is more challenging than it may appear at first reading. The key to the solution rests in an extension of a theorem in geometry concerning angles inscribed in a semicircle.

11. Develop a transparency sequence that can be used when teaching the Pythagorean theorem.

12. Prepare a demonstration using one of the contemporary software packages in geometry. Construct a right triangle with the altitude drawn from the right angle vertex. Measure the lengths of corresponding sides in the three similar right triangles and compute the ratios for each pair. Then find the corresponding areas of the three triangles and show that their ratios are the squares of those of the corresponding sides.

13. Prepare a report on some of the history surrounding the regular polyhedrons and the famous mathematicians, such as Pythagoras, Plato, Euclid, Archimedes, and Kepler, who studied them.

14. Read *Flatland* by Edwin Abbott, New York: Dover Publications, Inc., 1979. Reprints of this text originally published in the late 1800s are available. Prepare a plan for a short presentation to a middle-school class on Abbott's description of life in a two-dimensional world.

15. Read *Beyond the Third Dimension*, by Thomas Banchoff, New York: Scientific American Library, 1990. Select a chapter and use it to prepare a presentation appropriate for an upper-level secondary mathematics class.

16. Read *What Is Mathematics?: An Elementary Approach to Ideas and Methods*, by Richard Courant, et al., New York: Oxford University Press, 1996. Prepare a classroom report on the relationship between geometric constructions and algebra as described therein.

17. Read *The Penguin Dictionary of Curious and Interesting Geometry*, by David Wells, New York: Penguin Books, 1991. Select 10 interesting and unique geometry terms from the book and describe how they might be used to motivate the teaching of geometry in the middle school. Then repeat the process with another 10 terms suitable at the secondary level.

18. Geometry textbooks are likely to have major similarities as well as striking differences. Compare two current geometry textbooks, and comment on what you see as their basic differences. In particular, note the attention given to motivational activities, proof, geometric constructions, and technology.

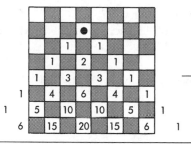

7

ACTIVITIES IN PROBABILITY AND STATISTICS

Probability and statistics are playing an ever-increasing role in society. This has come about, in part, because of the vast increase in data-handling and graphics capabilities of the computer. At the same time, educators are asking that the priorities in the instructional program be changed to include increased emphasis on such activities as collecting, organizing, presenting, and interpreting data, as well as on using collected data to draw inferences and make predictions. This chapter offers some suggestions on classroom aids and activities related to these recommendations.

7.1 MOTIVATION IN PROBABILITY AND STATISTICS

The subjects of probability and statistics tend by their very nature to be more motivating, concrete, and manipulative oriented than most other topics in mathematics. Related activities and experiments on these topics are more commonplace in the curriculum than most others, but the pressure of time often results in minimal attention to probability and statistics.

Use Actual Real-World Data

When computing and comparing the mean, median, and mode, look for examples that offer more than just the facts themselves. Consider the following table of the monthly rainfall in Bombay, India:

Monthly Rainfall in Bombay

Month	J	F	M	A	M	J	J	A	S	O	N	D
Rainfall in Inches	0	0	0	0	1	21	27	16	12	2	0	0

- Would you say the weather in Bombay is dry or wet?
- Does the mean of 6.6 inches, the median of 0.5 inches, or the mode of 0 inches best describe the monthly rainfall? Or is some other description needed here?
- How do these data compare with those of your own town or city?

Encourage Estimation

Have each student guess the diameter of a penny to the nearest eighth of an inch by choosing from these estimates:

Display the number of responses for each of the five choices. Ask the students how they think others would respond to the same question based on the collected results of the class. Encourage them to express their ideas in the form of probability statements. Only then let them measure a penny to find which of the listed estimates is best.

Choose Activities That Involve All Students

Ask each student to bring in three pictures of the same size, each cut in half vertically. Turn the pieces over, mix them up, and have another student select two pieces at random. What is the probability that the two pieces match?

First, have every student in class do the experiment once and record the combined results. Use them to establish the likelihood for a match based on the experimental data. Next, let each student list the different pairs of pieces that are possible (15) and how many match (3). Finally, let them use these numbers to compute a probability based on this list of possible outcomes ($\frac{1}{5}$).

Steer the discussion that follows around these two computed probabilities, one experimental and the other theoretical. Which do the students think is the better predictor and why?

For some classes, you may want to facilitate their listing of choices by suggesting matched halves be labeled A and a, B and b, and C and c.

AB   AC   (Aa)   Ab   Ac   BC   Ba   (Bb)   Bc   Ca   Cb   (Cc)   ab   ac   bc

Use Non-routine Problems

Exciting classroom discussions often surround the use of non-routine probability problems. Differences can arise from disagreements on what constitutes the correct listing of all possible choices in a sample space.

- A family has two children. You know that one of them is a boy. What is the probability that both children are boys?

What entries should go in the sample space for this problem? The answer lies in the two facts given in the problem. Thus, an appropriate listing might contain ordered pairs using B and G for boy and girl, respectively.

$$BG \quad GB \quad BB \qquad \text{Probability} = \frac{1}{3}$$

What error has been made in this incorrect choice of a sample space?

$$GG \quad BG \quad GB \quad BB \qquad \text{Probability} = \frac{1}{4}$$

Make Use of Familiar Things

Dominoes are not only useful teaching aids in the early grades for showing number relationships and fraction concepts, but they can make effective teaching aids in elementary probability as well.

- A domino is chosen at random from a complete set numbered 0 through 6. What is the probability that it contains a 5?

Show a single domino or two to establish the criteria for making and distinguishing dominoes. Cardboard models, cut out and punched, can be very effective on the overhead projector. Then challenge each student to make a complete list of all possibilities. Encourage a systematic listing, such as this:

```
00  01  02  03  04  05  06
11  12  13  14  15  16
22  23  24  25  26
33  34  35  36
44  45  46
55  56
66
```

$$P \text{ (five)} = \frac{7}{28} = \frac{1}{4}$$

At another level, extend the problem to sums and differences on individual dominoes. Construct frequency distributions. Compare and contrast the corresponding histograms.

Dramatize Action

Rule a transparency with lines 1 inch apart and place it on an overhead projector. Repeatedly drop pennies on the ruled surface. Let the class count both tries and successes as they search for a reasonable estimate of the probability that a penny will not land on a line. The projected images vividly dramatize the action for the whole class to see.

Compute a probability based on the experimental data collected. Then analyze the problem geometrically for another view of the probability.

The diameter of a penny is $\frac{3}{4}$ inch. If its center point falls in the quarter-inch strips in the middle of the one-inch spaces between the lines, the penny itself will not cross a line. This is $\frac{1}{4}$ of the total area and so a good prediction of the penny not falling on a line is $\frac{1}{4}$.

7.2 COUNTING AND PROBABILITY

In its simplest form, theoretical probability begins with a discussion of counting techniques. Counting is at the same time both one of the most trivial and most complex mathematical skills. The use of concrete models and manipulatives with some of the simpler counting problems can give the student a practical, geometric, visual approach that can be applied later on to more involved counting situations and probability problems.

Lettered Cards

Letter some 3×5 file cards to use as an aid in discussing counting techniques. Use the name of your school, a student's name, or your own, and build some counting and probability problems around it. The word "STATIS-TICS" is used here as an illustrative example.

Place each letter on a separate card. Use the cards to explain how each probability is found from a single random drawing.

$$P(A) = \frac{1}{10} \qquad P(S \text{ or } T) = \frac{6}{10}$$

$$P(S) = \frac{3}{10} \qquad P(\text{constant}) = \frac{7}{10}$$

Use the cards to contrast sampling with and without replacement. Two letters are drawn. What is the probability that both are S's?

$$P(2\ S's) = \frac{3}{10} \times \frac{3}{10} = \frac{9}{100} \qquad P(2\ S's) = \frac{3}{10} \times \frac{2}{9} = \frac{6}{90} = \frac{1}{15}$$

With replacement of the
first S before the second
is drawn

Without replacement of the
first S before the second
is drawn

Use cards to contrast permutations and combinations. How many permutations and combinations of 2 of the 5 letters in the word "COUNT" are possible?

$$_5P_2 = 5 \times 4 = 20$$

$$_5C_2 = \binom{5}{2} = \frac{5 \times 4}{2 \times 1} = 10$$

There are 20 permutations or *orderings* possible, but there are only 10 combinations or *choices* possible. Each pair of letters constitutes one combination or choice but two permutations or orderings.

Use cards to count more complicated letter arrangements. In how many ways can the eight letters in "EIGHTEEN" be arranged? Here the three duplicate E cards require dividing by 3!.

All possible arrangements

$$\frac{8!}{3!} = 8 \times 7 \times 6 \times 5 \times 4 = 6720$$

For all E's together, replace the three E cards with a single one and count the orderings possible with the resulting six cards. For each choice, simply replace the one E card with the three E's for the 8-letter arrangements with the three E's together.

 Arrangement with E's together

$6! = 6 \times 5 \times 4 \times 3 \times 2 \times 1$

$= 720$

- What is the probability that a random arrangement of the letters in "EIGHTEEN" have all E's together?
- What is the probability that no two E's are together?

Numbered Cubes

Numbered cubes or dice are especially useful teaching aids. Find empirical estimates first and then do the analysis with sample spaces for the theoretical probabilities.

- What is the probability of rolling a sum of 7 with a pair of dice marked 1, 2, 3, 4, 5, and 6 on their faces?

Have your students roll a pair of dice 100 times, recording the sum for each roll. Divide the number of times a sum of 7 occurs by 100, the number of trials. Use this as an estimate of the probability of rolling a sum of 7.

Then let the students construct and use a sample space to analyze all possible equally likely results. Mark sums inside the 6 × 6 grid as shown in the following figure.

SECOND DIE

	1	2	3	4	5	6
1	2	3	4	5	6	7
2	3	4	5	6	7	8
3	4	5	6	7	8	9
4	5	6	7	8	9	10
5	6	7	8	9	10	11
6	7	8	9	10	11	12

FIRST DIE

$P(7) = 6/36 = 1/6$

For variety, use a set of polyhedron dice consisting of a regular tetrahedron, hexahedron, octahedron, dodecahedron, and icosahedron numbered from 1 to 4, 1 to 6, 1 to 8, 1 to 12, and 1 to 20 respectively. On a given die, each face is as likely to occur as any other, but the probability of a given result changes from die to die.

$$P(3 \text{ on tetrahedron}) \quad = \frac{1}{4}$$

$$P(3 \text{ on hexahedron}) \quad = \frac{1}{6}$$

$$P(3 \text{ on octahedron}) \quad = \frac{1}{8}$$

$$P(3 \text{ on dodecahedron}) = \frac{1}{12}$$

$$P(3 \text{ on icosahedron}) \quad = \frac{1}{20}$$

- What is the probability of rolling a sum of 7 with the tetrahedron and octahedron as dice?

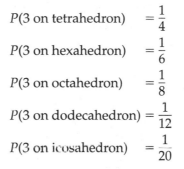

OCTAHEDRON

	1	2	3	4	5	6	7	8
1	2	3	4	5	6	**7**	8	9
2	3	4	5	6	**7**	8	9	10
3	4	5	6	**7**	8	9	10	11
4	5	6	**7**	8	9	10	11	12

TETRAHEDRON

$P(7) = 4/32 = 1/8$

There are 46,080 different ways of rolling all five of the polyhedron dice at one time.

$$4 \times 6 \times 8 \times 12 \times 20 = 46,080$$

- What is the probability of rolling a sum of 7 with all five of these dice? There are only 15 ways a sum of 7 can occur. Can you list them and then use them to compute the probability?

Tossing Coins

Make interesting probability activities centered around the use of coins.

- What is the probability that when two coins are tossed, both fall heads?

Repeated tosses emphasize the notion of probability *in the long run*. As more trials are performed the computed experimental probabilities tend to level off at the theoretical value. This is vividly illustrated by the line graph and by the cumulative fractions and percents in the following table.

Students first guess at the answer. Then, tossing two coins at a time, they compute the ratio of successes (2 heads) to trials, along with the corresponding cumulative percents. These percents are then plotted on a graph for each of 20 successive trials. Typical results might look like this:

Toss	1	2	3	4	5	6	7	8	9	10	11	12	13	14	15	16	17	18	19	20
Two Heads	X					X							X		X					X
Not Two Heads		X	X	X	X		X	X	X	X	X	X		X		X	X	X	X	
Rate of Successes to Total	$\frac{1}{1}$	$\frac{1}{2}$	$\frac{1}{3}$	$\frac{1}{4}$	$\frac{1}{5}$	$\frac{1}{6}$	$\frac{2}{7}$	$\frac{2}{8}$	$\frac{2}{9}$	$\frac{2}{10}$	$\frac{2}{11}$	$\frac{2}{12}$	$\frac{3}{13}$	$\frac{3}{14}$	$\frac{4}{15}$	$\frac{4}{16}$	$\frac{4}{17}$	$\frac{4}{18}$	$\frac{4}{19}$	$\frac{5}{20}$
Percent of Successes	1.000	.500	.333	.250	.200	.166	.285	.250	.222	.200	.181	.166	.230	.214	.266	.250	.235	.222	.210	.250

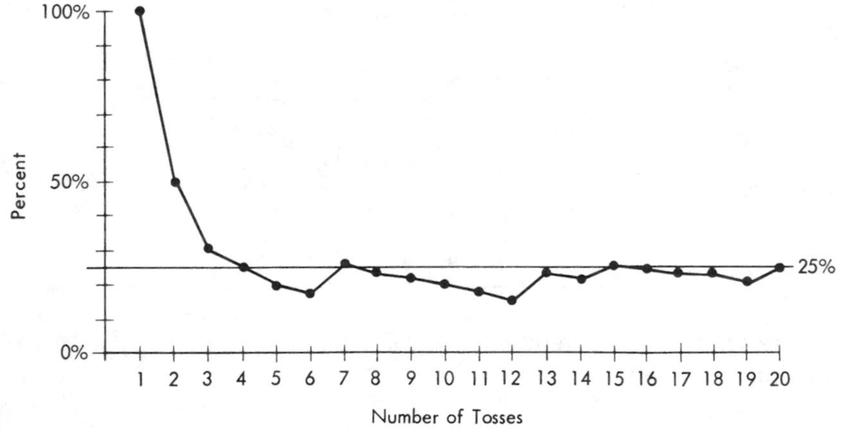

Percent

100%

50%

0%

25%

1 2 3 4 5 6 7 8 9 10 11 12 13 14 15 16 17 18 19 20

Number of Tosses

The original guesses can then be compared with the collected data and modified, based on the experimental evidence.

Students may first guess the probability to be $\frac{1}{3}$, arguing that the coins can fall 2 heads, 1 head, or 0 heads. However, the correct answer is $\frac{1}{4}$, since only one of these four equally likely possible outcomes is a success.

HH   HT   TH   TT

The greater the number of repetitions, the more likely the corresponding cumulative-percent graph will tend toward this value.

Of course, the assumptions are made throughout the experiment that these are unbiased coins randomly tossed. If these assumptions are in doubt, one might well find the experimental probability the better predictor.

Checkerboards

Pascal's triangle can be developed through the idea of a random walk by a checker on a board. Start with the checker as shown below, and repeatedly toss a coin. If the coin falls heads, move down to the left and if it falls tails, move down to the right. The path of the checker can be thought of as a random walk. The checker moves one square at a time diagonally down to either the left or the right. By counting the number of different ways it can move to various positions on successive rows, the numbers in Pascal's triangle are generated.

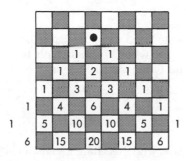

$$1 + 6 + 15 + 20 + 15 + 6 + 1 = 64$$
$$= 2^6$$

The sixth row of Pascal's triangle has a sum of 2^6 or 64, with some moves extended beyond the board. The probabilities of reaching the four white squares on the bottom row, starting from the position shown, would be

$$\frac{15}{64}, \frac{20}{64}, \frac{15}{64}, \text{ and } \frac{6}{64}$$

respectively, left to right.

If the checker must stay on the board and the coin is tossed only when a choice of moves exists, then these probabilities become

$$\frac{14}{54}, \frac{20}{54}, \frac{15}{54}, \text{ and } \frac{5}{54}.$$

The numbers in Pascal's triangle are combinations and can readily be derived from the binomial expansion. The numbers in the sixth row represent the coefficients in the expansion of $(H + T)^6$.

$$(H + T)^6 = 1H^6 + 6H^5T^1 + 15H^4T^2 + 20H^3T^3 + 15H^2T^4 + 6H^1T^5 + H^6$$

Each term also identifies the different six-step random walks to that position.

7.3 PROBABILITY EXPERIMENTS

Experiments in probability can be exciting and interesting to students with a wide range of ages and abilities. The element of chance and doubt, the close association with familiar games, and the active involvement of individual students all help to provide motivation. Here is an example of an experiment that might be used in class to introduce the topic.

EXPERIMENT 1   Random Walks

Material
Rulers, paper, and coins

Directions
Each student draws a number line from -5 to 5 and then, starting at 0, moves one unit at a time to the right or left depending on whether a tossed coin lands heads or tails. The first to reach -5 or 5 tossing his or her own coin wins.

Analysis
Reaching a 5 in five tosses requires 5 heads while reaching a -5 requires 5 tails. The chances of all heads are 1 in 32, as they are for all tails. So if you allow just 5 tosses, the chances are 1 in 16 that a student will reach -5 or 5. In an average-size class, then, at least one student should be expected to win in just 5 tosses.

In 5 tosses, $P(5) = \frac{1}{32}$, $P(-5) = \frac{1}{32}$, and $P(5 \text{ or } -5) = \frac{1}{16}$.

An interesting follow-up is to find how many in class landed at each number after 5 tosses and compare these results with those from a list of all 32 ways in which the 5 tosses could fall.

PROBABILITIES

1 way to stop at -5
TTTTT

$\frac{1}{32} = .03125$

5 ways to stop at -3
TTTTH TTTHT TTHTT   THTTT HTTTT

$\frac{5}{32} = .15625$

10 ways to stop at -1
TTTHH TTHTH THTTH HTTTH TTHHT
THTHT HTTHT THHTT HTHTT HHTTT

$\frac{10}{32} = .31250$

10 ways to stop at 1
HHHTT HHTHT HTHHT THHHT HHTTH
HTHTH THHTH HTTHH THTHH TTHHH

$\frac{10}{32} = .31250$

5 ways to stop at 3
HHHHT HHHTH HHTHH HTHHH THHHH

$\frac{5}{32} = .15625$

1 way to stop at 5
HHHHH

$\frac{1}{32} = .03125$

1.00000

Note how the numerators for these probabilities connect to row 5 of Pascal's triangle

$$
\begin{array}{ccccc}
& & 1 & 1 & \\
& 1 & 2 & 1 & \\
1 & 3 & & 3 & 1 \\
1 & 4 & 6 & 4 & 1 \\
1 & 5 & 10 & 10 & 5 & 1
\end{array}
$$

EXPERIMENT 2   Paths on a Square Grid

Material
Acetate copy of a large 4 × 4 square grid and a coin

Directions
Project the 4 × 4 square grid on the chalkboard and let it represent a 16-block area bounded by streets. Start at point *P* and take a random walk of 4 blocks. Determine your path by tossing a coin 4 times.

If the coin falls heads (H), walk one block to the right.
If the coin falls tails (T), walk one block up.

As a coin is repeatedly tossed, trace the path on the projected grid for the class. What is the probability that a four-block random walk takes you to the center point *C*?

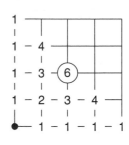

THTT

The path shown comes from the four tosses THTT. Experiment a few times, tracing out on the projected grid the four-block walks that result. Then analyze the problem mathematically.

Analysis
There are $2^4 = 16$ ways the coins can fall but only

$$\binom{4}{2} = 6$$

of them will take you to point *C*. Hence the required probability is $\frac{6}{16}$ or $\frac{3}{8}$. Note the connection between this problem and the five numbers in row 4 of Pascal's triangle.

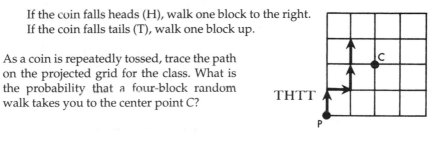

Some probability questions require predictions based solely on experimental data and the analysis of the results. These yield empirical rather than theoretical probabilities.

• What is the probability that a tack lands point up when dropped?

In this experiment the probabilities of various tacks falling point up are found by experimentation.

EXPERIMENT 3   Tossing Thumbtacks

Material
Thumbtacks of 3 different kinds

Directions
Three different types of thumbtacks are selected. Students first study their construction and try to guess which is most likely to fall point up and which least likely.

Ten tacks of one type are dropped on a flat surface 10 different times. Then the probability that a single tack would land point up is estimated using this ratio:

$$P(\text{up}) = \frac{\text{number falling point up}}{100}$$

The experiment is repeated with each of the other two tacks and then final results are compared with the original guesses.

Analysis
Experimentation is the best way to estimate probabilities here since no equivalent simple mathematical model can be designed. Some of the characteristics that increase the probability of landing point up are larger heads, flatter heads, heavier heads, and shorter points.

Many probability problems require much more than just counting and experimenting. Problem-solving skills come into play along with other aspects of the mathematics curriculum. This next experiment ties visualization and geometry to probability.

EXPERIMENT 4   Tossing Pennies on Squares

Material
Pennies and a large sheet of paper ruled in a $1\frac{1}{2}$-inch grid

Directions
Students first guess at what the probability will be that a penny, randomly tossed on the grid, will not fall on a line. Next, 10 pennies are tossed on the grid 10 separate times. The number n of pennies that do not fall on a line is counted and compared with the total number of tosses.

$$P = \frac{n}{100}$$

Answers are then compared with original guesses.

Analysis

A theoretical probability can be determined by comparing areas. Assume that the center of the penny lands anywhere within a given square. The radius of a penny is $\frac{3}{8}$ inch, so if its center lies more than $\frac{3}{8}$ inch from all sides of the square, the penny will not be on a line. Hence the only possible location for the center of the penny such that the penny itself is not on a line would be within a small $\frac{3}{4}$-inch square in the center. Compare this area to the total area of the original square for the correct theoretical probability.

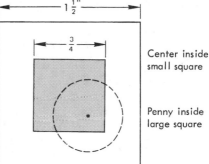

$$P(\text{not on line}) = \frac{\frac{3}{4} \times \frac{3}{4}}{1\frac{1}{2} \times 1\frac{1}{2}} = \frac{1}{4}$$

Center inside small square

Penny inside large square

- How big should the squares in the ruled grid be for there to be an equal probability of falling on or off the lines?

Here is a famous problem which was first presented by Count Buffon in the 1700s. Needles are dropped in a special way on a ruled surface such that the computed probability that one falls on a line gives an estimate involving π.

EXPERIMENT 5   Buffon's Needle Problem

Material
Toothpicks cut to a 1-inch length
A surface ruled with lines 2 inches apart

Directions
The toothpicks are randomly and repeatedly dropped from a reasonable height onto the ruled surface. The number falling on a line are counted along with the total number dropped. Their ratio should approximate $\frac{1}{\pi}$.

$$\text{To 10 places} \quad \pi = 3.1415926535\ldots$$

$$\frac{1}{\pi} = 0.3183098861\ldots$$

The latter value is always approximated as long as the distance between the lines is twice that of the length of the toothpicks dropped. Increasing the number of trials tends to improve the approximation.

Analysis
A detailed analysis of this problem requires calculus but yields the *exact* result, $\frac{1}{\pi}$.

Surveys often give data for initial experimental estimates of probabilities to problems that also have exact mathematical analysis.

- What are the chances that at least two people in a crowd have the same birthday?

EXPERIMENT 6   The Birthday Problem

Material
People to poll for birth dates and relevant reference sources

Directions
The problem is first carefully discussed. Students should guess what they think are the chances of a duplication with groups of say 15, 25, and 60. Next various groups are surveyed and records kept of the number of duplicate birthdays found in each group. The class itself should be surveyed first. Then fellow students, teachers in the school, parents, or families in the neighborhood can be surveyed along with other recorded data such as the birthdays of all the presidents of the United States. Finally, empirical probabilities can be computed based on the collected data.

Analysis
Omitting leap year's February 29, there are 365 possible birth dates. With just two people, the chances are 1 in 365 that they have the same birthday. However, with 3 people, the chances are greater since *any* two could have the same date. The greater the crowd, the greater the chance of a duplication of birth dates. For 366 or more people, a duplication is certain.

Here are the surprising results for various group sizes.

Size of Group	15	18	23	40	60
Chances of a duplication	better than 1 in 4	better than 1 in 3	better than 1 in 2	better than 9 in 10	almost certain
Approximate probability	$\dfrac{1}{4}$	$\dfrac{1}{3}$	$\dfrac{1}{2}$	$\dfrac{9}{10}$	near 1

For n people, the exact theoretical probability of at least one duplication can be found using the formula

$$1 - \frac{365}{365} \cdot \frac{364}{365} \cdot \frac{363}{365} \cdot \ldots \cdot \frac{365 - n + 1}{365}$$

Computing these probabilities can be an interesting exercise in and of itself.

7.4 STATISTICAL ACTIVITIES

Statistical activities in the classroom involve collecting, organizing, presenting, and interpreting data. They also involve drawing inferences from the data collected. Thus the important skills of listing, summarizing, graphing, and predicting are exercised and enhanced along with computational skills.

Estimating Length

Cut off a piece of string, hold it up for only a few seconds for the class to see, and then have the students write down their estimates of its length to the nearest inch. The activity calls for rough, quick estimates, so show the string for only a very short time before putting it away.

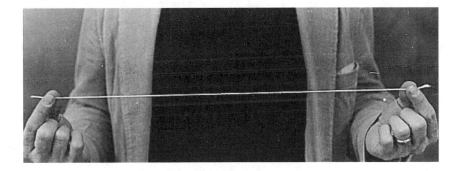

Have the class collect and tabulate the data in a frequency distribution. Have students draw a histogram of the results and comment on its shape. Let them compute the mean, median, and mode and discuss their merits as a typical estimate. Using these collected results, have the class make a final prediction of the actual length of the string. Encourage discussion by asking how confident they are in the prediction. Finally, produce the string and let the class measure it and interpret the comparison or contrast between their individual estimates, the class prediction, and the actual length.

The combined results of several actual class experiments with the piece of string shown in the photo above are given in the frequency distribution below. Estimates are to the nearest inch. The graphing calculator displays give the computed mean and standard deviation and the corresponding histogram using intervals of 1.5 inches.

Length x	Frequency f
12	1
13	0
14	11
15	15
16	18
17	7
18	23
19	6
20	10
21	3
22	3
	97

```
x̄=17.06185567
Σx=1655
Σx²=28699
Sx=2.192859781
σx=2.181527097
n=97
```

Here is a calculator generated display of a box plot along with the five values needed in drawing the plot. What would you guess was the actual length of the string based on these data and displays?

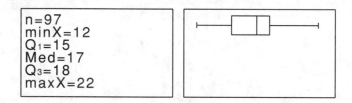

```
n=97
minX=12
Q₁=15
Med=17
Q₃=18
maxX=22
```

To add an element of suspense to this activity, put the string in an envelope after its first showing, seal the envelope, and give it to a student for safekeeping. Don't open it up to measure the string for several days. Have the students discuss and analyze the data and predict the actual length based on the collected estimates. Then, when the envelope is opened, make a big fuss about the process. The extra fanfare will be well worth it. Not only will it provoke attention and excitement, but it will help to build up to the surprise you can almost certainly expect. Most students, including those sampled above, tend to significantly underestimate such a length in this type of experiment. Despite the results shown for the estimates, the actual string length was 22 inches!

Comparing Heights and Arm Spans

Have students in pairs measure to the nearest inch their heights and their arm spans, fingertip to fingertip with arms outstretched. Let them collect the data and tabulate each set in a frequency distribution before computing the two means. Then compare the means and see what inferences they can draw in support of this hypothesis:

The average height is essentially the same as the average arm span.

Here is a set of actual data from an eighth-grade class. Note how closely the data supports the hypothesis.

Heights and Arm Spans in Inches

Height	f	Arm Span	f
56	3	56	4
58	6	58	6
60	7	60	7
62	4	62	2
64	1	64	2
66	5	66	2
68	3	68	4
70	0	70	2
	29		29

	Mean	St. Dev.
Heights	61.45	3.85
Arm Spans	61.66	4.54

Predicting Letter Frequencies

What letters are most frequently used in written material? Ask this question of your class and see how students suggest finding the answer. Some will suggest searching through references on the topic while others will suggest sampling written material. An ongoing study of this question can lead to some very interesting statistical experiences.

Begin by having each student guess the three letters used most often. Tabulate the results for the class in a frequency distribution. Discuss the degree of consistency that appears, finding the percent for the top five letters.

Next, have each student sample 500 successive letters from some randomly chosen portion of written material, recording the frequency and percent for each letter.

Here are the number of E's found in 20 samples of 500 letters each taken from sports pages of a newspaper.

```
2 | 8
3 | 3 8 9
4 | 2 5 6 7 7
5 | 0 0 2 2 3 5 6 7 7 9
6 | 1
```

They are displayed in a *stem-and-leaf* plot with the tens digits on the left as stems and the ones digits on the right as leaves. In these data, there were five samples in the forties:

$$42 \quad 45 \quad 46 \quad 47 \quad 47$$

Finally, see how the results compare, first with the student's initial guesses, second with the pooled results of the class, and third with the following percents for ordinary text material based on a very large sample.

A	B	C	D	E	F	G	H	I	J
8.2	1.4	2.8	3.8	13.0	3.0	2.0	5.3	6.5	0.1

K	L	M	N	O	P	Q	R	S	T
0.4	3.4	2.5	7.0	8.0	2.0	0.1	6.8	6.0	10.5

U	V	W	X	Y	Z
2.5	0.9	1.3	0.2	2.0	0.07

Similar activities can be constructed for typical word and sentence length. Valuable experience and insight can be gained by applying these results to new settings.

A computer printer prints out 80 characters to the line and 55 lines to the page. How many E's would you expect in 6 full pages, ignoring spaces and punctuation?

$$(6 \times 80 \times 55 \times .13 = 3432)$$

A long sentence contains 26 E's. Estimate the number of letters in the sentence.

$$\left(\frac{26}{.13} = 200\right)$$

A short essay contains 1329 words. How many E's would you expect?

(insufficient information)

Have students sample some material for an average word length and let them apply it to answer the last question above.

Surveying Preferences

Many interesting statistical activities revolve around collecting data on personal preferences.

- How many people in a randomly chosen group of 72 would you expect to prefer the color red?

Let each student ask 10 different people for their color preference from a selected list, record the results, and display the data in a circle graph using percents. Then have the students pool the results for the entire class and have each draw another circle graph for the total of all those sampled.

7.5 GAMES OF CHANCE

It was the study of games of chance that first led Pascal and Fermat to the invention of probability in the mid-1600s. So it is not surprising that probability plays a role in familiar card and dice games as well as other games of chance.

Poker

Interesting classroom discussion can come from counting the different possible poker hands and computing various related probabilities, such as the following.

- How many different 5-card poker hands can be dealt from a deck of 52 cards?

The answer is the combination of 52 things taken 5 at a time:

$$_{52}C_5 = \binom{52}{5} = \frac{52!}{5!\,47!} = 2,598,960$$

This may not seem like very many. However, if you were able to deal out a different 5-card poker hand every second, working day and night, it would take about one month to deal them all.

- Why is a flush better than a straight and a straight better than three of a kind in poker?

The ranking of the poker hands is based on the probabilities of their occurring—the better the hand, the lower the probability of its being dealt. These are the probabilities of the various hands:

straight flush	0.0000154	(1 in 64,974 hands)
four of a kind	0.0002401	(1 in 4,165 hands)
full house	0.0014406	(1 in 694 hands)
flush	0.0019654	(1 in 509 hands)
straight	0.0039246	(1 in 256 hands)
three of a kind	0.0211285	(1 in 48 hands)
two pair	0.0475390	(1 in 21 hands)
one pair	0.4225690	(1 in $2\frac{1}{2}$ hands)
no pair	0.5011774	(1 in 2 hands)

Here is a detailed solution for the probability of a fairly common poker hand, one pair (the probabilities of the other hands can be found in much the same way):

$$\text{Probability of one pair} = \frac{\binom{13}{1}\binom{4}{2}\binom{12}{3}4^3}{\binom{52}{5}} = \frac{13 \cdot 6 \cdot 220 \cdot 64}{2,598,960} = 0.4225690$$

Lotteries

A discussion of lotteries can be used to incorporate the concept of mathematical expectation. In games of chance, mathematical expectation can be thought of as the weighted mean of possible winnings, each weighted by its probability.

- Exactly 5000 tickets are sold in a fund-raising lottery at $5.00 each. The winning ticket holder wins a car valued at $15,000. What is the mathematical expectation of winning the car?

The probability that a single ticket is the winning ticket is 1 out of 5000. For this, you win $15,000 at a cost of $5.00. It follows that the probability that a single ticket is a losing ticket is 4999 out of 5000, and in this case you lose $5.00.

$$E[X] = \frac{1}{5000} \times (14{,}995) + \frac{4999}{5000} \times (\text{-}5) = 2.999 - 4.999 = \text{-}2.000$$

Your expectations for winning per ticket is a $2.00 loss. Since the lottery is a fund raiser, one should expect a modest loss on each $5.00 ticket purchased.

In a perfectly fair game, the mathematical expectation is 0. That is to say, the expectation of winning is exactly the same as the expectation of losing.

$$E(\text{winning}) + E(\text{losing}) = 0$$

With their increasing popularity, state lotteries offer the basis for some interesting counting and probability problems. In a PICK 6 lottery, 6 numbers from 1 through 46 are chosen at random. The probabilities of guessing 6, 5, or 4 correct are given here. Note how combinations are applied in each case.

$$P(6 \text{ correct}) = \frac{\binom{6}{6}\binom{40}{0}}{\binom{46}{6}} = \frac{1}{9366819} = 0.0000001$$

$$P(5 \text{ correct}) = \frac{\binom{6}{5}\binom{40}{1}}{\binom{46}{6}} = \frac{240}{9366819} = 0.0000256$$

$$P(4 \text{ correct}) = \frac{\binom{6}{4}\binom{40}{2}}{\binom{46}{6}} = \frac{11700}{9366819} = 0.0012491$$

Dice Games

A detailed discussion of the mathematics behind the dice game called craps can shed substantial light on the nature of conditional probability. The game is played with a pair of dice under the following rules.

If a 7 or 11 is rolled, you win.
If a 2, 3, or 12 is rolled, you lose.
If a 4, 5, 6, 8, 9, or 10 is rolled, you roll the dice again until a 7 occurs and you lose, or until the initial score occurs again and you win.

It is this third case that creates the conditional probability situation. Suppose the first roll is a 4, which has 3 chances out of 36 of occurring. Then the only subsequent roll that will end the game is a 4 or a 7. Of the 9 ways to roll either a 4 or a 7, only 3 are 4's. So having shown a 4 on the first roll, the chances of winning the game with another 4 are 3 out of 9. All other scores that may occur at this point are simply ignored.

Win on a 7 or 11	$P(7 \text{ or } 11) = \dfrac{6}{36} + \dfrac{2}{36} = \dfrac{8}{36}$
Win on a 4	$P(4) \times P(4 \text{ given } 4 \text{ or } 7) = \dfrac{3}{36} \times \dfrac{3}{9} = \dfrac{9}{324}$
Win on a 5	$P(5) \times P(5 \text{ given } 5 \text{ or } 7) = \dfrac{4}{36} \times \dfrac{4}{10} = \dfrac{16}{360}$
Win on a 6	$P(6) \times P(6 \text{ given } 6 \text{ or } 7) = \dfrac{5}{36} \times \dfrac{5}{11} = \dfrac{25}{396}$
Win on an 8	$P(8) \times P(8 \text{ given } 8 \text{ or } 7) = \dfrac{5}{36} \times \dfrac{5}{11} = \dfrac{25}{396}$
Win on a 9	$P(9) \times P(9 \text{ given } 9 \text{ or } 7) = \dfrac{4}{36} \times \dfrac{4}{10} = \dfrac{16}{360}$
Win on a 10	$P(10) \times P(10 \text{ given } 10 \text{ or } 7) = \dfrac{3}{36} \times \dfrac{3}{9} = \dfrac{9}{324}$

Add these separate probabilities to find the probability of winning on the first or any subsequent roll. The chances are just under $\frac{1}{2}$.

$$P(\text{win}) = \frac{8}{36} + \frac{9}{324} + \frac{16}{360} + \frac{25}{396} + \frac{25}{396} + \frac{16}{360} + \frac{9}{324}$$

$$= \frac{244}{495}$$

$$= 0.4929$$

7.6 MAKING CONNECTIONS TO OTHER TOPICS

Most topics in mathematics can be enhanced and enriched with probability applications. Some examples are given in this section. Notice how they require insight into and understanding of both the subject at hand and probability. Many also require good problem-solving analysis.

Factors and Primes

1. A factor of 60 is chosen at random. What is the probability that it is 20? that it has factors of both 2 and 5?
2. A counting number from 1 through N is chosen at random. What is the probability that it is prime, if $N = 10$? if $N = 50$?

Fractions and Decimals

The numbers 3, 4, and 5 are placed on three cards, and then two cards are chosen at random.

3. The two cards are placed side-by-side with a decimal point in front. What is the probability that the decimal is more than $\frac{3}{8}$?
4. One card is placed over the other to form a fraction. What is the probability that the fraction is less than 1.5?
5. Repeat the same two questions but starting with four cards numbered 3, 4, 5, and 6.

Polygons

6. A vertex of a paper isosceles triangle is chosen at random and folded to the midpoint of the opposite side. What is the probability that a trapezoid is formed?
7. A vertex of a paper square is folded onto another vertex chosen at random. What is the probability that a triangle is formed?
8. Three randomly chosen vertices of a regular hexagon cut from paper are folded to the center of the hexagon. What is the probability that an equilateral triangle is formed?

Measurement

9. A piece of string is cut at random into two pieces. What is the probability that the shorter piece is less than half the length of the longer piece?
10. A paper square is cut at random into two rectangles. What is the probability that the larger perimeter is more than $1\frac{1}{2}$ times the smaller?

Equations

The numbers 2, 3, and 4 are substituted at random for a, b, and c in the equation $ax + b = c$.

11. What is the probability that the solution is negative?
12. If c is not 4, what is the probability that the solution is negative?

Algebra

The numbers 1, 2, and 3 are substituted at random for a, b, and c in the quadratic equation $ax^2 + bx + c = 0$.

13. What is the probability that $ax^2 + bx + c$ can be factored?
14. What is the probability that $ax^2 + bx + c = 0$ has real roots?

Geometry

15. Two faces of a cube are chosen at random. What is the probability that they are in parallel planes?
16. Three edges of a cube are chosen at random. What is the probability that each edge is perpendicular to the other two?
17. A point P is chosen at random in the interior of square $ABCD$. What is the probability that triangle ABP is acute?

Trigonometry

Find the probability for each of these results:

18. The sine of a randomly chosen acute angle is greater than 0.5.
19. The cosine of a randomly chosen obtuse angle is greater than -0.5.
20. The tangent of a randomly chosen acute angle is greater than 1.

7.7 CALCULATOR SIMULATIONS

The calculator allows for the handling of real data from published reference sources and from classroom experimentation without the related tedious aspects of hand computation. Hence, the focus of such work can more easily be problem-solving oriented.

Technology also allows for convenient and interesting simulations that are both fast and accurate. They can make an excellent classroom follow-up to the hands-on aspects of statistical experimentation. Key to these activities is the random number generator conveniently available on both calculators and computers. Consider first the simple simulation of repeated rolls of a pair of dice.

Dice Rolling Simulation

Here are the sums from 72 simulated random tosses of a pair of dice.

2	9	10	9	6	11	10	5	9	3	7	9
9	2	7	11	11	7	6	11	3	11	7	7
3	5	9	5	3	7	8	8	7	6	5	5
9	8	7	7	7	6	9	9	11	10	6	8
7	5	9	7	8	7	9	7	8	8	7	8
7	7	6	12	8	9	6	7	8	2	8	9

A quick scan of the data may not spot anything unusual. However, a closer observation notes that there are no 4's. This is very unexpected for a sample this large, but that is the nature of randomness. These histogram displays from a graphing calculator contrast the data given above with that theoretically expected for the same number of tosses.

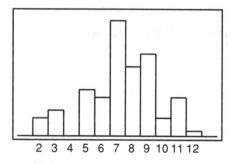

Distributions of sums from 72 simulated tosses of a pair of dice.

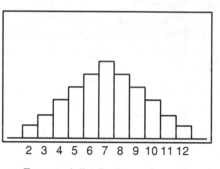

Expected distributions of sums from 72 tosses of a pair of dice.

Of course, in the long run the simulated results settle in on the expected values. Note how they compare with 3600 simulated tosses.

Sum	2	3	4	5	6	7	8	9	10	11	12
Simulated	107	227	279	382	489	562	488	412	315	243	105
Expected	100	200	300	400	500	600	500	400	300	200	100

Simulating Batting in Baseball

Batting averages of baseball players are readily available statistics and can serve as the basis for an interesting simulation activity. Select a player from one of your classes' favorite teams and simulate what his performance might be for the next few times at-bat.

Here is an example where the simulation is done two different ways on Babe Ruth's record for 2503 games over 22 years.

Compute the probabilities from the batting record.

	AB	H	2B	3B	HR
Record	8399	2873	506	136	714
Probabilities		.342	.060	.016	.085

Using Dice

Find the closest fractional approximation in terms of 36ths and assign dice outcomes that match these values. One such assignment is shown here but others are possible. Repeated rolls of the dice simulate successive times at-bat.

Batting Simulation	Dice Outcomes	Probability
single	9 or 10	$P(9 \text{ or } 10) = \dfrac{7}{36}$
double	11	$P(11) = \dfrac{2}{36}$
triple	12	$P(12) = \dfrac{1}{36}$
home run	4	$P(4) = \dfrac{3}{36}$
out	all other results	$\dfrac{23}{36}$

Using this method, probabilities cannot be matched exactly nor can outcomes always be conveniently assigned. But it is an easy way to simulate some additional at-bats based upon the records supplied.

Using Random Numbers

Assign decimals between 0 and 1 to match the probabilities of the various outcomes. Then repeatedly loop through the program that selects random numbers between 0 and 1 to simulate the successive at-bats.

Batting Simulation	Random Number Outcome	Probability
single	.000–.180	.181
double	.181–.240	.060
triple	.241–.256	.016
home run	.257–.341	.085
out	.342–.999	.658

In the calculator program, let N be a random number between 0 and 1. Then use these successive sorting statements to select a single, double, triple, and home run.

$$
\begin{array}{ll}
N < .181 & \text{Single} \\
N < .241 & \text{Double} \\
N < .257 & \text{Triple} \\
N < .342 & \text{Home run}
\end{array}
$$

In these simulations, the probabilities remain fixed. This is not unreasonable since a great many at-bats occurred and only a few additional ones will be simulated. Of course, the program can be modified so the probabilities change to reflect each successive at-bat.

Estimating the Value of Pi through Simulation

Simulation techniques can be used to find areas under curves. When appled to a unit circle, the simulation can be used to approximate π.

Imagine darts randomly thrown in a unit square in the first quadrant with a vertex at the origin. During the graphing of this simulation, the program counts those darts hitting inside the quarter-circle with radius 1 and center at the origin. The ratio of the number of hits (H) to the total number of tosses (T) multiplied by 4 gives an estimate of the area of the entire unit circle. Since the area of a unit circle is π, the value of $4\left(\frac{H}{T}\right)$ should offer a good approximation to π.

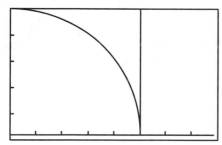

The dart board is a unit square   1000 randomly thrown darts.
with a quarter-circle drawn in it.   790 fell inside the quarter-circle.

Each run of the program produces a unique set of results and hence its own estimate of π. These are the results for the images shown above.

$$
\begin{aligned}
H &= 790 \\
T &= 1000
\end{aligned}
$$

Approximation to π: $4\left(\frac{H}{T}\right) = 3.16$

- Explain why the ratio of hits to tosses is multiplied by 4 to get the estimate for π.

EXERCISES

1. Suppose a person is chosen at random from the entire population of the world. What is a reasonable estimate of the probability that the person would come from the United States?

2. A person is chosen at random from the United States population. What is the probability that the person comes from your home state?

3. A factor of 72 is chosen at random. What is the probability that it does not have a factor of 3?

4. A special set of dominoes has faces that are numbered from 0 through 9. How many dominoes are in the complete set?

5. Three cards are numbered 4, 5, and 6 respectively. If they are randomly arranged to form a 3-digit number, what is the probability that the number will be divisible by 4? by 3?

6. Four cards are marked with the digits 5, 6, 7, and 8. They are arranged at random to form two different numbers. What is the probability that their sum is the greatest possible sum for two numbers formed from these four digits?

7. Two six-sided dice are numbered 1, 1, 3, 3, 5, 5, and 2, 2, 4, 4, 6, 6 respectively. What is the probability that, when randomly rolled, they will show a sum of 7?

8. What is the probability of rolling a sum of 7 using three regular dice?

9. Two coins are tossed at random. You win $10.00 if both coins show heads. What is a fair price for playing this game?

10. There are three cards in a stack. One is red on both sides and another is black on both sides. The third card is red on one side and black on the other. The cards are randomly shuffled and restocked. If the top of the top card is red, what is the probability that the other side is also red?

11. In how many different ways can the nine letters in the word "seventeen" be arranged?

12. The eight letters in the word "nineteen" are arranged at random. What is the probability that the E's are all together and the N's are all separated?

13. The numbers 2, 3, and 5 are substituted at random for a, b, and c in the quadratic expression $ax^2 + bx + c$. What is the probability that the resulting expression can be factored?

14. The numbers 3, 4, and 7 are substituted at random for a, b, and c in the quadratic equation $ax^2 + bx + c = 0$. What is the probability that the two roots are real numbers?

15. Find the probability that a randomly chosen acute angle has a tangent less than 1.

16. Two edges of a cube are chosen at random. What is the probability that they lie in two lines that are skew lines?

17. Two randomly chosen vertices of a paper square are folded to the center of the square. What is the probability that a hexagon is formed?

18. Two regular dice, one red and the other green, are rolled and the numbers of their faces multiplied. Draw a stem-and-leaf plot that shows a product for each possible roll of the dice.

19. If the letters in a newspaper article contain 315 T's, estimate how many letters were used in all.

20. Show how to set up and compute the probability of being dealt a full house—three of one kind and two of another—in a 5-card poker hand dealt from a regular deck of 52 cards.

21. What is the probability that a penny, randomly tossed on a grid ruled in 2-inch squares, will fall on a line?

ACTIVITIES

1. Sample 10 people for their estimates of the diameter of a quarter from these choices in inches.

$$\frac{3}{4} \qquad \frac{13}{16} \qquad \frac{7}{8} \qquad \frac{15}{16} \qquad 1$$

Interpret the results.

2. Create and answer five probability questions that relate to the possible arrangements of the eight digits in serial numbers on dollar bills.

3. A photograph is cut into four strips of equal size. The pieces are then reordered at random and the photograph is rebuilt in its original size. Describe how this activity could be used in a classroom to motivate a discussion on probability.

4. Repeat the coin-tossing activity described on page 214. Include in the table the cumulative percents and draw a line graph of the results.

5. Ask 23 people selected at random to give you their birth dates. See if you find at least one duplication.

6. Draw a 35° angle on a piece of paper and ask 15 people to estimate its measure in degrees. Compute the mean for the results. Do your sample results imply that people tend to overestimate, underestimate, or accurately estimate its size?

7. Sample 500 words from some ordinary newspaper text material. Find the mean and the standard deviation for the word length used.

8. A student showed this work in computing the probability of a two pair in a poker hand. Describe how you would use a deck of cards to identify the error for the student and give the correct method for finding the answer.

$$\frac{\binom{13}{1}\binom{4}{2}\binom{12}{1}\binom{4}{2}\binom{44}{1}}{\binom{52}{5}}$$

9. Find a source of numerical data that could be used effectively in the classroom as an example to demonstrate a stem-and-leaf plot. Supply the completed plot.

10. Simulate 36 rolls of a pair of dice by using the random number generator in a calculator. Compare your results with those expected.

11. Set up arbitrary probabilities, and describe how you can use a random number generator to simulate a bowling game to a high-school mathematics class.

12. Select a random sample of 100 words from a newspaper article. Collect data on the word length in the sample. Then use your graphing calculator to compute the mean and standard deviation and to draw a histogram and box-and-whisker plot.

13. Write and run a program on a graphing calculator to estimate the value of π using the method given on page 232.

14. Prepare a detailed description of the features available on a graphing calculator in the area of descriptive statistics. Describe how several might be effectively incorporated into the teaching of such a unit at the secondary level. Do the same for a unit on inferential statistics.

15. Prepare a lesson that could be used in introducing probability to a middle-school class.

16. Prepare a report on the early history of probability.

17. Investigate the use of probability by insurance companies in establishing their mortality tables.

18. *The Quantitative Literacy Series,* prepared jointly through the American Statistical Association and the National Council of Teachers of Mathematics, contains four books: *Exploring Data, Exploring Probability, The Art and Techniques of Simulation,* and *Exploring Surveys.* They are currently available through Dale Seymour Publications, Palo Alto, CA. Outline the key components in one of these publications, citing specific examples.

19. Search through a current middle-school textbook and a first-year algebra textbook. Report on the amount and type of statistics they contain.

8

ITERATION ACTIVITIES AND FRACTAL PATTERNS

The dynamics of change through iteration can give added motivation to many of the routine skills of arithmetic, algebra, and geometry. This chapter opens with some examples along this line. But iteration activities also offer new problem-solving arenas and visualization experiences.

Driven by today's technology, iteration has taken on added importance in the applications of mathematics. While the first classical fractals emerged at the beginning of the twentieth century, it was the power of computer graphics through enhanced imaging that really gave birth to the science of fractals. This chapter offers a wide variety of introductory classroom activities on fractals and their many interesting connections to the existing mathematics curriculum.

8.1 ITERATION ACTIVITIES

Mathematics is sometimes defined as the science of patterns. These patterns can appear in many ways, including numerical, algebraic, or geometric forms. They can be simple and obvious as well as complex and obscure. In many cases, they can be recognized, classified, analyzed, and generalized.

Mathematics teachers are encouraged to use patterns with their students as a vehicle both for practicing mechanical skills and for developing and expanding problem-solving skills. Numerous examples have already appeared earlier. We focus here on patterns that come from repeating processes. This is the concept of iteration.

Numerical Iteration

Couched in the right format, classroom activities with patterns can be highly motivating. For example, start by asking what events occurred on these dates in history? Then ask the students to discover the rules repeatedly being applied. Finally, use these rules on the year 1999.

Rule A

1492 → 16 → 7
1776 → 21→ 3
1812 → 12 → 3
1999 → ?

Rule B

1492 → 72 → 14 → 4
1776 → 294 → 72 → 14 → 4
1812 → 16 → 6
1999 → ?

Students who have difficulty counting or spelling may have trouble applying the rule used here on the word *seventeen seventy-six.*

zero → four
seventeen → nine → four
eighty → six → three → five → four

seventeen seventy-six → ?

- What pattern do you see here?

4   6   7   9   10   11   12   14   15   . . .

It is strange that for many, this sequence is baffling, while this next one is comfortably familiar. Encourage students to see beyond the obvious. Every student sooner or later is asked for the Fibonacci sequence. How many are ever asked for the counting numbers that are not part of that sequence?

1   1   2   3   5   8   13   21   33   . . .

Use an iteration diagram such as the one shown below to help students see the underlying iteration process used in generating successive numbers in the Fibonacci sequence. Arrows show the loop that repeatedly cycles the same process over and over.

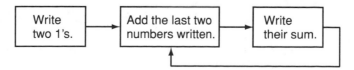

Arithmetic and geometric sequences can be expressed the same way. Successive values are plotted on a number line to show the dynamics of the processes.

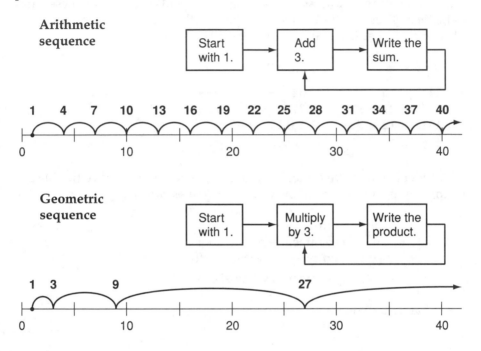

Arithmetic sequence

Geometric sequence

Algebraic Iteration

This iteration diagram generates the general infinite geometric sequence.

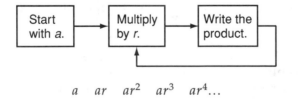

$$a \quad ar \quad ar^2 \quad ar^3 \quad ar^4 \ldots$$

Add successive terms for the corresponding geometric series.

$$a + ar + ar^2 + ar^3 + ar^4 + \ldots$$

For students first exploring converging, infinite geometric series, the calculator can be a convenient tool for discovery. Sums of successive terms can be easily computed on a scientific calculator, but they are shown here as tables on a graphing calculator. The fourth through tenth entries are displayed in each case.

Y_1 lists successive powers.

Y_2 lists sums of successive powers.

X	Y_1	Y_2
4	.00391	.32813
5	9.8E −4	.33203
6	2.4E −4	.33301
7	6.1E −5	.33325
8	1.5E −5	.33331
9	3.8E −6	.33333
10	9.5E −7	.33300

Y_2=.333332061768

$$a = \frac{1}{4} \quad r = \frac{1}{4}$$

X	Y_1	Y_2
4	.01235	.48148
5	.00412	.49383
6	.00137	.49794
7	4.6E −4	.49931
8	1.5E −4	.49977
9	5.1E −5	.40002
10	1.7E −5	.49997

Y_2=.499974597368

$$a = \frac{1}{3} \quad r = \frac{1}{3}$$

- What simple unit fraction do the decimals for the sums of successive powers of $\frac{1}{4}$ appear to be approaching? What about the successive powers of $\frac{1}{3}$?
- The answers should lead you to an interesting generalization. Can you discover it? Can you apply it to the sums of successive powers of $\frac{1}{2}$ and $\frac{1}{5}$? What about successive powers of $\frac{1}{n}$?

Later on, this magic of inductive discovery is replaced by deductive proof and the familiar formula for the sum of a converging, infinite geometric series.

$$S = \frac{a}{1 - r} \quad \text{for } |r| < 1$$

Repeating decimals also can be viewed through the eyes of algebraic iteration. Start by showing this iteration diagram to your students.

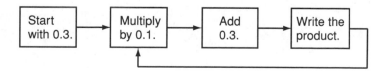

Have them generate the first few successive outputs. See if they notice where this sequence is going.

0.3   0.33   0.333   0.3333   0.33333   0.333333 ...

The limiting value in this sequence is, of course, $\frac{1}{3}$, which can be written as $0.\overline{3}$. The same process can be expressed algebraically using this equation.

$$f(x) = 0.1x + 0.3$$ Start with $x_0 = 0.3$.

Start the repeating process through the function with an initial input x_0. Take each output as the next new input. Successive values increase toward $\frac{1}{3}$.

$x_1 = 0.1(0.3) + 0.3 = 0.33$

$x_2 = 0.1(0.33) + 0.3 = 0.333$

$x_3 = 0.1(0.333) + 0.3 = 0.3333$

$x_4 = 0.1(0.3333) + 0.3 = 0.33333$

Clearly, iteration should be discussed when studying the composition of functions. Likewise, review the composition of functions when illustrating algebraic iteration.

$x_1 = f(x_0)$

$x_2 = f(x_1) = f(f(x_0))$

$x_3 = f(x_2) = f(f(f(x_0)))$

$x_4 = f(x_3) = f(f(f(f(x_0))))$

There is no magic here, only mathematics. However, be sure students understand the message. Repeating decimals can be generated through iteration by creating and using the appropriate functions. Have them try to do the same for the repeating decimals for $\frac{1}{11}$ and $\frac{1}{7}$.

Geometric Iteration

Students need to see iteration in many forms. Geometric iteration is important for a thorough understanding of fractals, discussed later in this chapter.

Example 1. Start with a 4" square piece of paper.
Repeatedly fold the four corners to the center.
How do the area and perimeter change from one stage to the next?

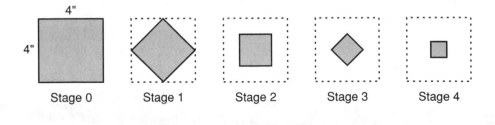

Stage 0   Stage 1   Stage 2   Stage 3   Stage 4

Stage	0	1	2	3	4	5	n
Area	16	8	4	2	1	$\frac{1}{2}$	2^{4-n}
Perimeter	16	$8\sqrt{2}$	8	$4\sqrt{2}$	4	$2\sqrt{2}$	$(\sqrt{2})^{8-n}$

In going from one stage to the next, multiply the area by $\frac{1}{2}$ and the perimeter by $\frac{\sqrt{2}}{2}$.

Example 2. Start with a strip of paper.
Fold in half, right to left.
Fold in half, left to right.
Fold in half, right to left.

Keep folding the top piece in half, alternating the direction, back and forth.

Watch how the marked edge moves. It starts at 1, moves to 0, back to $\frac{1}{2}$, and then to $\frac{1}{4}$. As the process continues, the marked edge converges on a fixed value between 0 and 1. What is that value?

$$1 \quad 0 \quad \frac{1}{2} \quad \frac{1}{4} \quad \frac{3}{8} \quad \frac{5}{16} \quad \cdots$$

- Show why the limiting value must be $\frac{1}{3}$.

Spirolaterals

Spirolaterals are geometric designs generated from number sequences through iterative procedures. They offer interesting opportunities for problem-solving exploration and discovery as well as valuable experiences in following patterns and rules. Spirolaterals also connect to a wide variety of other topics and have obvious applications when discussing symmetry, transformations, and coordinate geometry.

Start with a sheet of graph paper and a short number sequence.

From a starting point, move the first number of units to the right.
Turn and move the second number of units down.
Turn again and move the third number left.
Turn yet again and move up.
Keep repeating the number sequence when the digits run out.
Keep turning 90° clockwise, right, down, left, up, right, down, left, up.
Watch for something special to occur.

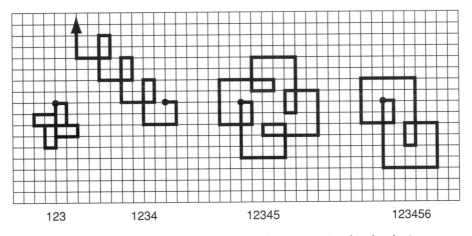

| 123 | 1234 | 12345 | 123456 |

Based on the examples shown, try to guess the properties for the designs generated by these number sequences.

112   1122   11223   112233   1122334   11223344

- Which will repeat after two cycles and which after four?
  Which will never return to the starting point?

Try some other number sequences on your own and study the corresponding spirolaterals. Look for the property of the number sequence that determines the general characteristic of the spirolateral? Make and test your conjectures.
    Spirolaterals can emerge from sequences of letters as well as numbers. Try giving them a special spin by using this conversion code.

A	B	C	D	E	F	G	H	I	J	K	L	M
1	2	3	4	5	6	7	8	9	1	2	3	4

N	O	P	Q	R	S	T	U	V	W	X	Y	Z
5	6	7	8	9	1	2	3	4	5	6	7	8

Let your students draw their own personal spirolaterals based on the number codes for their names. See if students can recognize the names of others in class by studying their corresponding spirolaterals. Here are four examples. Can you trace the repeating number patterns in the figures for these names?

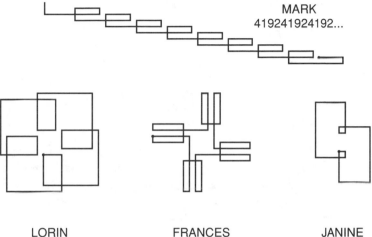

MARK
419241924192...

LORIN
3699536995...

FRANCES
69153516915351...

JANINE
115955115955...

For an extra added twist, bring in a bit of history of mathematics with your spirolaterals. See if your students can identify the three famous mathematicians that have these spirolaterals for their names.

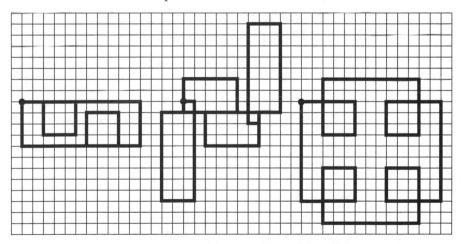

8.2 PATTERNS FROM TRIANGLES

Iteration activities in geometry can be used to connect the concept of structure with that of change. This combination can produce some very dynamic and powerful visual classroom experiences.

Folding a Paper Triangle

Start with an equilateral triangle cut from paper. Mark a vertex and fold it to the midpoint of the opposite side. Then unfold.

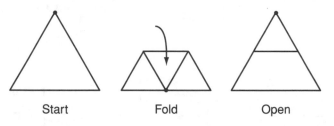

Start   Fold   Open

The crease forms a new, smaller equilateral triangle that contains the same vertex so the process can be repeated on it. Indeed, each time a fold is made a new triangle is created, allowing the iteration process to continue on and on. In a concrete sense, the new triangles quickly become too small to handle. In an abstract sense, the new triangles continue to shrink, converging to the limit figure, a point.

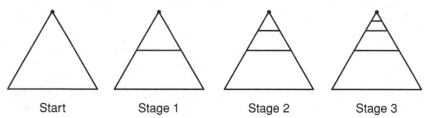

Start   Stage 1   Stage 2   Stage 3

In theory, the figure is forever changing as the iteration continues. Embedded in this changing structure lie many interesting properties worthy of investigation by your students.

- Have students find and count the triangles and trapezoids at different stages.

Stage	0	1	2	3	4	n
Number of triangles	1	2	3	4	5	$n + 1$
Number of trapezoids	0	1	3	6	10	$\dfrac{n(n+1)}{2}$

- Ask first if all the triangles are similar. Then ask the more challenging question about similarity for the trapezoids.
- Use the figure to stimulate your students' imaginations. Visualize the final figure as a ladder, where the folds are the steps. The number of steps

in this imaginary ladder is infinite, with each successive step half as wide as the preceding one. The triangular paper with its folds offers a nice model of a converging, geometric sequence.

$$1 \quad \frac{1}{2} \quad \frac{1}{4} \quad \frac{1}{8} \quad \frac{1}{16} \quad \frac{1}{32} \quad \cdots$$

If you cut at each fold, the same triangles and trapezoids can be formed by combining pieces. Students can do this at their seats or the pieces can be used to produce vivid displays on an overhead projector. For some, the different figures will be easier to see this way.

Subdividing into Triangles

Triangular arrays are useful when studying sums of successive odd counting numbers starting at 1. Build them from triangular pattern blocks where, as more rows are added, the triangular structure grows larger. Or, scale down the pieces so that the overall structure does not change size in going from one array to the next. The number pattern at each stage is easily seen in the structures as you count, row by row, from the top down. The numbers generated from stage to stage form the set of *square numbers*.

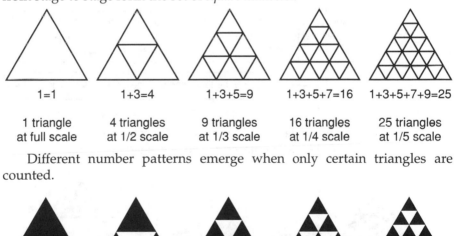

1=1	1+3=4	1+3+5=9	1+3+5+7=16	1+3+5+7+9=25
1 triangle at full scale	4 triangles at 1/2 scale	9 triangles at 1/3 scale	16 triangles at 1/4 scale	25 triangles at 1/5 scale

Different number patterns emerge when only certain triangles are counted.

1=1	1+2=3	1+2+3=6	1+2+3+4=10	1+2+3+4+5=15
1 triangle and 0 holes	3 triangles and 1 hole	6 triangles and 3 holes	10 triangles and 6 holes	15 triangles and 10 holes
1+0=1	3+1=4	6+3=9	10+6=16	15+10=25

This example shows how the *triangular numbers* can also be found in these triangular arrays. It also offers an opportunity for students to explore this underlying relationship between square and triangular numbers.

$$S(n) = T(n) + T(n-1)$$

Every square number is equal to the sum of the corresponding triangular number plus the preceding triangular number.

Many geometric patterns can be generated from triangles by following different iteration algorithms. One especially interesting example follows next.

The Sierpinski Triangle

This flowchart describes an iteration algorithm applied to an initial triangular region. The repeating loop is what generates the successive steps. In theory, the iteration process is endless. Some students will be able to construct the first few figures simply by following the directions.

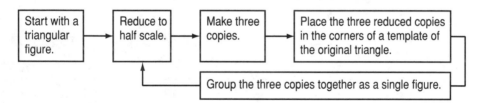

Other students will need to see you demonstrate the first step of the process by moving scaled down pieces on the overhead projector.

| Start with a triangular region. | Make three copies reduced to 50%. | Rebuild the triangular shape |

Still others may find it helpful to build several stages using manipulatives such as triangular pattern blocks.

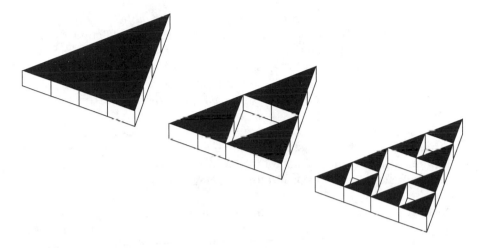

By repeating the process over and over, each time using the output figure as the new input figure, a surprisingly complex structure with powerful aesthetic and mathematical properties begins to emerge. The limit figure for this process is called the *Sierpinski triangle*. It is named after the Polish mathematician, Waclaw Sierpinski, who developed it in the early 1900s.

Many interesting numerical relationship can be explored and generalized by your students using these figures. Some are given in this table.

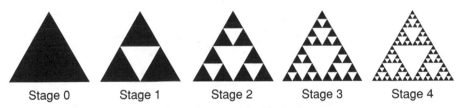

| Stage 0 | Stage 1 | Stage 2 | Stage 3 | Stage 4 |

Stage	0	1	2	3	4	n
Number of shaded triangles	1	3	9	27	81	3^n
Number of holes	0	1	4	13	40	$\dfrac{3^n - 1}{2}$
Area of shaded pieces	1	$\dfrac{3}{4}$	$\dfrac{9}{16}$	$\dfrac{27}{64}$	$\dfrac{81}{256}$	$\left(\dfrac{3}{4}\right)^n$
Perimeter around shaded pieces	1	$\dfrac{3}{2}$	$\dfrac{9}{4}$	$\dfrac{27}{8}$	$\dfrac{81}{16}$	$\left(\dfrac{3}{2}\right)^n$

Today, we know the Sierpinski triangle as a *fractal*, a class of geometric figures first named in the 1970s by the mathematician Benoit Mandelbrot. The primary characteristic of a fractal is *self-similarity*. Self-similarity occurs when a structure has a repeating pattern of smaller and smaller images of the whole embedded in it at different scales. Have your students study successive stages of the Sierpinski triangle until they see this recurring theme:

three reduced copies of stage 0 in stage 1,
three reduced copies of stage 1 in stage 2,
three of stage 2 in stage 3, and three of stage 3 in stage 4.

To form stage 5, reduce the linear dimensions of the stage 4 structure to one-half, make three of these reduced copies, and rebuild them within the same triangular template. Each iteration step is done in exactly the same way. It is the limit figure for this process that is *the* Sierpinski triangle.

Sierpinski triangle

At any finite state, the next stage will always have three times as many triangular pieces, so the figures are always changing. But at the limit state, the embedded, reduced images are *exactly* like the whole! Such an ideal figure is purely an abstraction. The best that can be shown is some finite stage where the triangular pieces are very small but not yet points.

8.3 PATTERNS FROM SQUARES

Squares are rather simple geometric figures. In fact, they are so familiar that it is easy to miss the many opportunities they offer for rich, rewarding classroom experiences involving iteration activities.

Getting Started

Pass out a paper square to each student and give these directions:

> Fold the square in half horizontally and then vertically.
> With the paper still folded, visualize the figure when unfolded.
> Count all the squares and all the rectangles seen in the mental image.
> Unfold the paper square and count again.

Fold in half both ways.   5 squares and 9 rectangles including squares

Searching for Number Patterns

Simple square grids offer interesting structures for investigation of number patterns. Imagine a grid subdivided into successively smaller and smaller squares.

> What can be seen when looking at these square arrays?
> What number patterns can be found?
> What generalizations can be made?

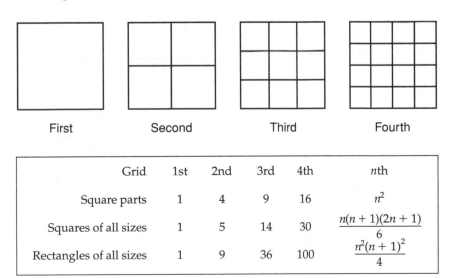

Grid	1st	2nd	3rd	4th	nth
Square parts	1	4	9	16	n^2
Squares of all sizes	1	5	14	30	$\dfrac{n(n+1)(2n+1)}{6}$
Rectangles of all sizes	1	9	36	100	$\dfrac{n^2(n+1)^2}{4}$

Careful counting will give the numbers in the first few steps of the process but may not reveal some of the interesting connections that can be found.

$$1 = 1^2$$
$$5 = 1^2 + 2^2$$
$$14 = 1^2 + 2^2 + 3^2$$
$$30 = 1^2 + 2^2 + 3^2 + 4^2$$

Sums of squares of
successive counting
numbers

$$1 = 1^2$$
$$9 = (1 + 2)^2$$
$$36 = (1 + 2 + 3)^2$$
$$100 = (1 + 2 + 3 + 4)^2$$

Squares of sums of
successive counting
numbers

This sequence of figures poses some interesting geometric questions as well. It is apparent that as more and more equal subdivisions are made, more and more, smaller and smaller squares are formed. But is there an end to the process and is there a limit figure?

The individual square parts continue forever to shrink. That process is endless. But the limit figure occurs when the four vertices of the square converge to a single point. The corresponding limit figure for these finer and finer grids must be a single solid square!

Iterating by Halving

A variation of the same sequence of figures occurs when successive squares are always cut in half in length and width. This is what occurs in the paper-folding activity that began this section. Clearly, different number sequences are generated through this iteration process of repeated halving.

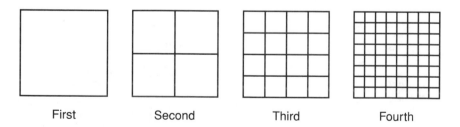

First   Second   Third   Fourth

Call the initial square stage 0 and watch only certain squares through successive stages of halving. Here are two examples.

Example 1.

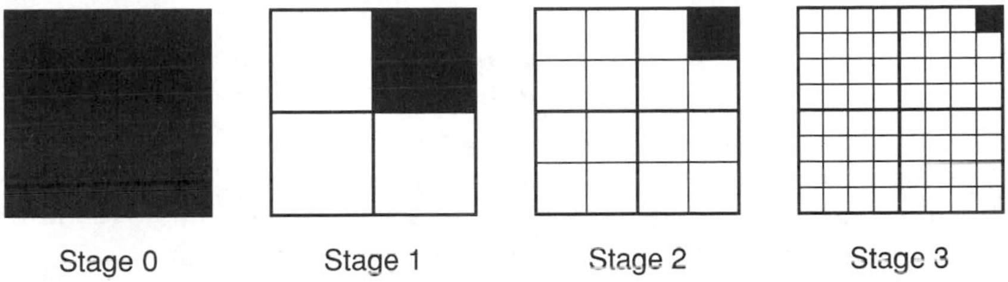

| | Stage 0 | Stage 1 | Stage 2 | Stage 3 |

Stage	0	1	2	3	4	n
Shaded squares	1	1	1	1	1	1
Area of shaded squares	1	$\frac{1}{4}$	$\frac{1}{16}$	$\frac{1}{64}$	$\frac{1}{256}$	$\left(\frac{1}{4}\right)^n$
Perimeter of shaded squares	1	$\frac{1}{2}$	$\frac{1}{4}$	$\frac{1}{8}$	$\frac{1}{16}$	$\left(\frac{1}{2}\right)^n$

Example 2.

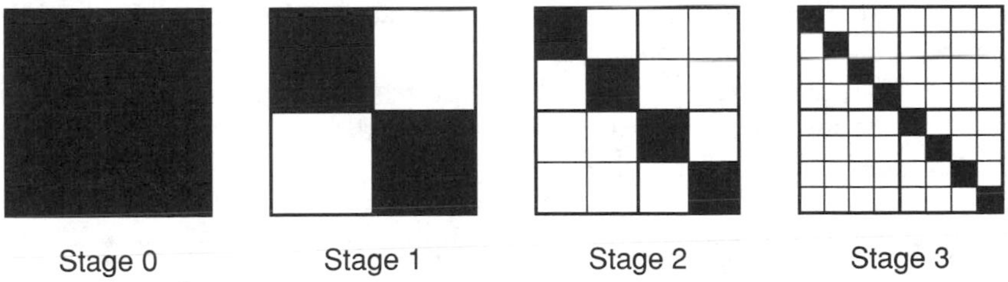

| | Stage 0 | Stage 1 | Stage 2 | Stage 3 |

Stage	0	1	2	3	4	n
Shaded squares	1	2	4	8	16	2^n
Area of shaded squares	1	$\frac{1}{2}$	$\frac{1}{4}$	$\frac{1}{8}$	$\frac{1}{16}$	$\left(\frac{1}{2}\right)^n$
Perimeter of shaded squares	1	1	1	1	1	1

Show your students these figures or have them draw the sequence on graph paper themselves. In either case, let them explore the corresponding number patterns. Then have them write down what they see happening in each case by answering these questions:

- How would you describe the two iteration processes?
  What are the corresponding limit figures?

The limit figures are a point and a diagonal, respectively. There are several different ways the iteration processes can be viewed. To set the stage for what is coming, suggest students view the processes this way:

For Example 1, reduce the linear dimensions of the entire figure to half and place a single reduced copy in the upper right corner of the original square boundary.

For Example 2, reduce the linear dimensions of the entire figure to half and place two reduced copies in the upper left corner and lower right corner of the original square boundary.

Revisiting the Sierpinski Triangle

A big surprise awaits those who try the same process using three reduced copies at each stage. First, have your students predict what the results will be. Then have them draw some successive stages on graph paper. Be sure they see three reduced copies of stage 1 in stage 2 and three reduced copies of stage 2 in stage 3. Something special emerges as this rebuilding with three reduced copies continues. After only a few steps, the complex Sierpinski triangle structure begins to appear!

Stage 0

Stage 1

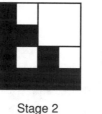
Stage 2

Stage 3

This time, of course, the Sierpinski triangle is in right triangle form. It is also emerging from smaller and smaller squares rather than from triangles as shown earlier. An enlarged copy of the fractal image is shown below. Whether the building blocks are triangles or squares, in the limit, both converge to points, resulting in the same complex fractal structure.

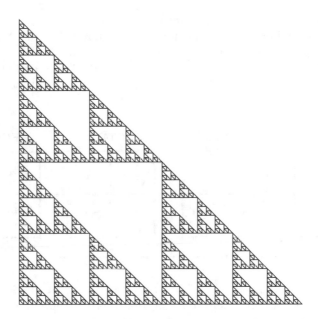

8.4 CONSTRUCTING FRACTAL PATTERNS

We have just seen how a common square can be changed into a complex fractal through a simple iteration process. If geometric transformations of the squares are made at the rebuilding step, a whole collection of fractals can be generated.

Rotations

There are eight symmetries of a square. That is, there are eight different transformations of a square that will bring it back into the original square template. Four are rotations and four are reflections. Start by reviewing the rotations with your students.

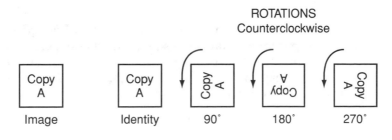

ROTATIONS
Counterclockwise

Image   Identity   90°   180°   270°

Suppose rotations are built into the iteration algorithm for building a fractal, as shown in the diagram below. Notice that two of the three reduced copies are rotated before they are regrouped as the single, square figure needed to begin the next stage. Copy A is rotated 90° and copy C is rotated 270°, both counterclockwise. Copy B remains in the identity position as determined by the initial figure.

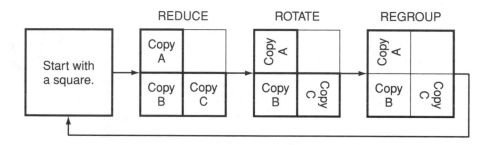

Have your students follow this process in drawing the first several stages on graph paper. Remind them that the rotations are applied to the reduced copies only, but they must be applied at every stage.

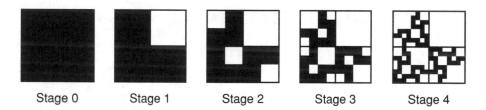

Stage 0   Stage 1   Stage 2   Stage 3   Stage 4

As with the Sierpinski triangle, make sure your students see the recurring theme of self-similarity. Only this time, rotations are involved.

Three reduced copies of stage 0 are in stage 1,
Three reduced copies of stage 1 are in stage 2,
Three of stage 2 are in stage 3, three of stage 3 in stage 4, and so on.

You may choose to supply your students with copies of the grids, each subdivided into the appropriate number of squares for that stage. Experience has shown that drawing the first several stages is often the hardest. This is where the students are learning to apply the process. Encourage students to see the underlying structure as it can help them draw successive stages much faster.

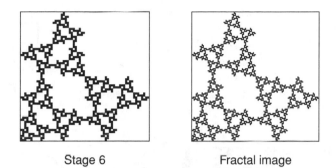

| Stage 6 | Fractal image |

The counterclockwise rotations of 90°, 180°, and 270° plus the identity transformation, or 0° rotation, make four different choices per copy. Any of the four choices can be assigned to each of the three reduced copies used in the grid. This gives 64 different building codes from rotations alone, all producing different fractal structures.

$$4 \times 4 \times 4 = 64$$

A Cooperative Construction

Thus far, the building algorithms given here for generating fractal patterns can be summarized by the three words in this iteration diagram.

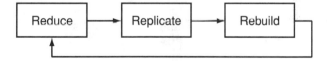

Reduce → Replicate → Rebuild

Specifically, the iteration involves repeatedly reducing to half scale, replicating three copies, and rebuilding in the same 2×2 square template using the appropriate rotations as needed.

A cooperative classroom version of this activity eliminates the reduction step.

1. The class decides on one of the 64 fractal pattern building codes using rotations.
2. Each student cuts out three stage-1 copies and arranges them on a larger stage-2 template using a glue stick.
3. Teams of three arrange and glue their three stage-2 copies on a still larger stage-3 template, following the same building code.
4. Three of these figures are arranged on a stage-4 template, three of those on a stage-5 template, and so on.

Follow the example below using the rotations shown in this building code. Watch how the fractal pattern grows as more and more students get involved in the process. A class of 27 students can build a stage-4 version using their 27 individual stage-1 parts. Larger versions can be constructed from more parts.

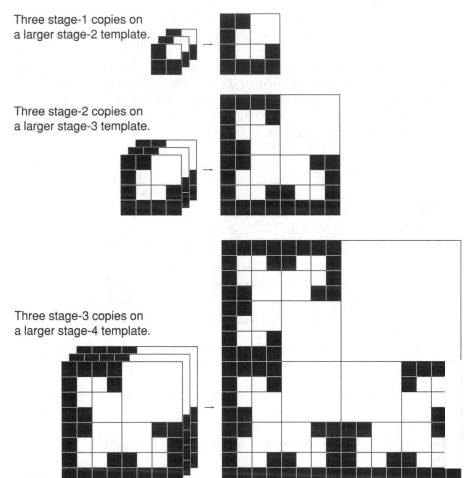

Three stage-1 copies on a larger stage-2 template.

Three stage-2 copies on a larger stage-3 template.

Three stage-3 copies on a larger stage-4 template.

This classroom activity gets everyone involved in the process of creating a single fractal pattern. Individual errors in following the chosen building code will quickly become apparent. Of course, students need to be reminded that reductions have not occurred. Thus, if 27 students have their parts glued into a stage-4 template, that template would be the size of the initial square at stage-0, had repeated halving occurred at each step.

For a more challenging variation, give students small copies of the fractal image itself. This way they must first identify the rotation code used before gluing up successively larger versions of the same fractal pattern.

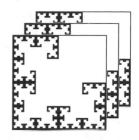

Tessellations from Fractal Patterns

Interesting designs can be formed by using fractal patterns. This example shows how small paper squares with this same fractal image can be arranged as tiles in a tessellation pattern that has quite a different overall appearance.

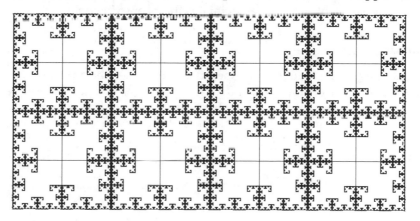

Reflections

Stay with the rotation transformations first. Let students gain sufficient experience building fractals involving rotations before they consider reflections. The best way to show the reflections of a square is with an overhead projector. Place an image on a square of acetate. Then show the four different ways the image can be placed in the template of the original square through reflections.

REFLECTIONS

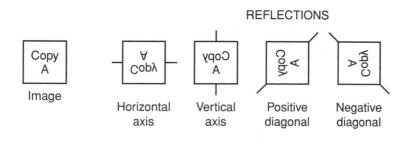

| Image | Horizontal axis | Vertical axis | Positive diagonal | Negative diagonal |

Combining reflections with rotations, there are eight different choices of transformations that can be assigned to each of the three reduced copies used in the 2×2 square grid. This gives 512 different possible building codes.

$$8 \times 8 \times 8 = 512$$

Encourage your students to investigate if these 512 different codes all give different fractal structures. It turns out that they do not.

8.5 FRACTAL CURVES

These activities center around fractals drawn by processes applied repeatedly to line segments. Dot paper facilitates their construction.

Spirolaterals

Spirolaterals can be thought of as special curves. When the alphabet code on page 242 is used on the word FRACTAL, you get the number sequence 6913213. The spirolateral appears very different when drawn on triangular dot paper as compared to square dot paper. Both spirolaterals exhibit special properties of symmetry, congruency, and rotation, but they are not fractals. There is no self-similarity.

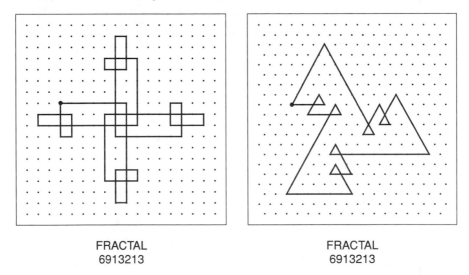

FRACTAL
6913213

FRACTAL
6913213

Show these figures to the class and let them do the translation. This forces them to see the congruent component parts in each structure. There are four congruent copies of the same pattern on the square dot paper, rotated successively through 90° clockwise turns. Only three copies are used on the triangular dot paper, rotated successively through 120° turns. Students need to see congruency in these two figures from this vantage point just as they need to see similarity in fractal structures.

Dot paper can be used to draw the scaled down images needed for the self-similarity in fractal curves. In each case, the initial figure is a line segment with length chosen for convenient subdivision.

Triangular Dot Paper

Triangular or isometric dot paper uses an equilateral triangle as its basic configuration. Thus, turning angles of 60° and 120° are easy to construct.

One fractal, called the *Koch curve,* was developed in the early 1900s and is used in constructing the snowflakes shown on page 23. You can see self-similarity begin to emerge in noting how four copies of each stage, reduced to $\frac{1}{3}$ size, are always used in the same way in building the next stage. Have your students draw the first few stages on triangular dot paper.

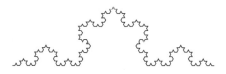

The Koch Curve

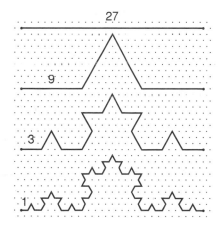

Square Dot Paper

Square dot paper facilitates the construction of fractal curves where 90° turning angles are required. This hat curve is generated through an iterative procedure that repeatedly calls for five copies, reduced to $\frac{1}{3}$ scale, in building the next stage from any given stage following this algorithm.

Notice how the five reduced copies are always placed in the same way at each stage, above and outside the hat. This generates the first fractal curve shown. Interesting variations are possible. The second fractal curve shows a variation that repeatedly places copies below and inside the hat instead of above and outside.

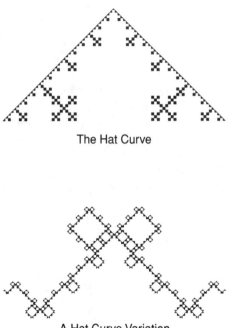

The Hat Curve

A Hat Curve Variation

Graph Paper

Regular graph paper can be used as well to create interesting fractal curves. This example takes an iterative procedure that generates a fractal curve and repeatedly applies it on the four sides of a square. Every segment at every side at every stage is replaced by 8 segments at half scale following this algorithm. View the center vertical portion as two segments.

Students start with a 2-inch square drawn on $\frac{1}{8}$-inch graph paper. This allows for a convenient stage-1 and stage-2 construction. For a stage-3 image, start with an 8-inch square.

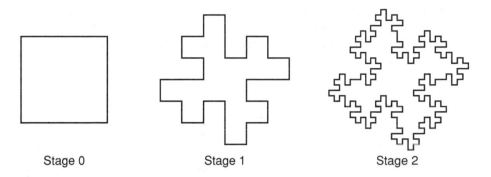

| Stage 0 | Stage 1 | Stage 2 |

One of the things that makes this particular building algorithm so interesting to study is the changing behaviors of the perimeter and area of the structure. Dimensions are given here in inches and square inches, starting with a 2-inch square.

Stage	0	1	2	3	4	n
Perimeter	8	16	32	64	128	2^{n+3}
Area	4	4	4	4	4	4

The perimeter diverges, getting large without bound, while the area remains fixed!

The Sierpinski Curve

One of the surprising characteristics of the Sierpinski triangle is that the fractal structure is the limit figure for a variety of different building algorithms. This time start with a line segment. Students can easily draw the first few stages on triangular dot paper. Select two points as shown. Make the distance between them a multiple of 2. In this illustration, the points are 16 units apart.

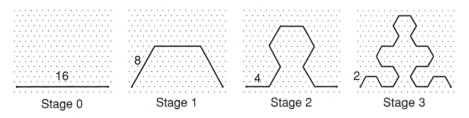

| Stage 0 | Stage 1 | Stage 2 | Stage 3 |

Do you see three reduced copies of stage 0 in stage 1, of stage 1 in stage 2, and of stage 2 in stage 3? Do you see the directions alternating back and forth? Think of each figure as a path from one endpoint to the other. The higher the stage, the more complex the path, but at no finite stage will the curve ever touch itself. The surprise is that, in the limit, this curve touches itself *everywhere*. And what is that limit figure? It is the Sierpinski triangle, the exact same fractal structure being generated earlier from the triangular pieces of paper.

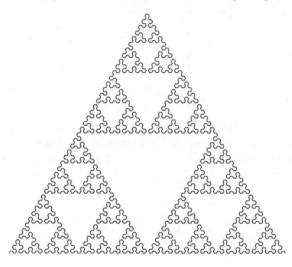

Stage 7 of the Sierpinski curve

Through these activities with dot paper, your students will gain a better understanding of how an iteration process can involve scaled-down versions of the whole embedded in the parts. This is, of course, the property of self-similarity, a characteristics of fractals. They will also begin to appreciate how simple rules repeatedly applied to an initial simple structure can quickly generate highly complex structures, another characteristic of fractals.

8.6 CONNECTIONS

Fractal structures often appear in strange and unexpected places. Students are surprised to see connections to Pascal's triangle, to games where moves are based on random rolls of a die, and to three-dimensional figures. They may also be unaware of the potential for creating fractal patterns using the drawing tools now found in most computer software packages.

Pascal's Triangle

Write down the first few rows of *Pascal's triangle* and then encourage your students to discover the generating pattern if they do not already know it.

Once found, have them use it to extend the array to include additional rows of numbers. The process is essentially numerical. Surprisingly, there is also an interesting geometric pattern hidden in the array of numbers found in Pascal's triangle.

Circle the odd entries in the triangular array of numbers. Do these circles form any special pattern? One would not expect to see a connection appear between Pascal's triangle and the Sierpinski triangle.

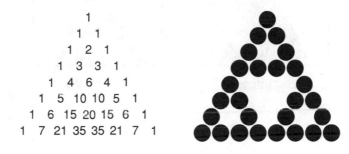

```
            1
          1   1
        1   2   1
      1   3   3   1
    1   4   6   4   1
  1   5  10  10   5   1
 1   6  15  20  15   6   1
1   7  21  35  35  21   7   1
```

The Chaos Game

Each student plays with a partner, using a pencil, ruler, and a die numbered 1 through 6. They play on a piece of paper with three points marked L, T, and R, corresponding to the left, top, and right vertices of an equilateral triangle.

- Start with a randomly chosen point on the triangle.
- Repeatedly roll the die, moving according to these rules:
    For a 1 or 2, move halfway to L.
    For a 3 or 4, move halfway to T.
    For a 5 or 6, move halfway to R.
- Trace the segments forming the path for 10 successive rolls.
    Use each midpoint as a new starting point for the next move.

Have students share their results. While no two paths are likely to be the same, their intuition will tell them that eventually all points in the interior of triangle LTR will be crossed.

Now have the students turn their papers over, mark the same three vertex points on the back, and repeat the process. But this time, have them mark only the midpoints, without actually connecting successive points. This is the chaos game.

Ask your students to predict what this image will look like after a great many more rolls. Students will likely predict again that all points in triangle LTR will eventually be covered. Surprisingly, whatever the location of the initial point and however the die may fall, in the long run, the midpoints will, for all students, form the Sierpinski triangle. Such is the deterministic behavior of this random process.

These graphing calculator displays show simulated results for both traces and points. Other fractal images can be drawn as well using the same chaos-game method.

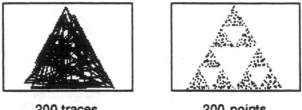

200 traces   **200 points**

Computer-Drawn Images

Students can create images of the first few stages of a developing fractal by using the drawing program found in most software packages. The built-in drawing features listed below allow for fast and accurate fractal image construction on a computer. By repeatedly going through the iteration steps, students gain a better insight into the role scaling and transformations play in the process.

Copying   Pasting   Rotating   Reflecting
Scaling   Grouping   Snap-on grid

This sample shows a computer-drawn, stage-by-stage, sequence generated by four repeated applications of a specific building algorithm. You can already see the self-similarity of the fractal beginning to emerge.

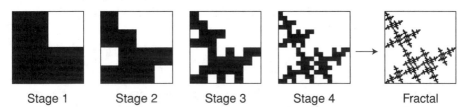

Stage 1   Stage 2   Stage 3   Stage 4   Fractal

The Sierpinski Tetrahedron

The *Sierpinski tetrahedron* is a fractal that exists in three-dimensional space with the same basic characteristics as the Sierpinski triangle that exists in a two-dimensional plane. Students will enjoy building models of the first few stages. The entire class can become involved in the construction of a larger model at some higher stage.

The building blocks are regular tetrahedrons of ever decreasing sizes. They can be made by cutting, folding, and taping paper using regular hexagons as shown on page 180.

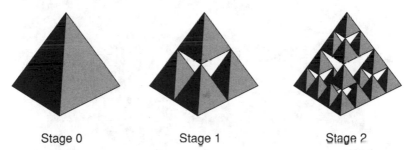

| Stage 0 | Stage 1 | Stage 2 |

Again, the iterative building process reveals the inherent self-similarity of the limit figure. Interesting numerical patterns can be explored using the first few stages.

Stage	0	1	2	3	4	n
Number of tetrahedrons	1	4	16	64	256	4^n
Volumes	1	$\frac{1}{2}$	$\frac{1}{4}$	$\frac{1}{8}$	$\frac{1}{16}$	$\left(\frac{1}{2}\right)^n$

Since the pieces at every stage are similar tetrahedrons, the construction process offers an excellent classroom opportunity to investigate how scaling affects the relationship among length, area, and volume of similar solids.

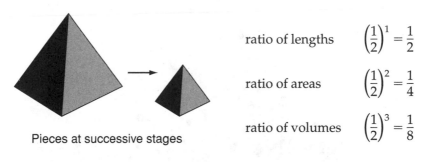

Pieces at successive stages

ratio of lengths $\quad \left(\frac{1}{2}\right)^1 = \frac{1}{2}$

ratio of areas $\quad \left(\frac{1}{2}\right)^2 = \frac{1}{4}$

ratio of volumes $\quad \left(\frac{1}{2}\right)^3 = \frac{1}{8}$

Ask students to identify the shape of the holes using a model of the first stage. Not everyone will see and recognize this shape as a regular octahedron.

Students familiar with the drawing package on a computer should be encouraged to use it to create images of some early stages of the fractal structure. This computer-drawn view shows stage 3 of the Sierpinski tetrahedron suspended in mid-air.

Here is another computer-drawn image of a structure not easily seen from the model itself. It shows, from a different angle, what all the stage-3 holes of the preceding figure look like when taken together.

Many interesting fractal sites can be found on the Internet. Encourage your students to search them out and learn more about this new topic in mathematics.

EXERCISES

1. Select a number with two or more digits. Multiply the digits in the numbers. Then multiply the digits in the product. Keep repeating the process until you reach a one-digit product. Show that both 76 and 77 yield the number 8 when this rule is applied. How many numbers between 10 and 100 yield the number 8?

2. Show that the infinite geometric series with initial term $\frac{1}{8}$ and common ratio $\frac{1}{8}$ has a sum of $\frac{1}{7}$. Write $\frac{1}{7}$ as a repeating decimal. How many terms in the geometric series are needed to reach the first block of repeating digits in the corresponding decimal?

3. The four corners of a paper square are folded to the center to form a new, smaller square for the next stage. Assume that at each successive stage the same process is applied, over and over. Find the ratios of the perimeters and areas, smaller to larger, at any two successive stages.

4. An equilateral triangle with 6-inch sides is cut from paper. A smaller, stage-1 triangle is formed by folding the three corners to the midpoints of the opposite sides. Assume successive stages of the triangle are formed in the same way. What are the perimeter and area of the resulting triangle after n successive iterations?

5. Refer to the paper-folding activity described in Example 2 on page 241. Where will the two ends of the folded paper strip be after ten successive folds?

6. Start with the equation $f(x) = 0.1x + 0.4$. Begin the iteration with $x_0 = 0.4$ and use the output as the new input x_1. Continue repeating the process for successive values of x. Express as a fraction the limiting value of this iteration process.

7. Iteration is performed through the function $f(x)$ using the special relationship $x_{i+1} = f(x_i)$. Write equations that can be used, through iteration, to generate the decimals for $\frac{1}{11}$ and $\frac{1}{7}$.

8. What geometric properties would appear in a spirolateral generated from the number sequence 12345 on a square grid?

9. The geometric properties of spirolaterals drawn on a square grid can be classified into three categories: repeating after two cycles (2), repeating after four cycles (4), and never repeating (N). Copy and complete the entries in this table. Look for a pattern in the numbers.

number of digits	3	4	5	6	7	8	9	10	11	12
cycle repetition	4	N	4	2						

10. Draw a spirolateral on a triangular grid for the word MATH using the conversion code on page 242. Use 120° counterclockwise turns. Then draw another using 60° counterclockwise turns.

11. A rectangular paper strip is folded in half repeatedly. What is the number of rectangles that would appear in the opened strip after n folds? How is the answer related to triangular numbers?

12. Prove algebraically the relationship $S(n) = T(n) + T(n - 1)$ for square and triangular numbers.

13. Express the number of triangular pieces that remain at stage n of the developing Sierpinski triangle both explicitly and recursively.

14. Express the number of triangular holes that appear at stage n of the developing Sierpinski triangle both explicitly and recursively.

15. At what stage of the developing Sierpinski triangle will there first be enough small triangular pieces to give one to each person in your state? in the United States? in the world?

16. Start with a region enclosed in an equilateral triangle with 4-inch sides. As you move from stage to stage in the developing Sierpinski triangle, the total perimeter around each and every piece of remaining region diverges. At what stage will this length first be greater than the circumference of the earth?

17. Prove that the area of the remaining pieces of the developing Sierpinski triangle converges while the corresponding perimeter diverges.

18. Prove that the nth term for the sequence 1 5 14 30 … is $\dfrac{n(n + 1)(2n + 1)}{6}$.

19. The rule for generating the hat curve fractal is given on page 259. How many line segments make up the hat curve at stage 5? at stage n?

Draw the first three stages starting with a shaded square and each building rule.

20.
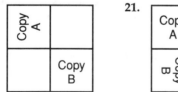

21.

22.

23. Identify the building code used to generate the fractal image shown.

24. Write the three sets of linear transformation equations needed to generate each new stage from the preceding one for the fractal shown in Exercise 23. Assume the figure starts as a unit square with origin at the center.

ACTIVITIES

1. Use the results of Exercise 1 as a starting point, and catalog all 2-digit numbers with the 1-digit numbers that result. Discuss the value of this activity in relation to the maintenance of computational skills.

2. Prepare a brief lesson reviewing repeating decimals and justify its use before introducing a unit on generating fractal images.

3. Enter a number greater than 1 in your calculator and repeatedly take the square root. Repeat again starting with a number between 0 and 1. Explain how this activity might be useful in introducing the notion of convergence in an algebra class.

4. Plan a short lesson that ties the use of spirolaterals to translations, rotations, and reflections.

5. Construct two spirolaterals for the name *Pythagoras,* using the conversion code on page 242. Make one on a square grid and the other on a triangular grid.

6. Prepare a brief lesson where students construct successive stages of the Sierpinski triangle and use them to review powers and exponents.

7. Develop a classroom activity where students generate the first four stages of the Sierpinski triangle using $\frac{1}{8}$-inch graph paper. Start with a 2-inch shaded square for stage 0.

8. Individual projects often add interest to a topic. Discuss how students might create the first several stages of different fractal images by using different rotations in their building codes.

9. As a team, do the cooperative classroom activity described on page 256 by gluing together a large fractal image. Display the results in an appropriate place.

10. Use the drawing package in your computer to create the first five stages of a developing fractal.

11. Draw stage 4 of the developing Sierpinski curve on triangular dot paper. See page 261.

12. Use a chaos-game program to generate the Sierpinski triangle on a graphing calculator.

13. Build a model of the Sierpinski tetrahedron at stage 2. Use tetrahedrons built from folded hexagons as described on page 180.

14. Find the volume of the holes of the Sierpinski tetrahedron at stages 1, 2, and 3, assuming a starting volume of 1 cubic unit.

15. Create a transparency sequence that can be used in teaching how the Koch snowflake is developed. See page 23 in Chapter 1.

16. Prepare a report on readings from Benoit Mandelbrot's first book, *The Fractal Geometry of Nature,* published by W. H. Freeman and Company, New York, 1983.

17. Read and report on the chapter titled "Images of Chaos" from *Chaos: Making a New Science,* by James Gleick, Penguin Books, New York, 1987.

18. Read about fractal dimension in *Fractals for the Classroom: Strategic Activities Volume One* by Peitgen, Jurgens, Saupe, Maletsky, Perciante, and Yunker, published jointly by the National Council of Teachers of Mathematics and Springer-Verlag, 1991. Then prepare a lesson for a senior high-school math class on computing the fractal dimension of several fractals.

19. Use a drawing program on a computer to create an image of stage 3 of the Sierpinski tetrahedron as shown on page 266.

EPILOGUE

This is the third edition of *Teaching Mathematics: A Sourcebook of Aids, Activities, and Strategies*. The first edition was published in 1975, and the second appeared in 1988, reflecting the combined teaching experiences of many years of both authors. Now, as we complete this third edition, it seems appropriate to look back at the many changes that have taken place in mathematics education as well as those that appear to be the trends for the years ahead.

The status of mathematics education in the United States has gone through many changes during the past several decades, and continues to be in a state of flux as we begin the twenty-first century. Indeed, each decade seems to have a new "battle cry" or theme, as we can see by reviewing the events of the past 50 years.

THE "NEW" MATH

In the post-war years there was great concern about developing and maintaining scientific power in our country as we watched Russia build up their nuclear power and send the first man into space in their space capsule named *Sputnik*. This provided the impetus for Congress to appropriate huge sums of money to retrain mathematics teachers as well as to develop teams of mathematicians and mathematics educators to develop new materials. The most famous of these was called the School Mathematics Study Group (SMSG), based at Yale University and then later at Stanford University. SMSG produced materials for the classroom, tested and revised them, and then released the materials so that they might be incorporated into commercial textbooks. During the decade of the 1960s this material, known as the "New Math," was generally accepted as the standard for the mathematics curriculum in our schools.

Although given the name "new," this body of subject matter can actually best be described under three categories as follows:

1. *Pushed-down mathematics*—Much of the SMSG material was similar to traditional programs but taught at an earlier level. For example, trigonometry and solid geometry had always been taught as twelfth-grade topics. In the new programs, trig was incorporated into second-year algebra courses and solid geometry was taught along with plane geometry. Many of the topics of elementary algebra were pushed down into the seventh and eighth grades, and topics such as signed numbers were found in some primary mathematics programs.

2. *New points of view*—Traditional topics were treated from different points of view so as to place emphasis on meaning and understanding. For example, in the new programs, it became important for students to understand why one "inverts and multiplies" when dividing by a fraction. The concept of a set was used as a unifying theme in both algebra and geometry. Such basic principles as the commutative, associative, and distributive properties were emphasized.

3. *New math*—Certain topics were introduced into the curriculum that had never been included before at this level, such as other number bases, modular arithmetic, and non-metric geometry.

Although many people like to say that the new math of the 1960s no longer exists, the actual fact is that many of the new topics have reduced emphasis given to them in contemporary programs. The material described as "pushed-down" mathematics and traditional mathematics from a new point of view certainly remains as part of most modern programs.

BACK TO BASICS

By the end of the 1960s, it became clear that our students were falling behind in their knowledge of basic skills. Thus one of the stories going around at that time was that most students knew that $7 \times 9 = 9 \times 7$ because of the commutative property of multiplication, but few knew that the actual product was 63! Parents began to complain that their children did not know the basic facts and that they were unable to help them with the new topics that they themselves had never studied! Thus the battle cry of the 1970s became "Back to Basics." Teachers, textbooks, and the general public wanted their children to know these facts rather than the fact that $1 + 1 = 10$ in the binary system of notation!

PROBLEM SOLVING

By the end of this decade, much progress had been made, but suddenly we became aware of the fact that students were unable to solve problems! One example given at the time was that the majority of students could find the distance around a rectangle if they were given a diagram with dimensions. But the number who could solve this problem dropped dramatically when the same situation was given in words, without a figure. The National Council of Teachers of Mathematics took recognition of this deficiency and published a document entitled *Agenda for Action* in which they stated "Problem solving must be the focus of school mathematics in the 1980s." This then became the battle cry of the 1980s as every effort was made to incorporate strategies for solving problems into the curriculum, using standard as well as non-standard problems.

TECHNOLOGY

By the end of the 1980s, our students had advanced their knowledge and their skills at problem solving, although once again students' achievement of basic skills seemed to have declined. However, the decade of the 1990s began with new emphasis being given to other approaches to the teaching of mathematics. Thus some of the new key words included "cooperative learning," an approach that suggested students work in groups to solve problems with some of these including "real-world" situations helped through the use of manipulatives. Technology became a major theme with the rapid introduction into the curriculum of calculators and computers. The role of technology in the teaching of mathematics is still evolving, although it is clear that we should not let technology drive what is in the curriculum!

THE TWENTY-FIRST CENTURY

As the decade of the 1990s ended and we moved toward the year 2000, controversy raged with numerous articles appearing in newspapers and journals concerning what was termed as the new "new math" or "whole math." The general public once again became concerned by the fact that so many students were unable to perform such arithmetic operations as long division, relying on calculators instead. A serious question arises as to whether we should stress such basic computational skills instead of relying on a calculator to do the job, so as to provide more time for such other important skills as that of problem solving. There does seem to be general agreement that there is an important role for technology in the curriculum. However, most educators would agree that students should not have to rely on calculators to find the product 7×9, nor to estimate the 15- or 20-percent tip required on a restaurant bill.

In order to prepare for the twenty-first century, the National Council of Teachers of Mathematics initiated a *Standards 2000 Project* to revise their *Curriculum and Evaluation Standards for School Mathematics* that had set the stage for curriculum development throughout the decade of the 1990s. This new document, entitled *Principles and Standards for School Mathematics*, has a publication date of spring 2000 and combines as well as strengthens the interrelationships among curriculum, teaching, and assessment for grades pre-K through 12. The revision reaffirms the current NCTM *Standards* while addressing new teaching and curricular challenges for the next decade in four grade bands: pre-K–2, 3–5, 6–8, and 9–12.

As we conclude this overview, one thing appears to be true: the item that remains invariant throughout transformations of the curriculum is the pedagogy used by effective teachers of mathematics. Thus the authors have attempted to include in this text those approaches to the teaching of mathematics that successful teachers continue to use throughout the changes that take place in the content being taught. Appropriate motivational techniques have been and always will continue to be important. As suggested on the very first page of this text, as teachers of mathematics we must learn to teach our subject artistically . . . with passion, with a clear demonstration of our love for the subject, and with the conviction that we can motivate our students to study and learn the subject matter that we teach. We trust that the suggestions for such artistic teaching that have been included in this text will prove to be helpful for those of you who continue your profession into the twenty-first century.

ANSWERS TO ODD-NUMBERED EXERCISES

CHAPTER 1 (PAGE 30)

1. Write the sum as $1 + 2 + 3 + \ldots + (n - 2) + (n - 1) + n$. Then consider pairs of numbers such as $(n + 1)$, $(n - 1 + 2)$, $(n\ 2 + 3)$, etc. There are $\frac{n}{2}$ such pairs and their sum is thus $\left(\frac{n}{2}\right)(n + 1)$.

3. Some representative sums are: $22 = 5 + 17, 32 = 25 + 7, 48 = 7 + 41, 50 = 3 + 47$.

5. Some representative answers: for $n = 4$: $4 < 5 < 8$; for $n = 5$: $5 < 7 < 10$; for $n = 10, 10 < 13 < 20$.

7. For the general array of nine numbers shown, the products of entries in diagonally opposite corners are $a(a + 22) = a^2 + 22a$ and $(a + 2)(a + 20) = a^2 + 22a + 40$.

a	$a + 1$	$a + 2$
$a + 10$	$a + 11$	$a + 12$
$a + 20$	$a + 21$	$a + 22$

The differences of these products is 40.
For an array of 16 numbers the products will be $a(a + 33) = a^2 + 33a$ and $(a + 3)(a + 30) = a^2 + 33a + 90$, with a constant difference of 90.

9. Limiting height $= 1 + \frac{\sqrt{2}}{4} + \frac{1}{4} + \frac{\sqrt{2}}{16} + \frac{1}{16} + \frac{\sqrt{2}}{64} + \frac{1}{64} + \ldots$
$$= \left(1 + \frac{1}{4} + \frac{1}{16} + \frac{1}{64} + \ldots\right) + \sqrt{2}\left(\frac{1}{4} + \frac{1}{16} + \frac{1}{64} + \ldots\right).$$
We have the sum of two infinite series whose sum is $\frac{4}{3} + \frac{\sqrt{2}}{3} = \frac{4 + \sqrt{2}}{3}$.
For the limiting breadth we can consider one side and double the result.

This gives rise again to two infinite series:

$$\sqrt{2}\left(\frac{1}{4}+\frac{1}{16}+\frac{1}{64}+\ldots\right)+\left(\frac{1}{4}+\frac{1}{16}+\frac{1}{64}\right) \text{ with sums } \sqrt{2}\left(\frac{1}{3}\right) \text{ and } \frac{1}{3}. \text{ Thus the}$$

total breadth is $\dfrac{2(\sqrt{2}+1)}{3} = \left(\dfrac{2}{3}\right)(\sqrt{2}+1)$.

11. Consider the products $0 \times 1, 2 \times 3, 4 \times 5, 6 \times 7, \ldots$ The next two will be $8 \times 9 = 72$ and $10 \times 11 = 110$.

13. Use the figure on page 10. Then the required point C will be at P_2.

CHAPTER 2 (PAGE 61)

1. (c); about 6 inches divided by 2.5 inches

3. (d); about 16 pennies per foot; $16 \times 5280 = 84,480$

5. (b); 10,000 minutes is about 167 hours, or approximately one week

7. Begin with 20 and remove n to obtain $20 - n$, or $10 + (10 - n)$. Add the digits in the remaining number of matches to obtain $1 + (10 - n)$ or $11 - n$. Then subtract: $(20 - n) - (11 - n) = 9$.

9. Possible answers:

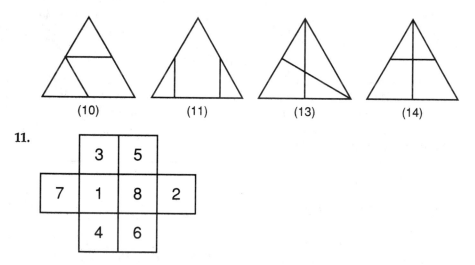

(10)   (11)   (13)   (14)

11.

	3	5	
7	1	8	2
	4	6	

13. Solve by trial and error.

15. Slide the horizontal match to the right and bring the one at the left down and to the right.

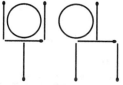

CHAPTER 3 (PAGE 85)

1. 19
3. 4
5. 1
7. Entries in the second row are 2, 1, 2, 0, 0
9. Entries in the second row for charts of numbers 0 through 6, 7, and 8 are:

```
0 through 6:  3  2  1  1  0  0  0
0 through 7:  4  2  1  0  1  0  0  0
0 through 8:  5  2  1  0  0  1  0  0  0
0 through 9:  6  2  1  0  0  0  1  0  0  0
```

There is no solution for a chart showing numbers 0 through 5.
11. "You won't give me the penny."
13. 1700 feet; note that when the boat meets for the second time, the total distance they will have traveled is three times the width of the river, and 2100 − 1400 = 700.
15. If x is the length of the square cut off, the volume is $V = x(12 - 2x)^2$ or $V = 4x^3 - 48x^2 + 144x$. The derivative is $12x^2 - 96x + 144$. If this is set equal to 0, then the maximum volume is formed when $x = 2$, and $V = 128$ cubic inches.
17. 15
19. 141 pages; page 5–6 is missing.

CHAPTER 4 (PAGE 125)

1. 64
3. $\frac{7}{4} + \frac{6}{5}; \frac{7}{4} - \frac{5}{6}$
5. $11 = 44 \div (\sqrt{4} + \sqrt{4}); 12 = 4 + 4 + \sqrt{4} + \sqrt{4}; 13 = (44 \div 4) + \sqrt{4};$
$14 = 4 + 4 + 4 + \sqrt{4}; 15 = (44 \div 4) + 4; 16 = (4 \times 4) + (4 - 4);$
$17 = 4 \times 4 + (4 \div 4); 18 = 4 \times 4 + 4 - \sqrt{4}; 19 = 4! - 4 - (4 \div 4);$
$20 = \sqrt{4}(4 + 4 + \sqrt{4})$
7. Assume a pay of $100. A 10% raise gives $110, and then a 10% cut gives $99. Beginning with a 10% cut gives $90, and then a 10% raise gives $99. In symbols, for a salary of x dollars: $(1.10x)(.9) = (.90x)(1.10) = .99x$.
9. 8
11. 5149
13. 1, 6, 15, 28, 45, 66; $n(2n - 1)$
15. 195; 39

17. $\dfrac{n^2(n^2+1)}{2} + 4n^2$

19. Consider the first n odd numbers: $1, 3, 5, 7, \ldots, 2n-1$. The sum of the first and last is $1 + (2n-1) = 2n$ and there are $\dfrac{n}{2}$ pairs. Thus the sum is $(2n)\left(\dfrac{n}{2}\right) = n^2$.

CHAPTER 5 (PAGE 159)

1. $\dfrac{n(n+1)(2n+1)}{6}; \dfrac{n^2(n+1)^2}{4}$

3. $x + 4 - 6 = 24,\ x = 26;$ $\quad 8(x+4) = 24,\ x = -1$ $\quad \dfrac{(x+4)}{10} = 24,\ x = 236$

$x - 6 + 4 = 24,\ x = 26;$ $\quad 8(x-6) = 24,\ x = 9;$ $\quad \dfrac{(x-6)}{10} = 24,\ x = 246$

$8x + 4 = 24,\ x = 2\frac{1}{2};$ $\quad 8x - 6 = 24,\ x = 3\frac{3}{4};$ $\quad \dfrac{8x}{10} = 24,\ x = 30$

$\left(\dfrac{x}{10}\right) + 4 = 24,\ x = 200;$ $\quad \left(\dfrac{x}{10}\right) - 6 = 24,\ x = 300;$ $\quad 8\left(\dfrac{x}{10}\right) = 24,\ x = 30$

5. $y = -\dfrac{x^2}{4}$

7. $y = -(x+2)^2 - 3$

9. $x = |y+2| + 3$

11. $16\dfrac{5}{8}$

13. 301; yes

15. V $\lessgtr$; $<$ WW $\lessgtr$; WWW $\lessgtr$ WWW $\lessgtr$ WW $\lessgtr$

17. $f(x) = 3x^2 - 8x + 5$

19. 2.718254

21. spiral in; $-\dfrac{1}{32}$; alternating series converging to 0

CHAPTER 6 (PAGE 204)

1. 10

3. 37.70 cu. in.; 75.40 sq. in.

5. 77.35 cu. in. and 120.89 sq. in.; 131.13 cu. in. and 130.92 sq. in.

7. 10

9.

V	4	8	6	20	12
F	4	6	8	12	20
E	6	12	12	30	30

11. 29

13. $\dfrac{x^2}{100} + \dfrac{y^2}{64} = 1$

15. $53\frac{1}{3}$ cu. in.; $48 + 16\sqrt{3}$ sq. in.

CHAPTER 7 (PAGE 233)

1. approximately 1 in 22

3. $\dfrac{1}{3}$

5. $\dfrac{1}{3}$; 1

7. $\dfrac{1}{3}$

9. $2.50

11. 7560

13. $\dfrac{1}{3}$

15. $\dfrac{1}{2}$

17. $\dfrac{1}{3}$

19. 3000

21. $\dfrac{39}{64}$

CHAPTER 8 (PAGE 267)

1. $76 \rightarrow 42 \rightarrow 8$; $77 \rightarrow 49 \rightarrow 36 \rightarrow 18 \rightarrow 8$;   22

3. $\dfrac{\sqrt{2}}{2}$; $\dfrac{1}{2}$

5. $\dfrac{171}{512}$

7. $f(x) = 0.01x + 0.09$ with $x_0 = 0.09$:
   $f(x) = 0.000001x + 0.142857$ with $x_0 = 0.142857$

9.

number of digits	3	4	5	6	7	8	9	10	11	12
cycle repetition	4	N	4	2	4	N	4	2	4	N

11. $1 + 2 + 3 + 4 + \ldots + 2^n = 2^{n-1}(2^n + 1)$;
for any counting number n, the answer is a triangular number.

13. 3^n; $F(n) = 3F(n - 1)$ where $F(0) = 1$

15. Answer depends on population of state of residence; stage 18; stage 21

17. Both successive areas and successive perimeters form a geometric series. For the areas, $r = \dfrac{3}{4}$. Since $|r| < 1$, the series converges.

For the perimeters, $r = \dfrac{3}{2}$. Since $|r| > 1$, the series diverges.

19. $5^5 = 3125$; 5^n

21.

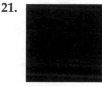   

Stage 0   Stage 1   Stage 2   Stage 3

23.

A Copy	
Copy B	Copy C

INDEX